VENICE

The Masque of Italy

The pleasant place of all festivity,
The revel of the earth, the masque of Italy !

Byron

General Editors: Elisabeth and Paul Elek
Translation: Neil Mann
Production: Stanley Freeman

VENICE

The Masque of Italy

Text by Marcel Brion   Photographs by Edwin Smith

Crown Publishers, Inc., New York

DG
676
B7

2/25/63 ctdpr 7.99

o.k. gck

45564

TABLE OF CONTENTS

LIST OF ILLUSTRATIONS

ILLUSTRATIONS IN THE TEXT

The illustrations on Pages 31, 64, 71, 79, 93, 102, 113, 126 and 140 are in the collection at Windsor Castle and are reproduced by kind permission of H. M. the Queen.

The illustrations on Pages 23, 37, 47, 57, 92, 115, 117, 147, 155, 200 and 201 are reproduced by kind permission of the British Museum.

The Publishers wish to express their appreciation of the advice and practical assistance so generously given to them by the Director and staff of the Ufficio Informazioni dell'Ente Provinciale per il Turismo, Piazza San Marco, Venice.

INTRODUCTION

THE BENEVOLENT deities who watched over the birth of Venice and saw it flourish, endowed the city from the very beginning with all the advantages conducive to the immortality (relatively speaking, for it is never wholly proof against some disaster) which is desirable in sublime works of art. Venice was, and indeed still remains, one of the masterpieces of human genius; one of those places on earth which are distinguished by their beauty and originality, where the natural lie of the land and the perseverance and ingenuity of the inhabitants have conspired with the invisible powers that keep guard over cities to achieve something splendid and unique.

It is because it is made up of a group of islands that Venice has preserved its specific character and charm more successfully than any other city in Europe. Providence protected it from war and invasion. A few recently added disfigurements have failed to make it ugly, and although Venice is threatened with ' modernization,' those who really love it will still find those silent, deserted parts, visited only by cats and occasional passers-by, where the very soul of the Middle Ages lives on. A few steps from the noisy thoroughfares, bustling with trade and full of jostling tourists, there are quiet streets and peaceful canals where gondolas pass now and then, with the silky swish of their shining black hulls through waters the colour of jade.

But Venice is no ' dead city.' Although today it no longer enjoys the haughty independence or the proud, fearless authority which made it the equal of all the great states of Europe, although the Arsenal is almost empty and the port used largely by tourist vessels, it still remains one of the spiritual and artistic capitals whose numberless treasures the visitor can never exhaust. Its population is one of the most active in Italy, and we need do no more than observe the quick, light step of Venetian men and women to recognize in them the true heirs of the enterprising, courageous and self-willed people who struggled long ago for mastery of the sea.

It is unnecessary to know the history of the Republic to enjoy the pleasures of Venice as they are enjoyed by the tourists from all parts of the world who throng there during the summer months; they are satisfied to glance over the most famous monuments in a few days or hours, and leave when they have barely touched the surface of a city which yields only to those who have the patience to conquer it. The facile exoticism of the Byzantine art, and the strange quality of thoroughfares used only by boats and strollers on the embankment, score a victory even over the most indifferent visitor. Yet it is only after a long stay and frequent revisiting that we can really win a city which offers to the hurrying passer-by no more than an outer appearance and reveals its secret charms only to those filled with the desire to discover them little by little.

Even the outer appearance of Venice will vary according to the route by which it is approached. The best way is still the one used until the time—bitterly regretted by some— when the island was first joined to the main-land by a railway and later by a motor road. If you leave Trieste by boat in the morning, or from Fusina in the late afternoon—the first of these routes will bring you to the Riva degli Schiavoni around noon, the second at sunset—you will gain an emotional experience which is denied to the trav-eller by road or rail. As a general prin-ciple, a maritime city should always be approached by sea, and this is supremely true of Venice, where a network of canals brings life to the city like the system of veins in a leaf. By the same token, it is only by strolling or, where necessary, by taking a gondola, that you can get to know the different quarters of the town (the Venices of Giudecca, Canareggio, Castelle and the Rialto are all quite distinct from one another) for then you can stop at leisure to glimpse the seemingly unlimited expanse of a crowded garden through a half-open trellis, you can gaze at a palace engraved with Byzan-tine dragons or Roman monsters, and enter one of the many churches, not one of which is like any other.

To know Venice, you must explore it slowly, patiently and untiringly, both by night and day—for a city is never the same at night as it is by day. You must talk with the inhabitants, see how they live, take part in their festi-vals and their work, and share in their enthusiasm for time-honoured celebra-tions, when the splendour and pomp of the Republic live briefly once again.

You must look in books, at pictures and other works of art, for evidence of the city's former life, and of its rise and fall, for you must know it at every moment of its existence. On the empty pages of memory you must conjure the picture of deserted muddy isles, lost in the middle of a lagoon; of ships bringing fugitives, driven from their lands by the Huns and Goths; and of the wooden houses built by these newcomers, who thought they were here only temporarily but were destined to remain through the limitless course of centuries. And as the picture continues to change, wooden houses are succeeded by stone ones, the cupolas and steeples of the *campanili* tower into the sky, Gothic arches rise up, and baroque domes whirl.

The history of Venice is that of a wonderful and enduring victory over the elements and men. Wrested from the sea, it had to be constantly safe-guarded against silting, which would flood the canals, and from the disin-tegration of the land, which was braced by piles. These weakening and destruc-tive factors had to be overcome, and constant vigilance was necessary for Venice to survive. In the same way, during the centuries which marked the city's rise and gradual decline, its ad-mirals, captains and statesmen main-tained cohesion among the classes of the city with a common ideal, just as the soil was strengthened with stakes driven into the silt in the water.

The art of Venice developed pro-portionally with its rising wealth and authority, with its awareness that it was a great power. For this reason, the simultaneous study of all the factors of its civilisation, and of all the evidence given by the city of its spiritual and aesthetic evolution, will alone explain the connection between innumerable elements which collaborate in preserving its being and promoting its growth like those of a human organism. Financiers play as important a part as artists in any explanation of the character of a city where, more than in any other in the world, there is a necessary blend of contrasts; it is quite impossible to remove any part of this blend without jeopardizing the equilibrium of the whole. The cult of beauty and trade for profit went hand in hand here, just as they did in all the great merchant capitals—Florence, Amsterdam or Antwerp—and the love for pleasure made its appearance when Venice came to its full flowering; it was the city's legitimate reward for the immense effort which its people had made to achieve and maintain mastery of the sea.

Later, when excessive waste was no longer compensated by the acquisition of new wealth, when a frenzied delight in pleasure was no longer counterbalanced by devotion to the common weal, the psychological, social and moral equilibrium which had been so strongly based on the political structure of earlier centuries gave way to disorder, a clear symptom of the fatal malady which affects declining civilisations. Venice brought about its own end in the eighteenth century, in the same way that it created its own impetus when it launched its galleys on the Mediterranean shipping routes. When the last Bucintoro was destroyed by fire in 1797, it was the symbol of the city's disappearance from the ' map of the seas ', over which it had for so long reigned supreme.

The way in which Venice's destinies rose and fell in the course of centuries is no mere titbit for the curiosity of a historian. Anyone who does not look at a city and listen to it in exactly the same way that he would look at and listen to a human being can only know it superficially. Because in Venice the past has more palpably survived into the present than it has anywhere else, because its modern role as an artistic and tourist centre helps it to oppose the change by which it is constantly threatened, it has remained almost completely intact, and the layout of its islands, canals and monuments preserves its imperishable character. Thus it is that here one has a sense of complete otherworldliness— both in place and time—which no other European city can equal; and whoever can offer himself to the city with the passion she demands if she is to offer herself in return, will quickly become a Venetian. Even if he does not share with the brilliant and eccentric Englishman who was known as Baron Corvo (Frederick Rolfe of *Adrian VII* and *Don Tarquinio*) the very rare honour of being received in the supremely exclusive guild of gondoliers, he is no longer a stranger. Once he has learned its familiar sites and become aware of its mysterious pulse, he is no longer merely passing through; he has come to stay.

Initiation in the history of Venice has its advantages for someone who would become a Venetian, for it helps him to live the life of the city in its continuity. To its external charms— and no one can remain indifferent to them—it adds the deep fascination of a great destiny which we are privileged to share, from the settlement of the fugitives in the empty lagoon to the last carnival of the Most Serene Republic.

THE PEOPLE OF THE ISLANDS

AT THE TIME when the Huns, kept at a respectful distance by an energetic and determined Chinese Emperor, and finding the fearless advance of their horses checked by the Great Wall, abandoned their escapades in Asia and turned back towards Europe, a great wave of terror passed over the Slav and Germanic peoples. The Mongols launched an attack on their closest neighbours, forcing them from their homelands and compelling them to flee. The latter were now left with no alternative but to invade those states which lay as a barrier to their flight. With the Huns spreading terror wherever they passed, both from natural ferocity and a calculated cruelty which was designed to fill other nations with dread, an extraordinary upheaval took place among the peoples of Europe—those whose lands neighboured Asia, at all events—and the period of the Great Invasions (or Great Migrations, as it is also known) began.

As the Huns hastened their advance the gulf before them increased, for experience taught that it was impossible to check the gallop of their little horses and the unerring flight of their arrows. In the face of this, hurried departure was the only means of salvation. Thus it was that the Vandals, the Visigoths and the Ostrogoths fled in panic from their own lands and fell back on Western Europe with the Mongols hot in pursuit of them. Great rivers and mountain chains were no brake for a savage onslaught. The barbarian hordes advanced in this way right into Italy, and as nature had been bountiful there, as the cities were rich and the people contented, the newcomers—whether Germans, Slavs or Mongols—forced their entry into the provinces of the Empire and no one was able to check them.

This happened at the beginning of the fifth century A. D. The innumerable tribes of the Huns, all once so jealous of their independence, were now firmly united in a single kingdom ruled by the warlord Attila, the son of Mundzuk, who was determined to conquer the whole of Europe. Having watered his horses in the Danube, he coveted the Tiber and dreamed of going on to Rome. Under his command, an invasion which had begun in hopeless confusion now proceeded according to an admirably conceived plan of operation. Among the German peoples conquered by the Huns, some entered into alliance with them; those who could not be subjected in this way were destroyed. Some tribes took service in the Imperial army, which was glad to gain these bold, courageous auxiliaries. The Empire's military strength was no longer what it had been at the peak of Roman glory. Softened by centuries of peace and an easy life of wealth and security,

15

the Italian peoples were stricken with terror by the onslaught of the barbarians, and because they knew that they were incapable of resisting them, they hastily retreated before the Germans, who were themselves fleeing before the Huns.

Where was this frenzied race to end? At the point where an impenetrable barrier halted both the Germans and the Huns. The barbarians had succeeded in crossing wide rivers on makeshift boats and even by swimming, but confronted by the sea they found that they could go no further. The nomads were ignorant of the art of navigation and they were unable to build ships. It was for this reason that the peoples of the mainland, as soon as the barbarians were known to be approaching, quickly took to their ships to find a refuge where they could never be overtaken: in the lagoon which extends along the coasts of the Adriatic.

The inhabitants of the coastal provinces between the sea and the Carso and Dolomite mountains were called Veneti, and they had given their name to the region in which they lived—Venetia. The Veneti were not native to this area and were thought to have come from Asia; legend even associated their arrival in northern Italy with the fall of Troy. Be that as it may, they had taken these lands, which were originally quite marshy, and made them among the most beautiful and fertile in the Empire. Splendid cities rose up on their territories— Concordia, Altinum, Aquileia and Heracleia—and even under the ancient Roman Empire, their virtues were proclaimed. Cicero declared on one occasion that the land of the Veneti was the flower of Italy. Small wonder then that this flower excited the covetousness of the barbarians, and that certain of them, Slavs, Mongols and Germans, had designs on it for themselves.

With the Germans it was possible to reach an understanding, but when the Huns arrived in sight of the Adriatic coast in 452, during Attila's great conquering sweep on Rome, the cities of Altinum, Concordia and Aquileia were abandoned by their inhabitants, who fled in disorder to the sea. They left their wealth, their houses and their lands to the mercy of the Mongols, who methodically ravaged this splendid region. The fleeing Veneti imagined that they would not be absent from their homeland for long; they hoped that the invaders would withdraw, as nomads usually did, when once they had taken all the booty they could carry. They did not foresee that after Attila's Huns, the Venetian mainland would be occupied by the Heruli of Odoacer, who arrived twenty years later in 476, by the Ostrogoths in 493, by the Franks in 548, and by the Lombards in 568.

Throughout Venice's history, a miracle has always happened at the right moment to turn the city's destiny in the direction most favourable to it, and now it occurred when the Veneti from the mainland were in flight from the barbarians and desperately seeking a refuge. They had reached the edge of the lagoon, and already it seemed to them that they could feel the Mongols' horses breathing down their necks. They were still hesitating whether or not to take to the water, although there were a number of boats available, when a supernatural sign was given to them. They heard a voice from the skies which told them in Latin ' to climb on a tower and look to the stars '.

And indeed there was a tower. Obedient to the mysterious command, they climbed to the top and saw the sea stretching out beneath them. Scattered over the water they saw green and brown patches, solid masses which they recognised as islands. They accordingly resolved to take their chance in the boats which Providence had apparently provided for them, and rowed towards the islands. The largest of them seemed to have the right conditions for a comfortable settlement. They stayed there, and to commemorate the supernatural voice which had commanded them to climb the tower, they called the island *Turris* (Latin for tower), then, noticing that it was not as large as they had at first believed, they called it *Torricellum* (little tower), or Torcello in Italian. [1]

Quite soon, and well in advance of Venice, Torcello became one of the most prosperous and powerful island settlements. Today, a visitor strolling in its meagre fruit gardens, cultivated by a handful of inhabitants, some of them subject to malaria, would have difficulty in believing that this was once an extremely active centre of economic and political life. Though today it is pervaded by an atmosphere of poverty, fever and neglect, Torcello was once a flourishing city of twenty thousand inhabitants. Of the former splendours recorded by tradition, there is nothing left today apart from two magnificent churches—evidence of the city's wealth and importance, and of the thriving population it once held. Raised to the dignity of a bishopric, it came under the special care of Bishop Paolo. It was he who called upon his flock, when the two churches were being built, to fetch from the mainland the stone which was lacking on the marshy island. It is fitting that Paolo Altino's relics still remain in the splendid Basilica dedicated to S. Maria Assunta, built in 639 (and extensively restored in the ninth and eleventh centuries) in the superb Veneto-Byzantine style whose restraint and harmony we admire so much today. Its mosaics are among the most beautiful in the world, and the huge picture of the Last Judgment which covers the interior of the south-west wall, and is contemporary with the Venetian mosaics of St. Mark's Cathedral, was well designed to impress the people of Torcello as they thronged in their thousands into the Basilica. Today the huge shell resounds only to the footsteps of occasional visitors who come to marvel at its art.

The other church of Torcello, Santa Fosca, circular in shape and not in basilica form like the Assunta, is of more recent date. It has its origins in the early twelfth century, and its grace and harmony prove how far Torcello still preserved its wealth and prestige among the peoples of the lagoon during this period. It achieved this in spite of the jealousy of Venice; she had applied herself to the systematic ruin of the rival island, whose power and prosperity cast a shadow over Venetian ambition. It was not to Torcello, however, that the empire of the seas had been promised, but to the cluster of islands of Rivoalto, so welcoming to the Paduans, which later became known as Rialto, and finally as Venezia: Venice.

Whilst the Altinians were building a new capital at Torcello, the splendid cities of the Veneti had been sacked, and for a century there was never a period long or stable enough for the Aquileians or the Altinians to accomplish the reconstruction of their destroyed cities. Eventually they grew accustomed to the life they led on the islands of the lagoon where they had found refuge. Though they were deprived of comfort, convenience or space, they still enjoyed complete security; they were safe from attack by the barbarians, and at an appreciable distance from the shore where the Mongols impatiently and angrily reared their horses at the sea which they were unable to cross.

The lagoon which lies between the mainland and the row of islands separating it from the sea was formed by a huge accumulation of muddy water shed along the coast by the great rivers of Italy, which appear to have arranged a meeting-place at this point: the Adige, the Po, the Isonzo, the Tagliamento and the Piave. For thousands of years the tide deposited silt along the coast, which became marshy, and at certain points the deposits gathered into masses which were stable and dense enough to form islands. Passage between the islands of the lagoon was very difficult for there were great stretches of shifting sand near the surface where ships easily ran aground, and it was necessary to have a very good knowledge of the channels where they could pass safely in order to escape the danger of being caught in the mud. [2]

The belt of small islands protected the lagoon from the storms of the high seas, though it was subject to the tide, and life there was quite easy as long as one's needs were not too great. During the period where the history of Venice begins, the habitable islands of the lagoon were occupied by peoples who had probably been settled there since time immemorial. They lived by fishing and hunting sea birds, and made up for anything they lacked by gathering salt, which they sold to their neighbours. In this way they foreshadowed the trade which was to become one of the fundamentals of Venice's economy, for the Republic imperiously asserted its claim to a monopoly in the production and sale of salt. [3]

The islanders were a hospitable people, and when the refugees from mainland Venetia came to them for help they allowed them to settle on their territory. The islands of the lagoon accordingly welcomed the citizens of all the great cities which were laid waste; the Altinians chose the island of Murano, the Aquileians that of Grado, and the Paduans the little archipelago of Rivoalto, later destined to become Venice. In a way, then, the Venetian mainland was in some measure rebuilt in the middle of the lagoon. The temporary settlement was in fact to be permanent: since time was passing and the barbarians were still occupying the lands where they had come to rest, the wisest course of action was to organize the community so that it could live in peace and harmony. Far more civilized than the fishermen, hunters and salt-makers of the lagoon, the newcomers from the mainland taught them the rudiments of the social life which they themselves had enjoyed in their ancient and splendid cities. The result was a curious racial blend of the refined and cultured mainland Veneti, and the primitive, probably still almost savage islanders of the lagoon.

The first principle which was firmly established by the maritime Veneti in their rudimentary constitution was a respect for liberty. It was in order to remain free that they had fled from the invading barbarians; and the original inhabitants had so far enjoyed complete freedom, with no restrictions on their fishing or hunting for sea birds. For the new Veneti, then, regardless of the peoples or reasons involved, freedom was a sacred necessity. They also declared that since the disaster had wiped out all social differences, those who had settled on the islands and their original inhabitants were to look on one another as equals. Hence, from her very earliest days, the fundamentals of Venice's political thought, and the constitutional precepts which were to govern the state for fourteen centuries were laid down.

With the hope of reconquering the mainland from the barbarians becoming increasingly remote, and faced with the need for defence against them in case they succeeded in fitting out a fleet and occupying the islands, the temporary settlement gradually became firmly established, built to last and to continue growing stronger. The Lombards, moreover, had really created a kingdom for themselves: it was strong, well organized and sought to increase its conquests. The Huns were nomadic; the Lombards were more disposed to settle down if the land appealed to them. The island state of the maritime Veneti was protected by its very poverty and apparent insignificance from the covetousness of the Germans who held the mainland. Having relinquished all thoughts of returning, the Veneti set to the task of rebuilding in the lagoon the social structure which was the basis of their state. Grado became the religious centre; Torcello assumed commercial supremacy; and at Heracleia there was a genuine government.

Within a century of settling on the islands, the refugees had adapted themselves to their new way of life. They had found an amicable *modus vivendi* with the original inhabitants, they had brought them a civilisation previously unknown to them, and they had developed the embryonic commerce which the islands already possessed. A letter which was sent to them by Cassiodorus, the Chancellor of the Empire, reveals the nostalgia for a simple life, free from all cares or ambitions, which was the Romans' dream.

'Where you live,' said Cassiodorus, ' the movement of the tide in turn reveals and conceals the surface of the fields. Your houses are like the nests of sea birds,

1. St. Mark's Square, showing the Cathedral and the Campanile. The Piazza—no other square in Venice is called by this name—is the hub of the city's life. From the eighteenth century onwards, the famous cafés there have been the favourite haunts of Venetians and foreigners alike.

18

which sometimes seem bound to the earth, and sometimes float over the waves. Your dwellings can be seen from afar; they are scattered over the hugeness of the seas, and this is no freak of nature but a product of human effort. You use interwoven rushes to secure the land and fearlessly offer this fragile barrier to the sea... One could even believe that your boats glide over the fields; their hulls can barely be seen. You have little use for the oar: you haul your craft with ropes; and rather than use the sail, you move your boats forward at the pace of your boatmen.'

It is intriguing to observe the mixture of precise detail and fancy with which this official of the Empire describes their way of life to the Veneti, who knew it, after all, better than anyone else. He refers to the methods they used to strengthen the soil of the islands, which were always threatened by the seas. The shifting soil did indeed have to be stabilized; it tended to be increased by the accumulating silt, and at the same time diminished by the movement of the tides. The interwoven bundles of rushes to which Cassiodorus refers, and which provided such inadequate protection, were replaced by trees imported from the mainland; these were for the most part larches and firs from Carso, which were proof against rot. These fine woods, together with cedars, when once they could fetch them from the East, were the materials the Venetians used to fortify their islands.

For the inhabitants of the Venetian islands, as for all typically seafaring peoples like the English and Dutch, the future lay in commerce. They had a means of exchange, the basis of which was fish and salt, and most important of all, they fitted out ships which transported their own goods and also proved serviceable in profitable barter arrangements. It was Cassiodorus once again who wrote, when chartering one of the fleets of the Veneti for the export of wine and oil: 'We have given instructions for the wines and oils of Istria, which are in great abundance this year, to be conveyed to Ravenna: as you have a large number of vessels within the area of this coast, do everything necessary to transport whatever the inhabitants of Istria can pass into your hands without delay. You will share the profits of this undertaking with them, since only your help could bring it to a satisfactory conclusion. Make haste to carry out this short voyage, you who are accustomed to making such long ones. Prepare your craft quickly, those boats which you moor at the very doors of your houses as we tether our horses, and make ready to leave as soon as my messenger, Laurentius, gives you the word.'

This description of the islands of the Veneti, where canals took the place of streets in a mainland city, and where gondolas were moored at the doors of houses in the same way that horses were tethered elsewhere, still holds good for present day Venice. From its very beginnings then, this city was destined for the maritime and commercial activity which guaranteed its wealth and power for so many centuries.

*
* *

Whilst the islands of the lagoon archipelago were inhabited by a native people of salt-makers, hunters and fishermen who were in any case few in number, foreign states showed little interest in having diplomatic relations with them or concern about what they did. When maritime Venetia became a social and economic fact, however, and when the republic of the islands showed itself active in its relationships with the mainland, it had to be acknowledged that a new power had come into being. The Byzantine Empire, which held a large part of Italy, immediately entered into relations with the Veneti. It proclaimed first of all

2. Bronze quadriga on the Cathedral. This masterpiece of fourth century B. C. Greek sculpture was taken by the Venetians from the Hippodrome in Constantinople in 1204.

21

that it was taking them under its protection; later it integrated them in the province under the Exarchy of Ravenna and considered them as subjects or vassals.

Venice's ties with the Empire did not in any way result in a loss of independence; these were two states in alliance to give each other protection against common enemies, and in the sixth century, this enemy was the German barbarian. Just as the Venetian fleet helped the Byzantine general, Narses, to check the Goths in 552, so the Emperor and the Doge united later on to create a barrier for the Lombards.

The Doge, whose name we now hear for the first time, was indeed a very important man; he was the Chief Magistrate in the Republic which united the islands of Rivoalto and was called Venice.[4] The Doge was chosen freely, and with the acclaim of the entire Venetian people: this method of selection was known as the *arengo*, and the plenary assembly of the people was called the *concilio generalis*. It was made up of all the free men of the city, who met on the main island of Rialto, in the largest square—later to be known as the Piazza San Marco. Their shouts of acclaim would indicate the most worthy of the candidates who were proposed or who proposed themselves.

Byzantium was not perturbed by the Venetians' free choice of their lord, who ruled in place of the normal imperial governor of a subject province. It was important to reckon with the Venetians' spirit of independence: they had taken refuge on the islands of the lagoon with the express purpose of preserving their freedom, and rejected all foreign domination, even that of the Basileus and the Empire of the East. Having agreed to remove the tribunes, who were the officials nominated by the Empire, Byzantium did try to reserve to itself the right of appointing the Doge, or at least of approving his election. The Venetians made it plain, however, that subservience of this kind was an affront to the pride of their young republic, and the Emperor gave way.

The different titles which were successively held by the master of Venice clearly reflect the city's evolution towards independence and complete self-government. Until the beginning of the ninth century, the Doge was styled *imperialis hypatos et humilis dux Venetiae*: this was the title which was borne by Giustiniano Partecipazio, the eleventh Doge, who reigned for only two years, from 827 to 829. The title changed after him, and in public records it became *gloriosus dux*, or even *Dei gratia dux*. The word *hypatos*, which was applied to Byzantine officials, disappeared.

In the duties of the Doge, as they were defined when the Republic first came into being, a distinctive feature of the Venetian way of thinking can be recognized: the Chief Magistrate could have sufficient power and prestige to govern for the public good but it was important to ensure that they did not arouse inordinate pride or ambition in him. The people were so very sensitive in this respect that on the slightest suspicion of a Doge's abuse of power he would be overthrown and even executed. Assuming personal power or attempting to create a hereditary office—these were major crimes. The object of this was indeed to ensure that the authority of the Doge was delegated by the people and controlled by them; the Doge was to be nothing more than the instrument of popular power, the people's representative in the fullest sense.

As Maranini wrote in his study of the Venetian constitution, [5] ' all who participated in its political life were Venetians, and what is more, citizens of Rialto: the dominant interests were those of the mother-island '. They would none of them relinquish the right to self-government through the institutions which they had bestowed upon themselves: the councils and the Doge. Throughout the history of Venice, we witness the silent struggle between the Doge and the councils—a consequence in fact of the deficiencies of the Constitution itself. This was drawn up in such a way that the Doge was to be the possessor of wide powers,

22

designed to cope with any dangers threatening the town, but the sensitive pride of the people continually asserted the right to subordinate him to the truly democratic organs, which were the councils. The more the Doge tried to increase the powers he received, the more the people strove to limit his personal authority and restrict him to his role as an instrument for the popular will. This fear of personal power can be traced back to the spirit of revolt which developed in them right up to 725 under the Byzantine *hypatos*, the Imperial official. In 740, regretting the concession which it had made to the Venetian spirit of independence,

The courtyard of the Doge's Palace

Byzantium tried to reintroduce the tribunate system, but such a violent revolt broke out that the Empire was forced to give way. It was content to arrange things in such a way that, without rousing the anger of the Venetians, the Doge remained—in theory at least—a vassal of the Emperor. Full recognition of the Chief Magistrate as head of the Venetian people was proclaimed in 742, and from that time on, relations between Venice and Byzantium varied according to the degree of prestige and power which the Empire possessed at a given time. When the Empire appeared to be on the decline, Venice loudly trumpeted its independence; when its strength revived, Venice resumed its role as a meek and respectful ally. [6]

The principal difficulties which the Doge encountered in exercising his authority came pre-eminently from his subjects; where ' monarchy ' was concerned, the Venetians' view was much like that of the Romans, who had Caesar assassinated on the suspicion that he wanted to ' make himself king '. It was unthinkable for a Doge to become king, and since he was no longer the vassal of Byzantium, he was called upon to remain the servant of the popular will which had brought him to power—this, in spite of the advantages which the state itself might have enjoyed if he had been permitted a wider measure of power, transferable to his descendants. The Venetian people were not, in fact, very enlightened politically;

this was still the time when the maritime tribunes of the various islands gathered in a kind of patriarchal assembly to allot special authority to whichever one of their numbers they thought the best. This made him the *primus inter pares*— the first among equals.

The solemn religious ceremony of the Doge's coronation, his investiture with the golden *corno* [7]—a symbol comparable in its significance to the crown—his mystic marriage to the sea, and the honours by which he was surrounded, isolated him more and more from the general body of magistrates: coins were struck in his name and image [8], and in all important matters concerning the political life of Venice, it was he who spoke in the name of the State. This distinction and all the ceremonial which attended it gratified the Venetians, for it demonstrated the power of their Republic. But they were always afraid that he might become too inflated by his own importance; thus, although they dressed him in purple, gold and other honours, periodically they would bring him back to a sense of true modesty. Ambition and 'the will for power' sometimes proved stronger than the instinct for security, and it happened not infrequently that the Doge was foolish enough to take unto himself absolute power, and claim the right to pass it on to his heirs.

This began with the Doge Orso, who bore the cognomen Ipato—a reminder of his position as a Byzantine *hypatos*. He reigned from 726 to 737 and sought to proclaim his family's hereditary right to authority. His ambition angered the people, who were willing to elect several successive Doges from the same family, but stubbornly refused to make the title a hereditary one. During the ninth and tenth centuries, the *corno* was bestowed upon seven members of the Partecipazio family and five Candianos, but the principle remained intact: the people had made their choice.

This choice had ceased to be the sole responsibility of the *arengo* and the *concilio generalis*, as it had been in the days when Venice was no more than a handful of families, settled on the small island group of Rialto. As the State grew and the problems of internal administration and relations with foreign powers became more complicated, acclaim by the free men of the land was no longer enough. 'Councils' were set up between the *concilio generalis* and the Doge. Unanimous consent was only possible where subjects were truly equal, but such equality can only be achieved in a very primitive society, and even then is unlikely!

As trade and sea travel gave new outlets to the islanders' industries and increased their wealth, class differences gradually emerged in a community which previously had none. Those who distinguished themselves most by their intelligence, courage, wealth and endeavour laid claim to a higher place in the social hierarchy. Perhaps the Veneti from the mainland had in some measure preserved some of their caste differences when they took refuge on the islands of the lagoon. At all events, an aristocracy quickly emerged in the very midst of the democracy which had wanted to preserve its right to elect the Doge. The *concilio generalis* soon became a mere formality, with the people meeting on the square to ratify the choice which the nobles had made.

Until the end of the Republic in the eighteenth century, this formality was respected, but the acclaim of the populace did not represent its choice, only its consent; whether it really approved or not was of little importance. The aristocracy, now impatient to concentrate all instruments of State control in its own hands, exercised constant surveillance over the Doge, lest he exceed his legitimate authority. The bodies charged with the duty of supervising, as well as governing by his side, were the Councils—the Minor Consiglio first of all, and then the Maggior Consiglio.

The designation of the councils as 'great' and 'small' arose from the distinction

3. Interior of St. Mark's Cathedral. Massive pillars and lofty cupolas lend mystery to the pervading atmosphere of contemplation and beauty.

already established in early lagoon society between the *majores* and the *minores*; in other words, those who were of high and low estate—the aristocracy and the people. And just as in all societies where class distinctions of this kind exist, a struggle arose between the two castes or parties, who were secretly moved by pride on one hand, envy and jealousy on the other, and the desire to wrest from one another as many privileges as they could. In Venice, however, there was nothing of a 'people's assembly' about the Minor Consiglio; quite on the contrary, it represented, as we shall see, an aristocracy of worth established side by side with the aristocracy by birth. The common people, the workers, fishermen, merchants and so on, had practically no part at all in the government. This did not trouble them unduly, for as simple, decent folk they had no political ambitions. Submissive, easily led, they were never at the root of revolutions, and when an insurrection against a Doge broke out, it was a faction of the aristocracy which instigated it.

The troubles of the Venetian people were therefore quite unlike those which shook Florence, where the rising of the Ciompi was a truly proletarian movement. The Venetian's characteristic indolence, his lack of concern, and his philosophy of live-and-let-live meant that excesses of the kind which were seen in other regions were almost completely unheard of there. Behind the mob which marched against Angelo Partecipazio in the ninth century, and against Pietro Candiano in the tenth, there was the oligarchy of the nobles and the rich. This submissiveness on the part of the people of Venice was partly due to their conviction that all the organs of the nation were important for the smooth running of the State and the common weal. The caulker, the waterman and the workman in the dockyard or *arsenalotto*, as it was called, knew that they were as indispensable to Venice's existence and prosperity as the nobles and magistrates. Fired by a devoted and ardent patriotism, every member of this shrewd, intelligent and gentle society worked in his own way for the common cause; and the fact that one might have greater wealth than another was never the occasion for a sense of enmity. The circumstances in which the people were called upon to voice their opinions in the running of the state were rare. All that was asked of them was that they remain faithful to an old and respected tradition.

* *
*

The function of the Maggior Consiglio was to make laws and appoint almost all the magistrates. It was the highest authority in the Republic, theoretically emanating from and representative of the people—the replacement for the *arengo*. At first it was made up of members of the true aristocracy, so that at the beginning of the thirteenth century it had no more than thirty-five members, elected by the electoral wards of Venice, which were known as the *trentacie*. In the course of the thirteenth century, however, the Maggior Consiglio was increased by a number of new members who were admitted to it, either for their merits, their services to the Republic or even for their fortunes. Factions were formed in it, and they would contrive the entry of their adherents in order to increase their power. Here, then, was the beginning of the demagogic exploitation of public authority, so fatal to the cause of the Republic.

To check the inordinate growth of the Maggior Consiglio, the Doge Pietro Gradenigo resolved to reduce it to its normal size, and at a historic meeting in February 1297, he decided that the Maggior Consiglio would henceforth be restricted. This is known as the *serrata*, or locking, of the Maggior Consiglio. The *serrata* did not lead to a smaller number of members, but it did establish

4. The bulbous cupolas and marble pinnacles which crown the Basilica are an odd mixture of Gothic and Byzantine. Of particular interest are the multiple crosses on the domes, which are of a kind seen only in Venice.

the conditions on which membership was possible. The *serrata* consolidated the position of those who had gained entry, but made it inaccessible to new members. Members had to have occupied a seat for four years before 1297 or else have had ancestors who had been members. The Maggior Consiglio thus became a repository of hereditary privilege and it was sanctioned by the institution of the Book of Gold; in this were written the names of all those who were worthy of membership. This was the famous Book of Gold of the Venetian aristocracy which Bonaparte burned in the name of liberty, equality and fraternity when he gained control of Venice in 1797. It was at this time that he also burned the Bucintoro, which Venice regarded as almost sacred.

The Minor Consiglio, originally consisting of ten members (while the Maggior Consiglio had as many as two thousand in 1542) was made up of men who were respected for their learning, their wisdom, and their political acumen. Their principal duty was to advise the Doge. The establishment of the *Sapientes*, the elders, was designed to create a legislative, constituent and executive hierarchy. The famous division of powers, so fashionable in modern states, did not exist in Venice, where, as Cessi has observed in his *Storia della Repubblica di Venezia*, ' every magistrate had duties in which all three powers could operate. ' [9]

As for the famous Council of Ten, whose formidable shadow weighs so romantically in the melodramas and novels about Venetian life, and which so incensed the French Revolution, it was created in 1310 with the object of protecting the State against sedition—a consequence of the plot hatched by Baiamonte Tiepolo, which created such a stir in the annals of Venice. In 1310, when Pietro Gradenigo was Doge, several of the representatives of the great families, with Querinis and Tiepolos at their head, resolved to seize power through violence. One night they gathered their followers for an attack on the Doge's palace. But an old woman who lived by the entrance to the Merceria, almost at the corner of St. Mark's Square, was intrigued by the noise and went to her window: she saw armed men passing. By accident or design, she allowed a metal vase to fall on them. This caused an outcry; the guard came running up, and the conspirators, thinking they had been betrayed, took flight. In memory of the old woman who saved the Republic that night, a bas-relief of her metal vase still adorns the façade of the house where she lived, just behind the clock-tower.

In contrast, the execution of Marino Faliero, which inspired so many poems and romantic pictures, represented the reaction of the aristocracy against abuse of power by the Doge. Elected Doge at the age of 70 in 1354, Faliero sought to strengthen his personal authority by gaining the support of the common people and thereby counterbalancing the power of the nobles. If he had succeeded, an extremely powerful Doge would have ruled over a democracy in which all class barriers had disappeared. The Council of Ten, which was specially created to watch out for any seditious movements after the plot of Baiamonte Tiepolo, discovered Faliero's scheme and denounced him. The Council, implacable whenever a Doge exceeded his authority, condemned Marino Faliero to death, and ordered that he be decapitated at the top of the great staircase, known as the Giants' Staircase, in the courtyard of the Palace; his name was to be struck from the list of Doges and his pictures was to be blackened wherever it had been painted.

5. Detail of the Pala d'Oro in front of the High Altar. Several generations of Doges and nobles enriched this extraordinary golden screen with precious stones, enamels and additional gold. The work was done first by Byzantine craftsmen, then by their Venetian pupils; the result is heterogeneous, but sumptuous.

The sentence was a terrible one, and it seems possible that it was rivalry between equally powerful families, as much as civic zeal, which led to Faliero's execution. In the collection of portraits which decorate one of the most sumptuous halls in the Doge's Palace, the place occupied by Marino Faliero's picture remains empty, as though he had never reigned—as though he had never lived. His foolhardy plotting had ended in his banishment from the memory of the people of Venice.

Such severity can only be explained by the absolute need to preserve complete cohesion at all times between the various organs of the State, and the strict subordination in which certain of them were to stand to the others. There was always a danger of treachery, and Baiamonte Tiepolo is known to have conspired with the enemies of Venice. The dread aroused by mention of the Council of Ten and the State Inquisition was often sufficient to maintain order, even among the most unruly sections of society. Today, on the Riva degli Schiavoni, separated from the Doge's Palace by the little canal which is crossed by the Bridge of Sighs, we can see the huge and awesome architecture of the Prisons. They were built by Antonio da Ponte in 1597, as the permanent seat of the magistrature, ' the Lords

The Libreria Vecchia from the Molo. Brownish-black ink over pencil; 7^1/$_2$″ x 10^3/$_4$″; Canaletto.

of the Night, ' who passed immediate judgment on those who had been caught red-handed. They stand as a reminder of how swift and terrible Venetian justice could be.

Informing was encouraged, and to save the informer from making himself known, openings were contrived in the Palace walls to connect with the boxes in which letters were delivered. Every accusation was followed up, even if the accused was an official of the highest rank. [10] In the same way, every imaginable precaution was taken when magistrates were being chosen, so that law and tradition could be rigorously observed. The election of the Doge by the Maggior Consiglio, for example, was only confirmed after nine different ballots. These were very complicated and very carefully supervised; they were introduced in 1172 in place of the popular assembly, following the trouble which resulted from the murder of Doge Vitale Michiel II.

The respective powers of the Quarantia Vecchia and the Quarantia Nuova, the Savi Grandi and the Savi di Terraferma, the Procuratori and the Pregadi, the Avogadori di Comun and the Inquisitors were determined in such a way

6. The Baptistery.
There are mosaics here which date from the Renaissance and even from the Baroque era; a clear indication of the extent to which this traditional Venetian technique continued to flourish. Many talented mosaicists still work in Venice today.

that every high-ranking citizen had a definite function within the state machine. Complete flexibility and precision were all-important in each of these bodies to ensure that the complex political system of the Most Serene Republic maintained maximum efficiency.

Institutions and different departments of the government were sometimes modified through the centuries, according to the changing needs of the Republic, but the essential structure of the State remained much as it was at the very beginning of Venice's political life. It was always a matter of major concern to preserve a balance of strength between the Doge and the Councils, and between the people and the aristocracy, to prevent one from gaining power which it could use at the expense of the other. In this way, during the twelve centuries of its existence as an independent state, Venice avoided the terrible revolutions which were the scourge of other countries. There were no brutal changes of régime, no military invasions. Up to 1797, no foreign soldiers, other than the city's own mercenaries, ever entered Venice. It was in this way that she preserved the fullest confidence in her wisdom, security and invincible strength. Storms raged round her but she was never troubled by them. Always ready for change, always adaptable to unforeseen circumstances, the structure of her political institutions was firmly rooted in the past yet ever prepared to face the future.

THE MOST SERENE REPUBLIC

FROM THE TIME when it entered the orbit of the Byzantine Empire, Venice, in its art, way of life and politics, became a kind of dependency of Constantinople. The latter, in its turn, assured its ally of friendship and protection. Venice was for all that strong enough to keep a comfortable distance between itself and its main enemies, the Dalmatian adventurers and their pirate squadrons, and the Lombard kingdom, which was equally hostile to the young republic of the lagoon and to the Exarchate of Ravenna—Byzantium's extension on Italian soil.

The capital of the young Republic changed places as its politics evolved. From Heracleia it was transferred to Malamoco, on an island situated between the lagoon and the sea; then, on the initiative of Doge Agnelo (or Angelo) Partecipazio, who reigned from 811 to 827, it was finally established on the island group of Rivoalto, separated from the sea by the stretch of the lagoon and by an island barrier which guaranteed its permanent security from attack and provided a safe port in which its ships could anchor.

It was Partecipazio's brilliant insight which recognized the advantages to be derived from strengthening the little island group with wooden piles and linking them to one another with bridges. Rivoalto thus became established on either side of the River Prealto, dividing the city into two and providing the broad navigable route which was to become the Grand Canal. The city fashioned in this way lost the name of Rivoalto, but it continued to be used—in the contracted form of ' Rialto '—for the bridge which was later to be built over the Grand Canal; before this it was crossed, as it is today, by boats connecting the two banks.

The custom of lining bridges with shops is not peculiar to Venice; it was known in Paris during the Middle Ages, in London, and even today in Florence, where the Ponte Vecchio still has its jewellers and goldsmiths. Until the thirteenth century the site of the Rialto bridge was occupied by a bridge of boats which could be opened for the craft passing up and down the Grand Canal. The wooden draw bridge which we see in the paintings of Bellini, Carpaccio and Mansueti was very convenient but unfortunately very prone to catching fire; it was burned down several times in the many conflagrations which broke out among the wooden houses huddled against one another in the narrow streets. It was called the Quartarolo Bridge at that time because a small coin had to be paid for the privilege of crossing it. One day, when a larger crowd than usual was thronging over it to see the cortège of the Marchese di Ferrara passing along the Grand Canal, it collapsed, and a number of people fell into the water.

33

It was then decided to rebuild it with fine Istrian stone and in such a way that it would stand for ever. It was to have very deep foundations, supported on piles made with twelve thousand larch trunks from the Carso Mountains. When the competition for designing the bridge opened in 1523, the famous architects of the sixteenth century, Fra Giocondo, Scamozzi, Sansovino and Palladio, all entered for it. It proved so difficult to choose between artists of such great talent, that after discussing, hesitating and arguing for nearly forty years, the authorities gave the commission to a man who lacked the reputation of his rivals, but whose name savours of predestination: Antonio da Ponte [11]. He accomplished a masterpiece with a daring single arch, lined with shops and always crowded with strollers.

* * *

The Venetians' first major concern had been to equip two fleets, one for trade, the other for war. Without trade, a city which has no hinterland, no agriculture and no industry is doomed to starve. Since it was separated from the mainland and compelled to live from the sea, the young Republic did its utmost to make the best of its unfavourable situation. The Emperor of the East demonstrated his magnanimity to his little ally by exempting her from customs dues and allowing her to trade in all the regions of the Empire except the Black Sea. This was a mark of his gratitude for the support which she had given him in the wars against his enemies, and especially against the Normans.

The merchant ships which sailed from Venice carried salt, wool, and some of the produce of the modest local industries. Those which returned were loaded with the merchandise of the east: spices, which the peoples of the Middle Ages consumed in great quantities, the cloths of Persia and Arabia, perfumes, silks and a variety of exotic wares. What Venice did not consume herself was re-exported to the mainland and made its way to the great markets of the Western Empire. Slaves were also imported from the east, and this was not considered either immoral or illegal at the time; the Venetians were particularly addicted to this trade, which was extremely lucrative.

As intercourse between the lagoon and the East became increasingly common, the Venetians established trade-posts in the countries with which they dealt. Caravans would go out from them, deep into the interior, and the inhabitants would visit them to buy Venetian products. At the same time, the peoples with whom the Venetians traded built warehouses and offices along the Grand Canal. Special hotels were opened for the foreign merchants who came on business: the Germans and Turks, who were the most important customers, had their own, and these had the benefit of many privileges, exemptions and immunities. They were called *fondachi*, from the Arab word *fondouk*, which was applied to this type of building in the East. Quite modest buildings to begin with, the Fondaco dei Turchi and the Fondaco dei Tedeschi became huge and magnificent. Famous artists were sometimes engaged to decorate them; Giorgione painted a fresco on the façade of the Fondaco dei Tedeschi, beside the Rialto Bridge, but the Venetian climate did not suit it and all that survived were a few almost indecipherable traces which have now been removed from the wall and placed in the Accademia.

Venice's activities were thus almost exclusively commercial ones. In contrast with other countries, she possessed no farmers and no *grands seigneurs* living on huge estates and reigning over vassals and serfs. Venice was quite oblivious to the feudalism which prevailed over the rest of Europe. Her aristocracy even practised the professions, which elsewhere would have meant degradation and loss of caste. Her most distinguished citizens were not ashamed to be shipping-owners, businessmen or merchants, and the ordinary people devoted themselves to the task of building ships and the manufacture of everything necessary for equipping them, as well as to the several crafts related to them. We have to remember that in Venice, all raw materials had to be imported: stone, first of all, for houses, wood for piles, and metals for tools and weapons. A state which has no mines, quarries, forests or cultivable land finds itself compelled to invent and apply quite exceptional ways of life. Venetian genius triumphed over all these difficulties and limitations. When we remember that the extraordinary power of the Republic was built up on a group of marshy islands where everything was lacking except salt, we can only marvel at a people who could accomplish such a miracle. If we may justly speak of the ' Greek miracle ', the ' Venetian miracle ' seems no less manifest or remarkable.

In the eighth century, the ' miracle' was so thriving that the Pope called upon Venice's naval fleet to recapture Ravenna from the Lombards who had settled there. Venice had held her own against the Franks of King Pepin, who, when he had conquered the Lombards, had tried to enter the lagoon and conquer the islands. In 899, she had repelled the Hungarian invasion which burst so violently upon Italy. She thus acquired a prestige with other states which strengthened her reputation as a ' great commercial power '. And by what was perhaps the most striking paradox in the entire history of the Middle Ages, this great power had almost no territory—at a time when territorial control, for states as well as individuals, was the criterion for wealth and authority.

It might almost have been said that the real Venice was represented by the ships that sailed the seas under her colours; the city's physical existence was limited to a handful of small islands, and to a few other islands scattered in the lagoon which were subject to her authority and strategically useful in her defence. The Venetians strove to increase the area of their city, joining the islands to one another by means of earthworks which were reinforced with rot-proof wooden piles. These were brought with considerable difficulty from the mainland. Houses were tightly packed together but a site was always reserved for the *campo*, in the middle of which stood the well. [12]

Because the Venetians visited the countries of Asia and Africa more often than those of Europe, they naturally adopted the customs, ways of life and styles of the East for their churches, their dwellings and their dress. It was, then, in the architectural style they had admired so much in Constantinople and Salonika that they built the church which was first to be the chapel of the Doge's Palace, then the Basilica, and finally—when the centre of the diocese was moved from S. Pietro in Castello to St. Mark's—the Cathedral. Venetian merchants were in the habit of acquiring relics from the East, either by purchase, trickery or violence. The galleys of the Republic would return home laden with the bones of many saints, as well as rare stuffs and sculptured marbles. These relics were distributed among the various churches which they were intended to protect with their supernatural powers. The more famous the saint, whether for his martyrdom or his eminence in the history of the Church, the greater was Venice's pride in placing the smallest piece of his skin or bone in her reliquaries.

It happened in the year 828 that two Venetian merchants (their names are recorded by tradition as Rustico of Torcello and Buono Tribuno of Malamocco) managed by stealth to seize the remains of St. Mark the Evangelist which were preserved in the Moslem territory of Alexandria. The body of an evangelist was sure to be a great safeguard for the future Queen of the Adriatic. Having escaped with the holy remains during the night, the two merchants wished to get them on to their ship. They met with Egyptian Customs officials, however, and were questioned about the suspiciously large bundle which was loaded on the back of their camel. Knowing the Moslems' horror of the pig as an unclean animal, they answered that it was a parcel of pork: the customs men were therefore careful not to touch it. According to legend (which has been depicted by Tintoretto in his wonderful painting of the *Translation of the Body of St. Mark* in the Accademia), such a terrible storm broke out that night that no one in Alexandria dared to go into the streets. The two Venetians were thus able to make their way to the port unhindered. [13]

Doge Giustiniano Partecipazio welcomed these holy relics with great joy and reverence, and placed them in one of the towers of his palace, which was at that time a fortified building. This tower was on the site of the magnificent Porta della Carta, which gives access from the Piazza to the courtyard of the Palace. The delight and wonder of the people were all the greater because an old tradition, very dear to the Venetians, said that St. Mark had once come to the islands of the lagoon. During one of his voyages, when he was spreading the Gospel in northern Italy, proceeding from Alexandria to Aquileia, a storm forced him to land on the very islands of Rivoalto. Whilst he was having some sleep, waiting for the opportunity to continue his journey, an angel appeared to him and told him that his body would come to rest in the very place where he was now lying.

It would seem that destiny had always intended the union of St. Mark, of the Lion which was his emblem, and of the young Republic whose standard was to bear its image. The merchants of Malamoco and Torcello had done no more than fulfill the designs of Providence in wresting these relics from the hands of the infidels and bringing them back to the place intended for them by the will of God. To provide the remains with a shrine which was worthy of them, Partecipazio began building a church in 829, and this was finished in 832. A century and a half later, this church and the Doge's Palace were destroyed by fire during public riots stemming from the reigning Doge's supposed ambition. Pietro Candiano IV was thought to be laying claim to the absolute powers denied him by tradition and the constitution. The building destroyed by the flames in 976 was built in the Roman basilical style, like the basilicas of Grado and Parenzo, and these were repeated in the new church, which was erected by Pietro Orseolo in 978. For its decoration, however, he called upon Byzantine artists.

It was Doge Domenico Contarini who sought to endow his city with a church which was worthy of St. Mark and of Venice's new power. There was an increasing tendency for Venice to become a second Byzantium as far as tastes were concerned, and it was decided to abandon the basilical style. The new church was to be in the style of St. Sophia and the Apostoleion—the great churches of Constantinople— and would rival them in beauty, wealth and magnificence. Unique in its perfect architecture and splendid decoration, St. Mark's Cathedral has been associated since the ninth century with all the great moments in the history of Venice. In the narthex, a red slab of Verona marble, bearing a lozenge of white marble, marks the place where Pope Alexander III and the Emperor Barbarossa met, when Doge Sebastiano Ziani brought them together in Venice on the 23rd July, 1177, in an attempt to reconcile them to one another.

It was arranged before the meeting that Barbarossa would bow before the Supreme Pontiff, but in order to preserve his self-esteem, the Emperor made the gesture less humiliating for himself by declaring, ' I am not kneeling before you but before St. Peter.' At this, the Pope replied drily: ' Before St. Peter and before me.' It was at St. Mark's again that the princes attended mass before departing on the fourth crusade. Instead of conquering the Holy Places, however, they ended by ravaging Constantinople.

Both in the course of its construction and after, the Basilica became a kind of museum, where the rarest and most beautiful things—the proceeds of profitable bartering in the markets of Africa and Asia, or booty from military conquest— were brought as offerings to the remains of the Apostle. To these remains were committed the destinies of the city; there they lay, and indeed lie today, beneath the High Altar, although they were lost for a time. There is an interesting story

A Palace on a Canal; Canaletto.

37

which tells of the disappearance of the Evangelist's body during some of the repair work which disturbed the old church as the centuries went by. The Holy Sarcophagus was mislaid during the repairs and was accidentally placed in the brickwork at the same time as some ancient marbles which were being re-used in this way. There was general dismay in the city when the loss was reported, but all efforts to find the relics were to no avail. This was true, at all events, until one day when an old woman praying in the chapel of the Holy Sacrament saw a light which seemed to shine through the marble plaques of the wall. This happened on the 25th June, 1094. The stones were dislodged from the place indicated by the miracle, and concealed behind them indeed was the precious coffin.

An incredible profusion of wonderful marbles, taken from the pagan and Christian buildings of Syria, Egypt, Greece, Palestine and Asia Minor, decorated both the interior and the exterior walls of the Basilica. Bas-reliefs inscribed with the ancient and holy themes of the Orient were embedded amid verd antique, cipolin, porphyry and breccia—all gleaming with a gentle, silky radiance. The floor of the church, paved with bold, magnificent mosaic designs, swelled as if it were rising on the surge of the sea.

Each of these treasures, so triumphantly wrested from the hands of the peoples of the East and offered to the Evangelist, has its own story. There is the Nico-peia, a Byzantine icon representing the Virgin, which was plundered during the sack of Byzantium. There too is the Painted Crucifix, which once belonged to a church in Constantinople and was taken from there in 1205. It received a dagger-blow from an inhabitant of the Canareggio district who was in a fit of blasphemous rage, and it suddenly began running with blood. The block of granite covering the altar of the Baptistery chapel, which originated from Mount Tabor, was brought back from Tyre in 1126 by Doge Domenico Michiel, and is said to be the very stone on which Christ mounted to preach. Two splendid columns of white marble, crowned with eagle- and lion-headed capitals, are said to have been brought from the Temple of Solomon. There is the ancient altar, once dedicated to Neptune, which was removed from a church in Asia and now bears the huge porphyry font of the Baptistery.

And round St. Mark's, as much as within it, there are marvels of Asian art: the two square pillars decorated with flowers and foliage, which Lorenzo Tiepolo took from the church of S. Saba of St. John of Acre and brought back as a magnificent trophy in 1256; the great shaft of a porphyry column, also from St. John of Acre, which is placed beside the columns of S. Saba in the corner of the Basilica and is known as the banishment column because it was from there that the magistrates pronounced sentences of exile; and the two groups of porphyry statues, fitted into the wall facing the Piazzetta, which represent emperors or soldiers; their severe but impressive style is a fine example of fourth century Byzantine sculpture. The fact that no one has been able to identify these figures precisely has been the source of a popular belief that they are four Saracens who were miraculously turned to stone when they were about to rob the Cathedral of its treasures [14].

This treasure, as it is today, after political changes of fortune and the plundering which sadly reduced it, is still one of the richest and most resplendent of all those to be seen in Western churches. The Sassanid flasks in rock-crystal, carved with branches and animals and mounted on enamels, the ivories from Egypt and Syria, the golden statues studded with precious stones, the gold-plated bindings of Gospels encrusted with pearls, intaglios and cameos, the silken materials which covered the relics of the martyrs, a reliquary of the Blood of Christ, which is perhaps the Holy Grail, and a profusion of magnificent sacred objects,

7. These carved marble screens, in the narthex of the Cathedral, once decorated a Byzantine church in Asia Minor. They were brought to Venice in the Middle Ages by merchants who took pride in giving their city, and particularly their Cathedral, the most beautiful treasures of Eastern Christianity.

MONTES · CVICOS·PREETOISCROS·VE RACIPINOECOZ BA·

O·ASRAM·OLNEIORE·ETITELLEXNOEICESSASETO·DILVVII· PONAMARCVINNVBIB· ETERITSIGRVEEDERIS VROSITVLRA AQ·VE OLLVVI·

CASTVDRO POLVLV

8

the gifts of emperors and patriarchs: these are no more than a small part of what the treasure of St. Mark's used to be, but what cathedral of a capital city would not be proud to possess it? Fortunately the Pala d'Oro has remained intact. Beyond the High Altar its sparkling wall of gold and jewels rises up as a symbol of the fabulous wealth won by Venice through trade and war.

In about the year 1000, Doge Pietro Orseolo decided to give the High Altar and the Apostle's tomb a crown which was worthy of them. Accordingly he commissioned the finest jewellers in Constantinople to make a solid 'wall' of sparkling enamel and gold, ornamented with thousands of pearls, precious stones and ancient intaglios. It was erected with great ceremony beneath the ciborium, between columns of cipolin which were brought from Istria and the East. This screen, because of the fine materials used in making it, was called the Pala d'Oro, and from the eleventh to the fourteenth centuries the Doges of Venice lavished their care upon it. They sought to immortalize their transitory reigns by adding more magnificent enamels, and larger and more precious gems to the original screen. In 1105 Ordelaffo Falier had some large pearls set in it; Paolo Ziani in 1209 inlaid some enamel plaques which had been stolen from the imperial palaces of Constantinople; in 1345, Andrea Dandolo enlarged the screen with a similar one which he had taken from some Byzantine church. In this way the continuing growth of the Pala d'Oro in size and wealth reflected, over four centuries, the history of Venice's growing power and prestige beyond the seas.

The dazzling wealth of the Pala d'Oro, with its pearls, its gems and the mass of gold in which its enamels are inlaid, is a reminder that the Venetian aristocracy who built it were originally corsairs when the occasion called for it, and merchants urged on by a greed for money. The enamels, on the other hand, represent the very peak, in beauty and excellence, of an art which the Middle Ages, both in the East and West, valued above all others; like mosaic, and for the same reasons, it has the power to perpetuate images in a material which neither time nor the elements can change. Of all the substances from which a work of art can be created, enamel is the most proof against decay, the one which loses nothing of its original lustre as centuries pass, and continues from generation to generation, exactly as it was on the day it was first made. The enamels in the Pala d'Oro come from different sources and periods which are still the subjects of scholarly dispute. There is no doubt at all about the dating of some of them: the plaques bearing the portraits of the emperor John Comnenus and of Basilissa Irene, for example, are contemporary with the period when they reigned in the second quarter of the twelfth century. They came from the monastery of Pantocrator, not far from the Apostoleion, which Dandolo plundered.

Stylistically it is easy to distinguish original Byzantine enamels from Venetian ones which were made by eastern artists or by European pupils of theirs in Venice itself. The oldest ones, those produced in Constantinople, date in all probability from the tenth century, and are in imitation of the famous altar of St. Sophia, whose splendours were so rapturously described by travellers. Enriched and enlarged by wonderful gifts and by plunder, the Pala d'Oro, like the Basilica itself, is thus a kind of summary of the history of mediaeval Venice.

Among the booty offered by the conquerors to the glory of the Evangelist, the rarest and most magnificent objects are the four horses in gilded bronze which are placed on the façade of the Basilica; they too have a complex and fascinating history. These horses were part of a quadriga on the monument of a god or emperor, and for centuries their beautiful workmanship tempted the covetousness of invaders. This work, whose origins and the monument to which it belonged are still unknown, dates from the fourth or third centuries B. C. After the conquest of Greece by the Romans, the bronze horses were erected on

8. Mosaics illustrating episodes from Genesis cover the arches of the narthex. This lively treatment of the story of Noah and the Flood dates from the twelfth century. St. Mark's magnificent array of mosaics has earned it the name of 'the golden Basilica.' The vivid colours of the figures glow against backgrounds of dazzling gold.

top of Nero's triumphal arch; Trajan took them down to have them placed on his own, and from there they passed on to Hadrian's mausoleum. When Constantine established his capital on the Bosphorus, he took the famous quadriga there with him, and it remained undisturbed until the Crusaders captured Constantinople and burnt it. Only the height of the base on which they were standing saved the horses from being consumed in the fire which swept the town.

Naturally they were included in the plunder which Dandolo sent, along with an amazing number of precious objects, back to Venice. They were then placed in the Arsenal, where the military strength of the Republic was being developed. Some forty years later it was decided that the most worthy place for this important trophy was the Basilica itself; the horses were raised on to the plinth where they still stand today, but from which they have often been moved during wars, invasions and occupations.

Whilst they were in the Arsenal, the horses had some Greek marble lions as their neighbours; they too had been brought to Venice at the proud whim of conquering captains. Two of them, from Delos, did not arrive until 1692, when Morosini, known as the Peloponnesian, carried them off from Greece. The other two, less archaic in style than those which once decorated the Temple of Artemis on the island where tradition holds that she was born, have been a part of Venetian life for much longer; generations of children have found pleasure in climbing on the backs of these gentle beasts. The recumbent lion was originally part of a temple or funerary monument on the road between Athens and Eleusis; the lion in a sitting position originally decorated a building dominating the port of Piraeus, which was called 'the Port of Lions' for this reason. Its changing fortunes through conquest and travel brought it to Constantinople; on its sides it is still possible to read a runic inscription, scratched there by the dagger-point of a Scandinavian soldier in the pay of the Empire. These palace guards, big fellows with blond hair, distinguished themselves by crushing a revolution which even came near to threatening the area round the Sacred Palace itself. They were congratulated and rewarded for their courage and daring, and it was to immortalize this exploit that the story of the revolution and the glorious part they played in ending it was inscribed on the marble sides of the lion.

* * *

Who was the architect of St. Mark's? No one knows his name, but a sculpture on an archway in the façade is popularly believed to be his portrait; this shows an old man biting his finger and is more probably intended to represent Saturn. Legend has it that the anonymous architect saw the plan and details of the magnificent church in a dream. On waking, he went to see the Doge and offered to build the church, boasting to him that it would be faultless. Once the building was completed, the architect saw that, contrary to his expectations, there were some small faults which it was too late to put right. He went to see the Doge once again to admit his mistake, and because of this, a part of the sum promised to him was withheld. According to the people of Venice, this caused him to regret his untoward honest speaking, and he endlessly bit his finger for having said too much.

Mosaic, which was developed to such rare perfection in Venetian art, was also a legacy of Byzantium and eastern tradition. This is clearly seen in the astonishing splendour of the Basilica of St. Mark, which is completely covered with sparkling gold over an area of more than four thousand square yards.

9. The church of S. Maria della Salute, seen from the Accademia Bridge. Longhena's Baroque masterpiece, the Basilica della Salute is an expression of the fear felt by the Venetians during the plague, and their gratitude to the Madonna whose intercession saved them from the scourge.

Mosaic existed in Roman times, but this was an opaque variety of marble and stone; the mosaic of St. Mark's is transparent, made from cubes of enamelled glass, which catch every ray of light and reflect it in a blaze of colour.

Mosaic is especially suitable in a country where damp can settle on painted frescoes and destroy them. Nothing is left of the wonderful frescoes painted outside buildings during the Middle Ages and the Renaissance; most bitterly to be regretted among the masterpieces lost in this way are the great works of Giorgione on the Fondaco dei Tedeschi. Had they survived, we should perhaps have been able to solve some of the mysteries still attached to this painter of genius.

In every part of Italy which fell beneath Byzantine domination, and more generally, under the influence of the East, technique and style in mosaic work achieved striking brilliance: in Sicily, in early Christian Rome, in Ravenna and Aquileia. For a long time Venice remained faithful to this way of decorating buildings, thus delaying to a considerable extent the evolution of its painting as compared to that of Tuscany and Umbria. Because enamelled cubes of glass were better suited than delicate, perishable frescoes to the solemn breadth and harmony of the Basilica's arches and cupolas, this was the way in which the Venetians continued to decorate it right up to the eighteenth century—whilst the rest of Italy had abandoned the genre almost completely. It was forgotten, however, that mosaic entails a certain style, and that to excel in it, even for great painters like Titian or Tintoretto, it is not enough to produce in terms of glass what is normally painted on canvas or panels of wood.

The finest mosaics in St. Mark's Cathedral are the ones which have preserved the hieratical forms and striking simplicity of colour which reflect the spirit of the technique and the subjects represented. From the period of the Renaissance, mosaic work grew closer to painting; this caused it to degenerate, and the Venetian government, fearing that the art might be lost, gave the command that the Basilica of the Evangelist was always to be decorated in this way, and that every master mosaicist was to take at least two pupils, so that the traditions and customs should not disappear. At first wholly dependent on Byzantium for design and execution in its mosaics, Venice soon had artists, former pupils in the schools of the eastern masters, who were able to equal and even surpass those who taught them.

* * *

In Italy it is customary for bells to be placed apart from the church in a tower known as the *campanile;* and one of the finest sights of Venice is that of the cupolas of her churches and the spires of the campanili, rising up amid the russet and yellow of her roofs. Each campanile has its own individual character, just as every Venetian bell has a distinctive ring—from the sad boom of the huge ' Marangona ' in St. Mark's to the delicate sound of the cracked convent bells, calling the sisters to morning Mass.

The campanile of St. Mark's was begun by Doge Giovanni Partecipazio at the same time that he was rebuilding the old church, towards the end of the tenth century. As St. Mark's was the Doge's chapel during this period, it was decided that its bell-tower should belong equally to the Doge and to the clergy of the church. Started in 1148—only the foundations had been laid before this date—construction work on the campanile was continued until 1189 under Adeodato, an architect from Val d'Intelvi. The work was so perfectly accomplished that it needed no alteration, and survived several fires, especially that of 1400, without

10. The Doge's Palace, and the Riva degli Schiavoni, seen from the Customs House.

45

suffering any serious harm. The top was damaged by lightning in 1417, after which the coping, originally of wood, was remade in stone. On a number of occasions during the years that followed, lightning made fierce attacks on the bell-tower, but it seemed to withstand it quite well. A large crack appeared in 1490, and in 1745 the campanile split from top to bottom; insufficient attention was paid to it at the time or subsequently, with the result that the building completely collapsed in 1902. As the campanile was a necessary adjunct of the Basilica and an ornament without which the Piazza San Marco was simply not the same, it was rebuilt; in 1912 it was standing again—exactly as it had been before.

* * *

Adjoining the Basilica, and sharing with it the glory of being the spiritual and physical heart of Venice, the Doge's Palace, like the church, represents the work of several centuries, and each period has left on it the characteristic mark of its own genius. St. Mark's Cathedral was built according to the original design of the architect and in a single style. The Palace on the other hand was a secular and functional building—the seat of government and administration; it was therefore modified several times whilst it was being erected in order to conform with changing tastes and needs.

Practical advantage plays as important a part as a feeling for beauty in every aspect of the building; if, for example, the visitor is surprised to find that the splendid staircase built by Rizzo and known as the Staircase of Giants, is situated in a corner of the inner court and not in the middle, he should remember that when the Doge was coming down the stairs, he had to be visible through the Porta della Carta, which opened on to the Piazzetta, to the crowd thronging the square, waiting to glimpse their ruler and acclaim him. Functional considerations play an equal part in all the interior features of the palace; entrance-halls, council-chambers, administrative offices, the arsenal and guard-rooms, like the exterior decorations, conformed more with the individual ideas of the architects who worked on them than with the rigid demands of symmetry.

The alterations in the residence of the Doge ran strictly parallel with those affecting the State and the City. During the days of Angelo Partecipazio, at the beginning of the ninth century, there was reason to fear an attack by King Pepin's Franks and the Palace was built as a fortress, with thick walls to ensure the complete safety of those within. There was no place for beauty in it as long as the occupants went in fear for their lives and it was only during the reign of Pietro Orseolo I that a restrained decorative element was introduced. He had it rebuilt when order had been restored after the popular risings which led to the death of Doge Pietro Candiano IV, and the burning of the old church of San Marco and the Partecipazio stronghold. It then became so magnificent that the Emperor Otho III, who was a guest there in 998, was overwhelmed by its wealth and beauty. Following the embellishments introduced by Doge Ziano Sebastiani, the Palace in which Frederick Barbarossa was accommodated in 1177 (when he came to Venice for his reconciliation with Pope Alexander III) was more splendid and comfortable than the one in which the Emperor Henry V had stayed a half century earlier.

Apart from certain not easily distinguishable features in the main walls, and the oldest parts now incorporated in the Basilica (the Treasure is still kept in what was once the sturdiest tower in the first palace), nothing of these ancient buildings remains. As Venice became increasingly rich and powerful, and no longer dependent on the thickness of the Palazzo walls for the safety of her government—the masts and hulls of her galleys were her ' floating ramparts '— she could afford to forget strategic precautions and engage her interest exclusively in lavish display. These were the circumstances in the fourteenth century which saw the rise of the Doge's Palace (in its general outline, at all events) as we know it today.

During the first half of the fourteenth century there were two men responsible for its construction—Pietro Bascio and Filippo Calendario, and a third was given to them as an assistant, a certain ' Master Enrico '. Calendario was foolish enough to become involved in Marino Faliero's famous plot and shared his downfall, for Faliero was beheaded and Calendario was hanged in 1355. Architects and decorators worked in the ornate Gothic style which was then fashionable, but with the Lamberti, who were concerned in the last stages of the work (after 1424), the spirit of the Renaissance came into the ascendant and prevailed until the Palace was completed, both before and after the fire which caused such terrible damage on the 14th September, 1483.

A view; Guardi.

Antonio Rizzo, an architect and sculptor of Verona, was then called upon to restore and improve what had been destroyed, and he built the wonderful Renaissance façade of the court yard and the noble Staircase of Giants. Unfortunately for him and for the Palace, Rizzo dabbled in shady affairs as much as Calendario had engaged in politics. When it was discovered that he had obtained twelve thousand ducats by fraud, he had no recourse but to abandon his work and save his life by taking refuge in the Romagna. There he soon died before a pardon could reach him. One might indeed have come, for his work was needed. Thus the composite appearance of the Palace is the work of many succeeding artists, each one of whom showed such a strong individual cast of character that it was quite impossible for him merely to carry on where his predecessor had left off. Pietro Lombardo, Giorgio Spavento and Antonio Abbondi—known as Il Scarpagnino—all left their mark.

In the sixteenth century there were two terrible fires (1574 and 1577) which caused so much damage that the Signoria began considering whether it would be better to restore the Palace in its former style or demolish what remained and rebuild it in the modern style of the period: in other words—should the Renaissance bow to the Baroque. Fifteen famous architects were summoned together to give their advice; had they acted on the opinion of Palladio, the brilliant master of Baroque Classicism (and these two terms are not absolutely contradictory, for every style carries the seed of its successor) the old building would have been pulled down and replaced by a palace in pure Renaissance style. Fortunately more heed was paid to Antonio da Ponte, who wisely recommended that the noble residence of the Doges be restored to its former condition; and this was the course they followed. This was accomplished so successfully that in external appearance the Doges' Palace remains with certain variations in detail just as it was built during the Gothic Middle Ages and the Renaissance to the undying glory of Venice—a never failing source of visual pleasure. The interior decorations are for the most part, of course, the work of the great Baroque painters of the seventeenth century—Tintoretto, Veronese, Bassano and their pupils.

* * *

Because aristocratic families followed the example given by the Republic's Chief Magistrate, they copied in their own houses the fashion set by the Doge's Palace and its changes in style. The improvements which were introduced in the palaces of the nobility accordingly combined several styles with striking originality and no concern for 'artistic purity', which would have been artificial. These were the circumstances which produced the composite architecture and eclectic decoration in which Byzantine tradition and traces of romanesque art are allied to Gothic forms.

Today there is no longer a truly Byzantine palace left in Venice, but the characteristic form of its arches, and the symbolic sculpture with monsters either interwined or facing one another, have survived the incursion of ogival art and floral ornamentation. Whether they are absolutely pure in style or varied and fantastic, the finest Romano-Byzantine or Byzantine-Gothic palaces of mediaeval Venice are pre-eminently personal and engaging works of art which have no equivalent in any other part of Italy. They retain a certain oriental character which relates them to the buildings on the shores of the Bosphorus and in the Christian East —in Cyprus and Rhodes. Wherever Venetian commerce penetrated, artistic osmosis happened at the same time; Europe and Asia exchanged their art forms as well as their merchandise.

Venice's special situation as a cluster of little islands in the lagoon, and her established contact with all the ports of the Levant, gave her a blend of artistic styles of which no other country would have been capable at this time, and which is supremely evident in her public buildings. Churches, indeed, followed more rigid designs, for from the first introduction of Gothic forms, the Dominican and Franciscan orders initiated the construction of Venice's 'Venetian' Gothic: SS. Giovanni e Paolo, which the lisping Venetian dialect softens to San Zanipolo, [15] S. Maria Gloriosa dei Frari, S. Maria dell'Orto and S. Stefano.

Whether they were the work of the Franciscans or the Dominicans, these Gothic

11. Exterior of the Ca' d'Oro. This enchanting building, which richly deserves its name of 'House of Gold,' was built at the beginning of the Renaissance for a young couple of noble birth. Its grace and elegance are characteristic of the Venetian aristocracy's taste at that time.

churches all have huge naves, high vaults, slender columns, and wide windows. While the Basilica of San Marco is like a huge shell enclosing its treasure of mother-of-pearl, gold and jewels, and itself the most precious treasure of all, the convent churches are open to the light. And because the Doge and the nobility gave their protection and support to the mendicant orders who lived by charity, it was quite natural that they should be buried in the very churches where Mass was said for the repose of their souls. Thus SS. Giovanni e Paolo and the Frari in particular saw the rise of an extraordinary funerary architecture. Its developments and variations make an intriguing study: from the simple, undecorated sarcophagus, dating from the beginning of the Middle Ages, to the Gothic luxuriance of scrolls and pinnacles; to the calm, logical beauty of the Renaissance; and to the extravagant paradox of the Baroque. These tombs furnish us with very valuable information about Venetian sculpture; statuary there was far less advanced than painting.

In this respect Venice differs again from Tuscany; whilst the latter is above all a land of sculptors, the Venetians prefer painting. The geography of Florence and Venice to some extent explain this difference; the solid forms of stone encourage the plastic arts, while the perpetual motion and constantly changing colours of the water, here as in England and Holland, produced painters rather than sculptors. That is why a great many of those who worked in Venice show their origins in their names: the Pisani during the Middle Ages and the Lombardi in the Renaissance. But Paolo and Giacobello delle Massegne, who carved the figures of the apostles at the entrance to the chancel of St. Mark's were true Venetians who had accepted the discipline of a foreign school. The Bregnos were from Verona.

*
* *

Because mosaic technique used a hieratical stylisation of figures, denying perspective and placing forms in a world without depth or duration, Venetian painting continued—long after it had displaced the enamelled glass cube—to conform with the same ideal, forswearing any tendency towards realism. For a long time the painters of the Middle Ages remained blind to the natural beauties of the landscape and placed their figures against abstract golden backgrounds or skies starred with gold. They understood the limitations of mosaic, but although they were no longer enslaved by it, they made no effort to move out of its purely spiritual world.

In 1365 Doge Marco Cornaro, who believed that mosaic should be restricted to religious art, summoned Guariento, one of the mainland's greatest fresco painters, to Venice to decorate his Palace. The work done by Guariento was considered by his contemporaries to be superb, but the ravages of time and damp have effaced it and to-day there is not enough left of it to form a true estimate of its value.

As for Paolo and Lorenzo Veneziano, their art was still quite close to that of Byzantium and the icons. Paolo worked for some time in Constantinople where his work acquired a stiffness which was full of dignity and distinction. Lorenzo's work has certain affinities with the Czech painters—especially the Master of Treborn. They did not aspire to the great monumental and decorative art of Guariento, but preferred to follow the path of the Byzantine and Byzantine-Venetian icon-painters who were highly esteemed in Venice. In the Museum of Icons, which is attached to the Church of St. George of the Greeks, it is now possible to study the transition from the complete anti-realism of Eastern figure-painting to the softening of the face and the gentler expression. This is recognizable in panels

12. Exterior of the Ca' Foscari. This palace, built for the Doge Francesco Foscari, is a remarkable example of fifteenth century Venetian Gothic architecture.

51

by Giacobello del Fiore, his *Saint Chrysogones on Horseback* in the church of S. Tro-vaso, for example, and his *Crowning of the Virgin* in the Accademia—and by Michele Giambono, an eclectic painter, responsible for the mosaic work in the Mascoli chapel in St. Mark's Cathedral, and for the very different, almost modern style of another *Crowning of the Virgin* in tempera; an interesting work to compare with that of Giacobello.

In the mysterious Semitecolo, there was a touch of folk spirit, and a certain dramatic realism. In the second half of the fourteenth century, he began to break free from the hieratical tyranny of mosaic, thus preparing the way for the Bellinis. At the same time, on the island of Murano, probably in the midst of the famous glassworkers and despite the distracting proximity of mosaics, a new art was developing. Engaged in it were the old Antonio Vivarini—whose work, though Byzantine in style, yet fell under the influence of Masolino da Pani-cale—his brother-in-law Giovanni of Germany, who brought echoes of the great Nordic revival to Northern Italy, and his two sons, Bartolomeo and Luigi.

The great screen in the church of S. Zaccaria, by Antonio Vivarini, and the Screen of St. Mark, by Bartolomeo, which is in the Frari, show the huge step for-ward which was taken in the studios of Murano, where the new Venetian paint-ing was developing under the influence of mainland Venetia, Tuscany, Lombardy and Umbria. The Vivarinis, it should be remembered, belong to the fifteenth century—a period in which there was a radical aesthetic revolution throughout Italy, far in advance of that of Venice, which seems backward by comparison. Alvise Vivarini died in 1503, and Luigi in 1507. The Renaissance was by then well under way and had made its greatest conquests.

There was still something mediaeval in fifteenth century Venetian painting, as well as in the architecture of the time, but this was not because the artists of the lagoon were indifferent to the discoveries being made elsewhere or because they deliberately avoided the new current of change. But for the artists of this island-state, separated from the mainland, inspiration naturally came to a very large extent from the East. Antonio Negraponte, a native of one of the Greek islands dominated politically and economically by the Most Serene Republic, as his name indicates, has more in common with the artists of Asia than Europe, and his *Virgin Enthroned* in the church of S. Francesco della Vigna is more like a Chinese or Indian image than a Christian Madonna. This spiritual and material bias towards Asia even affected the curious but delightful work of Carlo Crivelli. It belongs entirely to the Renaissance, but yet it seems at times to be stiffened and hardened by the desiccating influence of mosaic and the ikon's absence of any really human quality. Venice's aesthetic character had been so strongly marked by the thought and techniques of her early art that she had to make an effort to throw them off and focus attention on the great contribution of the Bellinis, who gave humanity to the faces they painted, and realism to their landscapes.

13. The church of S. Barnaba, seen from the Ponte dei Pugni. In the eclecticism of styles which is one of the charms of Venice, this church's classical façade, verging on baroque, harmonises with its Roman campanile. The Bridge of Fists was the scene of a traditional battle between two rival districts of Venice.

14. The Ponte delle Turchete, with a dilapidated house reflected in the water— a typical sight in this city of strange contrasts, where riches and poverty mingle in exciting disorder.

* *

It was an astonishing sight that greeted the visitor arriving in Venice. This great island, composed of many small ones, was reached by sail and oar. From the distance, as one drew closer to it, it offered a view of cupolas and campanili, rising above the iridescent waters of the lagoon. On landing, one was absorbed in the colour and tumult of a busy throng, hurrying in all directions, engaged in their crafts and trades. In the Middle Ages there were about a hundred thousand inhabitants who were almost completely occupied in business connected with the

13

14

sea and commerce. Unlike the city we know today, at that time Venice had many horses, for the aristocrats and the wealthy were afraid of soiling their clothes and shoes by walking about in the muddy lanes. Indeed, it was only in the thirteenth century that the work of paving the streets began—with flag-stones specially brought from the mainland, and for this reason reserved for the more important parts of the town. A whole century passed before the Piazza San Marco was paved with Istrian limestone, and was at last freed from the earth which had made it muddy in winter and dusty in summer.

The little islands were connected to one another by means of many bridges; these bridges were arched so that boats could pass under them easily. As they had no balustrades at this time, and for the most part were narrow and slippery, horsemen often had their work cut out to prevent their mounts from falling into the canals. Men more advanced in years, such as the city magistrates, were particularly conscious of this danger; they consequently preferred to ride on mules or even donkeys—slow in tread and sure of foot. Their preference was made all the stronger by the custom at this time of allowing one's pigs and poultry to roam at large in the streets, to seek their food in the rubbish thrown into the alleys during the night.

Certain bridges served as battlegrounds for the inhabitants of rival districts. On the Ponte di Santa Fosca, which crosses the 'Rio' of the same name[16], the shapes of feet carved in the stone can still be seen as a reminder that this was the site of the famous *lotte di pugni*; these were the occasion for battles between the inhabitants of the Castellani quarter and those of S. Nicolo—respectively known as Castellani and Nicolotti. There is another *lotta di pugni* bridge over the Fondamenta Gherardini.

The Castellani and Nicolotti represented the two factions into which the common people of Venice were divided. The Castellani were very envious of the parishioners of S. Nicolo dei Mendicoli because their head, the *gastaldo*, was the chief dignitary in the guild of fishermen; he had the privilege of escorting the Bucintoro in a special boat during the *Sposalizio del Mare*—the ceremony of Marriage with the Sea. Although it was nothing more than an honorary title, and carried no special privileges with it, the *gastaldo* was called the 'Doge of the Nicolotti'; the Castellani, who had no Doge of their own, were extremely jealous of this.

The *lotta di pugni* was fought as follows: the champions representing the two sides faced one another on opposite sides of the canal, and, at a signal from the referee, hurled themselves at one another in the middle of the bridge, trying to force their opponents back with kicks and punches. Since the bridge had no parapet, the heated battle soon forced most of the contestants into the water. When all had been well and truly beaten or soaked, and one side was in control of the bridge, the victory was duly acknowledged and both the Nicolotti and the Castellani celebrated it with feasting, illuminations, singing and dancing.

There was yet another sporting occasion on which the rival factions vied for superiority: the regatta. Still held with much pomp and ceremony on the first Sunday in September on the Grand Canal, the regatta was originally regarded as a competition of very considerable importance because of the opportunity it provided for a display of strength, skill, speed and agility—all of them very important qualities in seamanship. Light craft like gondolas and *sandali* competed with one another, and were followed by large, magnificently decorated *bissoni*, often manned by crews of as many as a hundred oarsmen.

It must have been a wonderful sight to see these vessels skimming like arrows over the shimmering water of the canal with their fine fabrics and gilded sculpture, whilst on the palace balconies, fine ladies leaned on Turkish carpets and Indian

15. Exterior of the Palazzo Contarini. This charming staircase, built in the shape of a snail shell, has given the palace the nickname 'del Bovolo.' The architect, Giovanni Candi, probably wished to imitate the 'leaning tower' of Pisa.

brocade, applauding their champions as they passed. The winner of the race received a banner as his prize, and he would return with it triumphantly to his home, where it became an object of positive veneration. Whoever came fourth was given a live sucking pig; it was placed squealing and wriggling in his arms, amid the laughter and banter of the crowd. These prizes still exist in Venetian everyday speech in describing some success or failure; a man who succeeds is said to have *arrivato in bandiera*, and a man who fails has *preso il porchetto*.

From these games it can be seen that in Venice, as everywhere else, the favourite sports were the ones which were most useful in everyday life. The *gara di pugni* and the regatta were the typical exercises of a seafaring people; they were specifically intended to preserve the perfect physical condition of the seamen who sailed in the warships and merchantmen of the Republic.

In spite of the tendency the Venetians had to throw their kitchen refuse in the canals, this was not such an unhealthy practice as one might suppose, for the tide crossed the waters of the lagoon and made itself felt, faintly but clearly, even in the *rii*. To prevent these from being blocked, the canals were periodically dredged and cleaned of mud.

Specially appointed officials were responsible for the sanitation of the town and the safety of its inhabitants. Venice was thus the first city in Europe to take the health measures now considered essential for a civilisation which is worthy of the name. Three *savi*, that is, officially appointed experts, were entrusted with the task of ensuring that no epidemics broke out—very difficult in a port where ships from all parts of the world unloaded goods which were obviously not examined by any board of health. The thought of the plague, which was the scourge of Europe in the Middle Ages—in Siena alone the epidemic of 1348 led to the death of one inhabitant in every three—caused the Venetians to tremble with fear. The *savi* thus had to ensure that no danger of the contagion was permitted to enter, and to remove it at once if by some chance it did.

Other officials, known as ' Lords of the Night ', had it as their duty to ensure the safety of their countrymen, and to protect them from murder or robbery in the night. Venice, like other European cities, did not have street-lighting until quite late in its history. Anyone taking a walk after nightfall needed a lantern or torch, for the lamps piously placed before holy images in the squares only gave a weak light. It was also wise to be armed and, if possible, escorted. As the title indicates, the Lords of the Night sat throughout the night in their own palace adjoining the prisons, which were close by the residence of the Doge. Criminals caught red-handed were brought before them, and if they were proved guilty, the appropriate sentence was passed immediately and they were despatched to a cell or the executioner. [17]

The law and order which reigned in Venice, and which was strictly enforced although the population was naturally pleasant, obedient and easy to govern, was a democratic one; at least, so it was claimed to be. In fact, the richest families acquired considerable influence by their wealth, and their dependants assured them preponderance in public debates. Naturally, as the population increased and the problems of government became more complex, the great body of the people was called upon to express its views with diminishing frequency. The subdivision into classes according to a certain hierarchy developed functionally, with each citizen occupying the post for which he was most suited.

In Venice the democratic spirit was not dependent on an impossible equality of condition and fortune, but on equal devotion to the common good. For a long time entry into the Maggior Consiglio was open to all—theoretically at least— and even into the Serrata and the Book of Gold. It is always in the interest of a financial oligarchy to establish itself on a semblance of democracy, and there

The Campanile, after being struck by lightning on the 23rd April 1745. Brown ink and grey wash; 18″ x 11³/₈″; Canaletto.

were certain situations in which the whole Venetian people felt itself to be one
—a single body animated by a single soul; this was true during the city's great
traditional festivals like *Giovedi Grasso*, the *Sposalizio del Mare*, and the *Festa dei
Matrimoni*, which commemorated epic moments in the nation's history. [18]

57

The festival of *Giovedì Grasso* was instituted in memory of the victory over the Patriarch of Aquileia, in 1185, during the reign of Orio Malipiero. According to the peace treaty which ended the war, the Patriarch had to send the Republic a bull and twelve pigs on every Shrove Tuesday. For the waggish Venetians, this curious tribute represented the prelate himself and his twelve canons. The animals were very solemnly received in the courtyard of the Doge's Palace, where they were then slaughtered in the presence of the Doge and the Lords by the *massaro*, or head of the guild of butchers. This ceremony was accompanied with great public rejoicing in the Piazza and Piazzetta. Among the entertainments most enjoyed by the people, there were the Labours of Hercules—often portrayed by Venetian painters—which consisted of an astonishing human pyramid, with a child at the top waving a flag. The end of the ceremony would be followed by the 'Turk's Flight': a young man would come down a smooth rope running from the top of the Campanile of St. Mark's to the loggia of the Doge's Palace, where the Doge himself would be sitting with the Chief Magistrates; he would then give the Dogaressa a bouquet and a poem. There were also *moresche*—dances by mountebanks disguised as Saracens, interspersed with fencing displays and comedy shows, which made the festival complete.

Ascension Day, abbreviated to *Sensa* in popular speech, commemorated one of the Republic's most resounding victories—the defeat of the Dalmatians in the year 1000 by the fleet of Doge Pietro Orseolo II. Following this success, the squadrons of the Republic took possession of Istria and Dalmatia and established the undisputed dominion of Venice over the Adriatic. This day remained one of the most important ones in the history of Venice and was celebrated with great pomp every year. First there was a huge fair on the Piazza and Piazzetta, where the stages set up by the mountebanks and singers were intermingled with the crowded stalls of the tradesmen. But the major event of the day was the Doge's symbolic Marriage to the Sea.

Lo Sposalizio del Mare was celebrated for the first time by Pietro Orseolo II after his victory over the Dalmatians. It was repeated in every succeeding year by the reigning Doge and it was as though Venice's sea power were magically bound by the consecration of this mystic union between the element which gave the Republic its prosperity, and the Chief Magistrate, who represented the State as a whole. It accordingly became customary for the Doge to board a splendid boat called the Bucintoro which conveyed him to Mass at the church of S. Nicolo on the Lido. Pietro Orseolo II had stopped there, when returning from his successful campaign, to pray to God and offer thanks for His help in the battle.

On his return from the Lido, the Doge removed the wedding-ring from his finger and threw it into the sea, uttering the ritual words, *Desponsamus te Mare, in signum veri perpetuique dominii*—'We marry thee, O Sea, as a sign of real and perpetual dominion'. The entire population of Venice, in a variety of boats ranging from the humblest to the most splendid, accompanied the Bucintoro amid cheers, singing, shouting, fanfares and the thunder of cannons. The Bucintoro itself was renovated a number of times through the centuries, always in the most characteristic style of the period; it was successively Byzantine, Gothic, Renaissance and Baroque. The last one, Rococo in style and dating from 1729, was burned by the French when they were occupying the city in 1794. Because it had become the very symbol of Venetian power, the invaders destroyed it, and with it the Book of Gold. The conquered people were shown, in this way, that their era of independence and wealth had come to an end.

Though every alteration of the sacred vessel brought with it a change in the style of its decoration, its dimensions never varied; perhaps because they were the *optimae* for a man-of-war or because there was some symbolic meaning attached

16. This superb palace in classical style, which once belonged to the Grimani Doges, is now the Court of Appeal. It was built in 1550, by the great architect Sanmicheli.

17. The Palazzo Dario. The façade of this lovely Renaissance building is encrusted with precious polychrome marbles. It is named after the nobleman Giovanni Dario, who had it built in 1487.

18. Along this part of the Grand Canal, between the Rialto and the Station, there are several old palaces which still bear traces of Byzantine decoration.

19. This statue of St. John, one of Jacopo Sansovino's finest works, stands upon the font in the Baptistery of the Frari Church.

16   17

18

to them. The boat was a hundred feet in length, twenty-one feet in breadth, and had two decks; the rowers sat on the lower one, and there were armchairs of scarlet and gold for the chief magistrates on the upper. The departure of the Bucintoro for the Lido was a signal for tremendous excitement in the *baccino* of San Marco, and this has been very well described in a book by Bailly:

'Over the whole area of the lagoon, from San Marco to the Lido, warships and merchantmen were lined up and decked with flags. When the clock at last struck the hour of departure the Doge left his Palace amid a sudden clangour of bells. Before him went his squires, fife-players, trumpeters, standard-bearers, mace-bearer, Master of the Horse, sword-bearer and curule chair. He was escorted by the lords; then came the Lord Chancellor, the Papal Nuncio, the Ambassadors and the high magistrates, and from the quay of the Piazzetta, this glittering throng in purple and gold made its way on to the ceremonial craft. The roar of a cannon gave the signal to get under way, the guns of the ships anchored in the dock thundered, the rowers bent over their oars, and the Bucintoro set off for the Lido. Behind it came the three large gilded craft belonging to the Doge, the *peatoni*, then the gondolas—also gilded—of the Ambassadors, the Nuncio and the Patriarch. These were followed by six large galleys, magnificently painted and decorated, their banners unfurled, and with Dalmatian soldiers aboard them. Fanfares of trumpets rent the air all the while. A second group of twelve vessels, large galleys, feluccas, and brigantines, was reserved for troops of the Republic, most of them Dalmatian. In the third rank of the procession, there were the guild barges, fringed with gold, their banners of painted silk, and bearing their bands of musicians. And finally, in their wake came a great host of boats and gondolas —crowded with men and women, with flags, flowers and garlands. The lagoon echoed to the sound of instruments, singing and shouts of jubilation; and from the Riva degli Schiavoni, those who were watching the spectacle greeted it with joyful clamour amid the repeated salvos of the ships' guns.' [19]

The third historic festival was the *Matrimonio*, which commemorated a victory over the Narentine pirates in 900 by Doge Pietro Tribuno. The Venetian coasts were periodically attacked by hordes of Slav pirates, who sometimes even penetrated as far as the city itself. The Republic waged a long war against them for mastery of the Adriatic. Whenever they had carried out an attack, the raiders took shelter along the Istrian and Dalmatian coast in river mouths which were well known to them, and where it was unwise to follow. The Narentines were able to act with almost complete impunity: they even went so far as to carry off young Venetian brides from church as they were about to be married.

There was an old custom which brought all classes together in truly democratic unity, and this dated from the period when the people from the mainland had been put to flight by the barbarians and sought refuge among the people of the islands. The tradition was that all marriages were to be held every year on the same day, the 2nd of February (the Festival of Purification), and in the same church —S. Pietro in Castello. This was the metropolitan church until its place was taken by St. Mark's.

In the year 900, early in the morning on the Day of Purification, and in accordance with custom, all the young brides gathered in the church with their relatives and maids of honour, richly dressed and wearing fine jewels, in order to receive the marriage blessing. Unhappily, the church was situated in a fairly remote part of the town, and during this period it was surrounded by small uninhabited islands, covered with bushes and undergrowth. The pirates had concealed themselves in these bushes and as soon as the ceremony began, a crowd of them rushed into the church, seized the young women and carried them off to their ships. They planned to sell them in the East, where Venetian girls were evidently at a premium in Moslem harems.

20. Statue of an archangel by Pietro and Tullio Lombardi, on a balustrade in the church of S. Maria dei Miracoli.

21. The chancel of the Frari Church. The light which streams in through the huge Gothic windows illumines the glowing beauty of Titian's famous 'Assumption of the Virgin.'

As soon as the alarm was given, all the men present, and those who had answered
their calls for help, took to their boats and gave chase to the raiders. They rowed
so hard that they caught them up and recovered the womenfolk. They brought
them back in triumph to Castello, where the waiting crowd were already in despair.
In memory of this remarkable feat of bravery, the custom arose of choosing

A Beggar. Pen and bistre over black chalk; Sebastiano Ricci.

twelve young girls every year to represent the brides carried off by the Slavs.
They were presented to the Doge, who gave them presents and entertained
them to supper in his palace. The charming custom of collective marriages continued for a long time, and in order to preserve its democratic nature and popular

64

appeal, it was decreed that all couples should be identically clothed, so that there could be no way of distinguishing their class, degree or fortune. Very simply clad, so that the poorer ones were not ashamed or worried by heavy expense, they gathered according to tradition at S. Pietro in Castello, no longer in any fear of attack by the Narentines. [20]

It was on such occasions, when the people were really united by the memory of victories they had achieved together that the democratic unity of Venice was manifestly confirmed. It was an artificial unity, perhaps, but it was still enough to prevent social inequalities, which were becoming increasingly marked as the wealth of the town increased, from creating the friction and hostility which might jeopardize the balance and security of the State.

The pleasant good-nature of the Venetian character, so highly praised by foreigners, tended to minimise social inequalities. Similarly, Venice opened her doors wide to all who would trade with her. The *metoiki* (or aliens) as they were called in Greece, were generously received and often succeeded in gaining important posts: the fact that the Moor, Othello, was commander-in-chief of the army of the Republic is sufficient evidence of this. Today, in the quarter of the Madonna dell'Orto, it is still possible to see the palace once occupied by three eastern merchants from Morea; they were three brothers, Rioba, Sandi, and Afani, and their statues still decorate the façade of their palace overlooking the Campo dei Mori, which was named in their honour. The people living in this district refer to the palace of the three Moors as the ' Palace of the Camel ' because a bas-relief depicting this animal is set in the façade overlooking the canal.

The motley crowd of foreigners who lived in Venice during the Middle Ages clung to their own customs, dress, and language. No one was surprised, when passing through the streets of the city, to meet majestic turbanned Turks in long flowing robes, bright-eyed gesticulating Slavs, or Germans in the costumes of Franconia and the cities of the Hanseatic League. This mixture of nationalities created a babel of different languages and an extremely cosmopolitan atmosphere; Venice was thus quite different from other Italian towns, such as Florence, Milan or even Rome, where the city's individual character was jealously guarded from foreign influence.

More than any other city of the age, Venice was physically, morally and intellectually wide-open to the outside world, and it was here that syncretism between East and West had its most salutary effect. Continuous intercourse with foreign countries stimulated curiosity, a spirit of enterprise, a passion for discovery, a need for the unending enrichment of knowledge. Life in Venice was thus always open to fresh surprises. Unlike other mediaeval cities, enclosed as they were by walls, and full of distrust for foreigners, Venice's only battlements were provided by the water, which was her constant invitation to daring and the longing to venture far afield which is the driving force for all great explorers.

*
* *

In the Rialto quarter, already cluttered with shops, banks, money-changers and warehouses, behind the old church of S. Giovanni Grisostomo and not far from the Bragadin Palace (still associated with the glorious memory of the martyr of Famagusta) in the Corte del Milion, there was a house occupied by a merchant family who were renowned for their courage, their enterprising spirit, and their taste for long voyages to the East. In this house, in 1254, was born the son and nephew of these bold, determined men—the famous Marco Polo.

65

The figure of Marco Polo is one of the most representative of mediaeval Venice and the spirit of adventure by which the Republic was inspired. Dalmatian in origin but settled in Venice for more than two hundred years, the Polos were held in very high esteem in the world of commerce. They belonged to a breed of intelligent men with inquiring minds who understood that the future of the Republic depended upon her expanding trade and that this trade had to be encouraged in every country that it was possible to reach. The history of exploration in the Middle Ages shows us that there were many men who ventured into unknown or little-known countries—moved by the deep desire both to win new souls to Christianity and to establish new trade between Europe and Asia, that land obscured by mystery and legend.

In the thirteenth century Asia was almost unknown; its attraction was for none but the foolhardy, who were drawn by the fabulous wealth of India and China, which was then called Cathay. Like so many Venetians whose travel took them less far afield, the Polos were not explorers or ambassadors in the modern sense but they acted as such to a considerable extent. Though they were not travelling in any official capacity, they carried presents and messages for the rulers of the countries they visited; they tried to establish friendly relations between them and the Republic, and when they came home, they provided very accurate reports on the geography of the countries, the ways of their inhabitants, their religions, trade and political conditions.

Marco Polo's father and uncle spent fifteen years in the Far East, and when they left again in 1271, he begged them to take him as well. He himself spent twenty-four years away from Venice. Young, and possessed of a lively imagination, he was fascinated by the extraordinary sights that met his eyes. He visited Armenia and Persia, spent some time in India, crossed the Gobi Desert, and settled in Mongolia, where he became a high official in the service of Kubla Khan. His descriptions of the ruler's residence in Chang-tu, and of the battle between Hulagu, the King of Persia, and Bereke, the Khan of the Golden Horde, are wonderful pieces of reporting. During the three years that he governed Hiang-Chu for the Mongols, the merchant was transformed into a very remarkable administrator.

In everything Marco Polo says of China, Indonesia, Japan and Central Asia, there is evidence of his acute observation and remarkable foresight in recognizing the importance which the men and things of these unknown countries were to have for Europe. He draws attention to the use of coal in China and of petrol in Armenia, and demonstrates the absurdity of the accounts given by armchair travellers of far-off lands peopled by strange monsters. Marco Polo's essentially Venetian character equipped him with the lucid objectivity which still seems such a remarkable feature of his memoirs. They were entitled *The Book of Marco Polo*, and were referred to by his contemporaries as *Il Libro del Milion* owing to the frequency with which he mentioned this number when speaking of the peoples and treasures in the fabulous lands he visited.

Three years after returning to Venice, he took part in the naval battle of Curzola between the Republic and the Genoese. The famous traveller was captured and thrown into prison. Whilst he was being held, Marco Polo overcame the boredom of his enforced idleness by telling the story of his travels to his cell companion. This man, a Pisan by the name of Rusticien, was so fascinated by the accounts that he convinced Polo of the benefit he would derive from having them published, and began to take them down at his dictation. And this was how the *Libro del Milion*, which was destined to immortalize the name of the Polos, became the chosen reading of the Middle Ages and of all succeeding generations. It was an exciting tale of adventure, a true picture of the political situation

22. Exterior of S. Simeone Piccolo. Called 'little' to distinguish it from S. Simeone Grande, this church was built by Giovanni Scalfarotto in 1718. Its classical style was inspired by the Roman Pantheon.

22

in the Far East in the thirteenth century, and the charming personality of the author himself is evident on every page.

* * *

Venetian politics in the Middle Ages were exclusively controlled by two equally powerful necessities, and it was on them that the life of the city depended. The first of these necessities was the mastery of the seas. The Doge affirmed this in the ceremony of Marriage with the Sea: ' As a sign of real and perpetual dominion.' Proud dominion was in fact the essential condition for political security and prosperity in trade. The second necessity, which was just as important, concerned trade on land; for this it was essential to have free communication with the interior, whether by roads or river routes.

Every island-state can be condemned to death by an efficiently carried-out blockade. It was all important for Venice that her goods and capital should circulate freely between her European customers and her suppliers in the East. To this end she had to be strong, so that none of her competitors could paralyse her by placing physical obstacles or customs barriers in her way. Since trade was the life-blood of the Republic, her entire policy was conditioned by her economic interest. The conquest of power, prestige and authority was a means and not an end in itself; her policy had to be handled with skill and resilience, so that it could be readily adapted to changes in the economic situation.

Throughout the Middle Ages, Venice was compelled to do battle against powerful enemies in order to keep her dominion over the seas. First she came into conflict with the Normans, who began by settling in Southern Italy during the first quarter of the eleventh century. Encouraged by their success in Sicily and Apulia, they sought to advance as far as the Northern Adriatic, take possession of Albania and threaten the Venetian coast from there. As descendants of the Vikings, the Normans were bold seamen, more reckless than the Venetians; they lived from conquest rather than from trade. Their plan was to block the channel of Otranto and close the port of the Adriatic in such a way that Venice and Northern Italy would be placed at their mercy.

The danger was a serious one: the Normans were unscrupulous adventurers, bold to the point of foolhardiness, ready to win or lose everything like the soldiers of fortune they were. They began by placing themselves in the service of the Lombards, but as soon as they felt strong enough to work for their own gain they declared themselves free of all allegiance and conquered Calabria and the neighbouring provinces for themselves. A threat to Albania was a threat to Venice, for the Republic was bound to be affected by the fate of the Eastern coasts which were so near to her own, but even more than this, it was a provocation to Byzantium, which held dominion over the territory.

At first the Empire reacted mildly, not fully realizing the danger. Venice was more clear-sighted and in 1075 she attacked and destroyed a Norman fleet which had made its way up the Adriatic and aimed at the Dalmatian coast. This was no set-back for such enterprising and stubborn fighters. Six years later, in spite of the efforts of Venice and Byzantium, they took control simultaneously of Durazzo, which occupied a commanding position in the northern Adriatic, and Corfu, the key with which access to this sea could be opened or closed.

To rid herself of the Normans was a vital necessity to Venice, and she was accordingly willing to accept the offer of alliance made to her by the Emperor Alexis Comnenus. By skilful diplomacy, however, she managed to give her

23. North aisle of S. Nicolo dei Mendicoli, ' St. Nicholas of the Beggars.' This parish is one of the poorest in the city, but its church is magnificently decorated in carved and gilded wood.

consent to a combined operation which was of equal benefit to both allies as though it were a concession on her part: to all intents and purposes, it was Venice who came to the aid of the Empire. It was therefore only fitting that the Empire should pay her the price she demanded. This price consisted of exorbitant economic advantages which Byzantium would never have granted if she had not been so afraid of the Normans: a free Venetian enclave in the port of Constantinople, exemption from taxes and customs dues on all goods exported or imported throughout the territories of the Empire, as well as substantial tribute and a few concessions to personal vanity in the shape of dignities conferred upon the Doge and the Patriarch.

Having got what he wanted, Doge Domenico Selvo [21] launched his fleet against the Normans in a joint action with the Byzantine squadron. For three years, however, victory remained undecided; it was only in 1085 that Selvo's successor Vitale Faliero, a bold, determined man, defeated Robert Guiscard, who died in the battle. Having lost their leader, the Normans asked for peace—or rather, were compelled to accept it. For the Doge this meant the acquisition of the Dukedom of Croatia.

The Narentine pirates—it was a clan of theirs which carried off the Venetian maidens on their wedding day—were Slavs settled on the other side of the Adriatic in almost impregnable strongholds; from these they would set out on raids. Their swift and daring fleets plied their way through the seas, attacking merchant shipping and presenting a grave threat to communications. The Venetians found it was impossible to catch them and force them to submit, so they first resorted to buying the Narentines' neutrality for a large sum of money, but encouraged by their impunity, which the Republic was compelled to acknowledge, they began increasing their demands. This was nothing less than blackmail, and around the year 1000, Doge Pietro Orseolo II set about the task of bringing such a humiliating pact to an end.

The destruction of the pirates sheltering in the mouth of the Narenta was nothing less than a spur for even larger scale operations. The government of the Republic realized that Venetian prosperity could never be guaranteed until access to the Adriatic was free and unhindered. To this end, the sea had to become a kind of Venetian lake; in other words, the eastern coast had to be in the same hands as the western coast. The Slavs who inhabited Istria and Dalmatia were a turbulent people, much given to plundering, in whom there were still many of the Asiatic elements brought by the invasion of the Huns. They were related to the Scythians and Sarmatians, and like these nomads, inclined to make frequent and profitable raids on the territory of their neighbours.

The corner-stone of the policy of Pietro Orseolo II was the conquest of the Eastern shore of the Adriatic, which would bring him the Dukedom of Dalmatia and convert disputed waters into an inner sea, entirely controlled by Venice. Orseolo took advantage of Byzantium's inability to maintain a number of Dalmatian coastal cities which were theoretically subject to the Empire. Venice substituted herself for the Empire and defended them against the Slavs. These cities, the most important of which were Zara and Ragusa, yielded enthusiastically to their liberator. The Italian fleet, based at Pola, gradually gained control of the coast of Istria and Dalmatia. It followed the pirates right up to their hide-outs and compelled recognition, with a due proportion of brutality, from cities such as Curzola and Lesina, which were reluctant to show their obedience.

Orseolo's victory was willingly approved by Byzantium; she was content to see territories which were no longer of any use to her passing into his hands. The Empire put no obstacle in the way and the Adriatic became a 'Venetian

Lake.' According to tradition, Venice's mastery of the sea, and its symbolical confirmation in the Ascension Day 'marriage,' was proclaimed by the Pope himself, who sent the Doge a ring for his 'betrothed.' 'Marry her every year,' advised Alexander III, 'so that future centuries may know that the sea belongs to you, as the bride belongs to the groom.' The Emperor also wished to show his recognition of the importance of the new ducal power, and he gave his niece, Maria, in marriage to Giovanni, Orseolo's son. It was by this means that the

The Abate Urbani at Cards. Pen and brown ink; Antonio Maria Zanetti.

elected Head of the Republic entered by a royal route into the ancient family of Porphyrogenetes.

By ties which bound East and West, Venice was struggling to establish a stable situation which would be beneficial to trade. This delicate balance was then imperilled by the curious social and religious phenomenon which shook Europe to its foundations: the Crusades. Trade depends on peace; a declaration of war on Islam, even for such a just and noble reason as the recovery of the Holy

Places, brought with it an upheaval in which commercial relations were inevitably to be disturbed. What attitude could Venice take when the western princes took their Cross into battle for the first time in 1100? It would be foolhardy to enter with blind enthusiasm into this holy adventure, but there was no absolute security in remaining remote from it.

Only the great maritime cities of Italy, Pisa, Genoa and Venice, had fleets large enough to carry the crusading armies into Syria. Fearing that she would be forestalled by her two rivals, who were challenging her trade in the Mediterranean, the Republic promptly fitted out two hundred ships which she sent to the aid of the Eastern Christians. The King of Jerusalem rewarded her for this by granting territorial rights in Palestine in the shape of trade-posts, and a third of the city of Haifa, one of the busiest merchant cities, as a free port.

There was another Crusade in 1122, at the instigation of the Pope, who requested the Venetians to go to the help of Baudouin II, but the expedition took an unexpected turn. In the meantime, relations between Venice and Byzantium had deteriorated. This was the fault of John Comnenus, who had threatened not to renew the privileges accorded to the Venetians by his predecessor's Golden Bull. Worse still, he conferred on the Pisans all the friendship and benevolence which the Venetians had previously enjoyed at the hands of the Basilei. The Pisans had, for instance, been granted a free port on the Bosphorus at the very time when the privileges of the Most Serene Republic were brought into question.

The Venetian squadron sent to reinforce the King of Jerusalem set out for its home port as soon as its mission had been accomplished, but it stopped *en route* to sack a number of Greek islands belonging to Constantinople. As a result of these skirmishes, the lion of Saint Mark flew over Samos, Lesbos, Rhodes, Chios and Andros. The Empire was not strong enough to engage in a war with the sole purpose of driving the Venetians out. Doge Domenico Michiel and John Comnenus therefore reached an agreement by which Venice's old privileges were restored and she was acknowledged as legitimate owner of the territories she had won by violence. On the face of it, there was harmony between the two states, but they were no longer true allies. On several occasions they were united in action against the Normans, but they were really two hostile powers, treating one another with animosity and distrust. The Empire was already in decline; the young Republic of Saint Mark was flying straight as an arrow towards the peak of its glory.

Their relationship was so precariously balanced that the slightest blunder from one side or the other could provoke a serious outburst. In 1171 a thoughtless, stupid action on the part of the Emperor Manuel Comnenus was responsible for a further war, from which Venetian trade drew an immense profit.

It seemed a tragedy at first, for all the Venetian inhabitants of Constantinople were arrested, and some of them roughly handled, their property was confiscated and their ships were blockaded. Possibly these brutal and clumsy measures were to some extent justified by the way in which Venetian merchants had abused the privileges they enjoyed. The chroniclers of the period, Nicetas Acominates in particular, claim that there were more than 80,000 ' Latins ' in Constantinople (and by Latins we should understand Italians) who monopolised trade, and offended the imperial power with their arrogance. Some hold that Manuel Comnenus needed money and resorted to this robbery in order to fill his treasury.

Matters were soon settled, but the seed of discord continued to grow, and barely eleven years after the disorders in Constantinople had been allayed, a new conflict arose. Provoked by the Emperor, it endangered the very lives of the Venetian colony on the Bosphorus. Serious insurrections broke out this time,

24. Burano: Fondamenta de Cao Molecca. A typical view on the island of Burano, where the women still work at the ancient traditional craft of lace-making.

25. Torcello: exterior of the Cathedral. When it was built in 638, the Cathedral was Veneto-Byzantine in style, but it was altered in 864 and 1008. On the right is the round, cloistered church of S. Fosca, built at the beginning of the eleventh century.

26. Some of the Cathedral's heavy stone shutters are still in position, like this one in the clerestory. They were perhaps a necessary protection against the sea-squalls which might have broken the transparent alabaster window-panes, and also against the pirates and marauders who were tempted by the riches of the Cathedral.

25   26

threatening the Sacred Palace itself; the Venetian merchants were perhaps only indirectly involved. The uprising was mainly against the successor of Manuel Comnenus, the weak Alexis II, who was unfit to reign. Constantinople was at the mercy of the mob's vengeful fury. As in all revolutions, they took advantage of the disorder to plunder shops and dwellings, regardless of nationality, and to seize the property of the Venetians along with that of the other rich people of the town.

Order returned when the instigator of the riots, Andronicus Palaeologus, seized the Sacred Palace and ascended the throne, which had been hastily abandoned by Alexis II. A long period of palace revolutions, conspiracies, assassinations and usurpations followed; after Andronicus, these brought Isaac the Angel, then his brother, Alexis III, to power.

Isaac the Angel's son was also among those who laid claim to the throne. He entered into an intrigue with Pope Innocent III, promising that if he gained the throne, he would end the schism and the Church of the East would be reunited with the Church of the West under the authority of the Supreme Pontiff. This was how matters stood when the Fourth Crusade began.

* * *

The three preceding Crusades had been more or less beneficial to Venice in that they brought her many trade centres in the East. The failure, or rather, the inadequate success of the previous campaigns led the Papacy to wage this new holy war on an utterly unprecedented scale. The flower of Christianity was mobilized against Islam; kings and princes set off with their armies and the people followed in a crowd, inspired with burning zeal. To transport such a huge number of men-at-arms across the sea, the leaders of the Crusade turned to the Venetians, not the Pisans or Genoese. They revealed their plans and needs to the *savi* first of all, and then to the *arengo*, which was specially convened.

It was a very moving scene when the Crusaders' petition was presented, and the old historian Villehardouin has left a striking description of it [22]. It seems that the Venetians were almost moved to tears by the sufferings of Christianity in the East, and they promised their help in a great surge of selfless enthusiasm. In fact things happened quite differently; the Magistrates of the Most Serene Republic drove a very hard bargain with the leaders of the Crusade. Doge Enrico Dandolo, who was a farseeing businessman and a statesman, recognised the advantages which Venice could derive from this expedition. As he was providing much of the money for it, he was made commander-in-chief: he was to be the 'Lord of the Host.' And as the fate of the Kingdom of Jerusalem was of less interest to him than that of the Empire, he planned to divert the Crusade at the right moment to Byzantium instead of wasting time in Palestine.

The financial clauses of the agreement were to bring substantial profits to the Republic: 85,000 silver marks for the ferrying of the army, its upkeep and protection during the voyage. For its protection alone, fifty galleys were to be armed. Nearly forty thousand men and five thousand horses were to be embarked. The private docks and shipyards worked furiously to get the ships which were to be used in working order. On the agreed day, the fleet was ready but the Crusaders had not yet raised the amount fixed for the first payment according to the contract. How could this confused situation be resolved?

A number of princes made certain requests to Dandolo; he listened to them sympathetically, and it is even possible that he had 'suggested' the requests in

27. The interior of the Cathedral at Torcello is majestic. Ancient pillars support the ceiling of the three naves and Byzantine screens of carved marble enclose the chancel.

28. South-west wall of the Cathedral, entirely covered with a mosaic representing the Last Judgment. It was the work of Byzantine, or Byzantine-trained, craftsmen and includes iconographic subjects typical of Eastern Christianity.

the first place. Between them, they decided that it was possible to benefit from the troubles in Byzantium and return Isaac the Angel to the throne. He would pay generously for the help he received, supplying the total amount of cash required by the Venetians. The latter also asked the Crusaders to help them check sedition in Zara before they left for the Holy Land, allowing a considerable reduction in the transport fees for this.

When once it was accepted that the urgent departure for the Holy Land could be delayed merely to please the Venetians, the very spirit of the Crusade was seriously attacked and weakened. Although priests sang the *Veni Creator* as the oars touched the water and the wind filled the sails, the truly religious meaning of the expedition had become subordinated to purely commercial considerations. Instead of making straight for Palestine, the Crusaders' fleet was bent on a different objective—one which was certainly unknown to most of the leaders themselves: the conquest of Constantinople, and not the Holy Places.

The ships were supposed only to call at Constantinople. Over forty thousand men disembarked there; among them were many devout crusaders but also quite a large number of adventurers. The form taken by the army's ' halt ' there is well known: there was shameless pillage and devastation on an unprecedented scale. As far as Venice herself is concerned, suffice it to say that the destruction of the capital of the Eastern Empire and the degradation of its imperial might served the interests of the Republic as completely as Dandolo, in his ambition, could have hoped.

It was with his counsel that the Crusade took Constantinople as its objective and not Egypt or Syria, and he himself was at the head of those who attacked and plundered the city. The old Doge was seen making his way up the ladders which were placed against the towers and forcing in the bronze gates of the Sacred Palace. His allies, the crusader princes, were so clearly impressed by his political and military worth that they even proposed to proclaim him Emperor. Dandolo, however, was too well aware of the sensitivity of his fellow citizens and the suspicion which attached itself to all those who aspired to ' caesarism ', to accept this flattering offer. What interested Venice in the paradox which concluded the Crusade was the material profit to be drawn from it, and this profit was vast. In the spoils of the Byzantine Empire, Venice found plenty to satisfy her covetousness and ambition.

In the division of the Empire's possessions on the Mediterranean coasts, Venice gained what she wanted most: coastal cities where she could establish trading posts, free ports where she could unload her merchandise before proceeding into the interior, and islands where her ships could harbour in every part of the eastern Mediterranean. Like the Adriatic, the Mediterranean became a Venetian lake. The old historians were not indulging in flattery when they said that the Most Serene Republic now possessed a ' quarter and a half ' of what had once belonged to the Roman Empire. Candia, purchased from the Marquis de Montferrat, Crete and Cyprus guaranteed even more definitely the key-positions which would make it possible to control Mediterranean trade and keep out rivals—or at least, raise obstacles which greatly diminished their competition.

Venice's policy toward her colonies was both strict and flexible. Her more important possessions were given governments based on her own; they were partially autonomous but subject to the supervision of Venetian officials. In Constantinople itself, the Venetian quarter stretching along the Golden Horn was withdrawn from the control of the Imperial Magistrates and administered by a *bailo* [23] chosen by the Senate from among the most distinguished Venetians.

The Republic's prodigious rise angered her competitors, and Genoa in particular, for she also aspired to mastery of Mediterranean trade. The Genoese

A Sarcophagus Reliquary in the North Transept of St. Mark's Cathedral. Brownish-black ink over pencil; $10^5/_8''$ x $7^3/_8''$; Canaletto.

intervened on a number of occasions in the internal political life of Byzantium, to attack the privileges enjoyed by the Venetians. Genoa supported the claims of Michael Palaeologus, and when he came to the throne in 1261 he accorded her all the advantages formerly enjoyed by the Venetians. The main dispute

79

between Venice and Genoa was access to the Black Sea and the chance this gave of settling colonies from which it would be easy to trade with Russia, Central Asia and the Far East. The main object of Marco Polo's travels had been to find the best routes for reaching Asian markets.

For more than two hundred years the war between the two great trading cities continued, with alternating victories and defeats for both of them. The Genoese and the Venetians were equally ruthless in their struggle for profit, bold in the schemes they undertook, and stubborn in their resolution. It even happened during the so-called War of Chioggia in 1379 that the Genoese fleet made its way up the Adriatic and came very near to Venice itself, threatening a blockade of the Republic's ships in their own harbours. The peace of Turin failed to allay the hate which always divided the two States, but it provided them with a reasonable *modus vivendi*. A victory won by the galleys of Carlo Zeno in 1380 and the surrender of the Genoese troops in Chioggia brought an end to a wasteful and wearing conflict.

***

The possession of the river routes leading to the interior of the Continent was as important as mastery of the sea for the free circulation of Venetian goods. It was to guarantee her security here as well that Venice pursued an extremely skilful continental policy in addition to a maritime and colonial one. Her nature was not really warlike, and she was not disposed to interfere in disputes between Italian potentates. Furthermore, she did not have any real colonial ambitions on the mainland. But passage rights were indispensable to her and sometimes, in order to have them, she was compelled to win control of the lands through which she wished to pass.

The Doges' great shrewdness, the generous terms on which they entered into alliances or won support, barter and trade through power, these were the main elements in Venice's cold, clear and practical continental policy. The Republic's intervention in the struggle of the Italian Free Cities against the Empire, her consistent opposition to the growth of the temporal power of the Holy See, and the steadfastness with which she maintained a balance of power between the great states of the peninsula so that no single one of them would ever be strong enough to threaten her—all these testify to the wise and firm line of action adopted by the Senate. The Republic supported Frederick II of Hohenstaufen, although she had no direct interest in the dispute, because of her *lungimirante*, or far-sighted policy, as it is described in Venice. She foresaw the danger which could threaten her as a result of the Swabian Emperor's lust for power.

Although it was natural for her to look towards the sea which was the source of her power, Venice was compelled to keep secure hold on mainland possessions in order to prevent her rivals from reaching the lagoon and blockading the islands. She also had to contrive passage-ways for herself across the chess-board of Italian principalities. The conquest of the March of Treviso in 1339, the defeat of Francesco da Carrara, who yielded Padua to the Venetians in 1406 and the capture of Udine and Friuli in 1420: these were pointers to the infiltration of Venice's power in Northern Italy, and to the patient, tenacious methods which she used to gain the territories she needed, one after the other, so that nothing could hinder the free upsurge of her European trade.

The produce of the East came along the caravan routes to her warehouses on the Black Sea and the Mediterranean, and she was the great turn-table for

29. Porphyry bas-relief on south corner of the Treasury of St. Mark's Cathedral. Much discussion has taken place between archaeologists as to the identity of these figures which, from their dress, could be either kings or warriors. It has been suggested that they represent the Basileus of Constantinople and the Emperor of the West embracing, but popular tradition had it that they were robbers who had tried to steal the Treasure from St. Mark's and been turned to stone as a punishment.

30. The gondola is the symbol of Venice. It is elegant, swift and beautifully balanced. The iron prow, balancing the weight of the gondolier who stands in the stern, is said to represent the various districts of the city by the number of its indentations.

29

30

distributing it in Europe. She was the main driving-force in a kind of circulatory system which conveyed silk, furs and spices from Turkestan to the Baltic, and from China to the English Channel. Ghent, Bruges and Antwerp were rich clients as well as the Hanseatic League, Amsterdam and London. Along the roads which wound through the mountain passes (particularly the Brenner), trains of mules and horses made their way towards Germany, taking up their burdens from the camels of Asia.

The movement of the fleets and caravans, stretching over a vast spider's web in which the Rialto, the Piazza San Marco and the Riva degli Schiavoni were focal points, was strictly controlled by the Senate. Centralized power and the democracy's rigid supervision compelled merchants and their shipping to comply with a departure time-table which was determined by law. What follows is an example of the precise, imperative rules which were to be observed by a ship-owner sending a ship to Aiguesmortes in Languedoc:

'The galley will load cloths and spices at Venice up to the 13th January next; she is to leave Venice on the 15th of the same month. These terms may not be extended, suspended or broken under penalty of a fine of five hundred ducats. No silken goods may be loaded or shipped on this galley anywhere in the gulf of Venice or outside it apart from veils, taffetas and Saracen cloths. If the master of the galley loads or permits the loading of any silken goods, he will be suspended for a period of five years, during which time he may not command any of the galleys of the State or of private persons.' [24]

The people of Venice willingly submitted to this discipline, knowing that it was initiated for the good of the State and to everybody's advantage. The influential citizens of the town, despite their huge fortunes and their resulting power, were as tightly bound by the law as any ordinary seaman. They all watched constantly over one another's activities, and the meticulous articulation of the administrative machine ensured that no one, whether he be the Doge or a councillor, would be tempted to overstep his authority or abuse his office.

Magnificently dressed for their duties, and wreathed in dignity, the Senators were basically no more than merchants, for the Venetian aristocracy was an aristocracy of wealth. The *numerus clausus* fixed by the Book of Gold and the Serrata prevented parvenus from entering the Senate, but those who belonged to it by birth were themselves ship-owners and merchants. In Venice, then, there was nothing to compare with the feudal nobility, the true aristocracy of other European countries, who led their lives according to a code of rights and duties which had little significance in the banks of the Rialto. Chivalry, that strongly based, intimate institution of the feudal nobility, was quite unknown to Venetian businessmen, who were not above indulging in slave traffic when they were also shipping spices and selling cloths. The ethics of Venetian policy were inspired by other ideals and conformed with other principles; this explains its complete efficiency and the fundamental immorality of its pragmatic approach.

31. A gondolier negotiating
a narrow canal. The gondoliers
are extremely dexterous
in handling their long craft,
and give warning of their approach
with cries which date back
to the far distant past.
' *A oel!* ' means ' Look out! '
' *Sia de longo!* ' means ' Pass
on the right! ' ' *Sia stali!* '
means ' To the right! '

VENICE AND THE RENAISSANCE

THE TRANSFORMATION which the city underwent with the advent of the Renaissance was the visible manifestation of deep changes which were affecting the character of the Venetians, their artistic and social life, and to some extent their customs. The successes which they had achieved by warfare during the previous century, their consolidated commercial supremacy in the East, and the prestige which accompanied the Ambassadors of the Republic to all the courts of Europe; these were the justification for the new sense of pride and security which Venetians now experienced. For several hundred years they had fought a hard, bitter struggle to assert themselves over their rivals; their triumph was now complete.

A few days before he died, Doge Tommaso Mocenigo made a moving speech in the Palace which can be looked upon as his political testament. From the sculptured figure lying on his tomb, the work of Niccolo Lamberti and Giovanni di Fiesole, we know the severe, almost mournful features of this great Magistrate of the Republic. His face is thin and narrow, his forehead strongly accentuated, his nose sharp and hooked. We can recognize the man of action and daring, the wise and cautious politician; the face might well be that of a ship's pilot as much as that of a warrior: Tommaso Mocenigo was all these things in his time. And this is how he addressed the Senators:

' Our city sends more than ten million ducats of merchandise all over the world in her ships, and gains almost two million ducats in profits a year. Furthermore, there are a thousand gentlemen whose incomes range from seven hundred to four thousand ducats. If you continue to maintain present methods, affairs will continue to improve; you will become the lords of Christendom and all will fear you. Everyone knows, indeed, that the war against the Turks has made you brave and experienced; you have six captains who can hold their own against any great army, and the past years have seen you to be the best mainstays of Christianity. You have able ambassadors and men who are pastmasters in the government of the city. You have scholars distinguished in many different spheres of knowledge, and especially in law. Every year a million golden ducats are struck and two million in silver.'

The prosperity which the Doge justly proclaimed, since it had been achieved by all his people, was nonetheless not as stable as he described it, and he would have done well to tell his audience that wealth and glory can only be preserved at the cost of unremitting effort and continuous sacrifice. The Republic had become what it was because the Venetians, from the Doge to the humblest boat-man, all worked and fought for the good of the State. The united and selfless effort of every citizen remained a daily obligation, so that the wealth already acquired would not be lost through a lack of foresight, or through indifference.

In the same way that the unstable land of the islands would disintegrate if it were not periodically reinforced, just as the canals would become clogged with mud if they were not constantly dredged, so the commercial and political supremacy attested by the Doge's enthusiastic account was always at the mercy of changing circumstances and needed untiring vigilance. It was not enough to be rich and powerful to keep dangers from the city for some of them, indeed, threatened Venice from without. There was the threat to which her monopoly in the spice trade was subjected by the Portuguese discovery of new sea routes, and the superiority of the national army in some European states over the com-panies of *condottieri* on whom Venice depended for her security. Another danger which was even more difficult to expose and ward off, arising as it did within the people itself, was the taste for luxury, a natural and inevitable consequence of commercial prosperity.

In the fifteenth century as in the time of Marco Polo, the spirit of daring, the taste for adventure, and the desire to conquer new commercial outlets for the Republic perpetuated the great tradition of voyages of discovery over all the seas of the world. 'The brothers Niccolo and Antonio Zeno,' writes Bailly, 'explored the northern seas as far as Labrador and Greenland. Pietro Querini, in 1432, entered the Arctic Ocean. Niccolo da Conti, at the beginning of the fifteenth century, visited Arabia, China and Indochina, and provided the first precise information about the size and shape of the Indian Ocean. Cristoforo Fiorovanti and Niccolo Michiel reached the North Cape. Alvise Cadamosto rounded Cape Verde in 1456 and reached the Bissago Islands. Caterino Zeno explored Persia. Giosafatte Barbaro, in 1472, passed through Muscovy and Armenia to the shores of the Caspian Sea. Ambrogio Bembo, at the dawn of the sixteenth century, visited Persia and India, and has left a detailed description of them, whilst Giovanni Batista Soderini explored the Congo, and brought back enough objects of interest to found a museum.' [25]

This brief summary of the achievements of the great sailors proves that the spirit of enterprise was still alive in the Venetian people, but it did not belong to them alone: the Spaniards and, even more, the Portuguese, went in search of unknown lands. During the fifteenth and sixteenth centuries, in fact, the desire for exploration and conquest became so pressing and was the cause of so much rivalry that Pope Alexander VI acted in advance by dividing a sphere of influence, which was open to the conversion of its pagans and to the greed of merchants, between the Spaniards and Portuguese. No other nation derived any benefit from the division; France and Britain were not considered as candi-dates, and Venice, which had the largest fleet and the most active overseas trade, was not included either.

In this there was a serious warning, and for more than a century before it happened, the Venetians were disturbed to see Portuguese ships seeking a route to the spice lands which was quicker and more certain than the one normally taken. The route to which the Republic had had almost exclusive rights since the Crusade disrupted communications between Europe and Asia, had long ceased to be in dispute, but in 1498 grave changes were heralded in international commerce by Vasco da Gama's voyage to India round the Cape of Good Hope.

In theory it seemed that this discovery would complicate rather than simplify trade in spices. Hitherto they had been transported across the Asian continent to Alexandria, where the Venetians took charge of them and distributed them all over Europe. Henceforth, Portuguese ships which took on cargoes of pepper, cinnamon and ginger from Indian ports delivered them direct to Lisbon, and from there they were sent forthwith to European customers. The voyage was long, difficult and dangerous, but it had the advantage of being from port to port; it cut out the intermediaries who imposed large freight charges on the goods they carried and could raise their terms whenever they felt so inclined.

Being committed to the Arabs, who were the intermediaries, Venice could only view the rise of Portuguese power with alarm; there was virtually nothing to be done, fon Venetian seamen were not accustomed to the long-range voyages at which Bartolomeo Diaz Magellan and Vasco da Gama excelled, and it was too late to try to beat successful competitors on their own ground. The Venetians were therefore compelled to watch the spice trade, which had always been so profitable, deflected from its traditional route and making its way round Africa direct to Portugal. Since it had been possible to dispense with all the many intermediaries, spices could be sold there for one fifth of the price on the Venetian market. It was consequently very much to the advantage of the English, the Germans, the French and the inhabitants of the Low Countries to take their supplies straight from Lisbon. [26]

It was not long before the effect of the change in the spice route was felt in the warehouses and banks along the Rialto. The Germans bought no more for they were now able to deal on more favourable terms with Lisbon. The Flemings cancelled their orders with Venetian merchants when they heard of the arrival in Portugal of a huge ' spice-fleet' in July 1501. Girolamo Priuli observes in his journal that no trade was carried out on the spice market—not even a ducat's worth, and ' no one could conceal the fear and apprehension he felt.'

Spices, it is true, made up an important part of Venetian trade, but not the whole of it, and the prosperity of the Republic was not in such very great danger. The really serious thing was the way in which the people had grown accustomed to riches, to the luxury and pleasures which they procured and the weakness which almost inevitably followed. An easy life for all classes of society, the immense wealth of those who were occupied in trade, and the spectacle of success without effort: these were the things which destroyed the essential qualities of the race—energy, endurance, daring and devotion to the common good. What happened in Venice may well be compared to the change seen in Rome when the Republic was succeeded by the Empire; by the eighteenth century, the decline in the civic spirit which had begun two hundred years earlier was complete.

To all outward appearances, Venice's energy, daring and invincible strength remained unchanged. Her fleet, the basis of her power, was still very impressive. She possessed forty-five large galleys whose combined crews totalled 11,000 men; 25,000 others sailed on 3300 smaller craft. This fleet entailed huge repair and maintenance expenses, for scholars tell us that the ships of this period only lasted about five years—the stouter ones lasted perhaps as long as ten years—owing to faulty methods of construction and poor facilities in the ports. [27]

To keep the fleet in good working order, a host of workmen were kept labouring on construction and repair. At the beginning of the fifteenth century, there were more than 6,000 men in their guild. 36,000 seamen and 6,000 workmen in a population of 170,000 is quite a heavy proportion and was unequalled in any other country. Naval construction and repair were of prime importance in the life of the community, and there were very strict laws relating to them, especially where the supply of ships to foreign countries was concerned. The number of ships intended for export was controlled by law, and the States

wishing to place an order with a shipyard were compelled in the first instance to obtain the authorisation of the Grand Council. This was a measure taken in 1266, and it remained in force; potential enemies and competitors of the Most Serene Republic were thus prevented from using her facilities to her own ultimate detriment. The naval dockyard, which belonged to the State, was exclusively reserved for naval vessels; commercial shipping was built in private yards but these were nonetheless closely supervised by the Council of Ten, for matters relating to the sea were viewed with the utmost concern by the Magistrates. [28]

They accordingly made a point of encouraging builders to ensure that their men were never out of work, and that there was always a supply of competent and experienced manpower. Ship-owners who experienced heavy losses at sea and were not in a position to renew their merchant vessels were given loans by the State, which had an interest in ensuring that the fleet was not reduced in tonnage or quality. In 1558 the State made an advance of fifty-four thousand ducats to two patricians who had lost a large ship; this was a considerable sum for the period. The fitting out of ships of heavy tonnage was also officially encouraged. When the Senate recognized that there were not enough of them it ' instituted a competition for two ships of a thousand tons to be built and fitted within two years, the fitters to receive four ducats per ton. In 1490 there was an order for four ships of the same tonnage '. [29]

There was no lack of bankers on the Rialto who were willing to make offers to shipowners in need of funds, and Shakespeare has given a lively and accurate picture of the kind of transaction which occurred in this sphere. He also demonstrates the exorbitant rates of interest sometimes asked by money-lenders, even if they did not go to the extreme of demanding their pound of flesh like Shylock. Round little tables on the bridge, in the street, or on the embankment, heated discussions were carried on, and without being accused of usury, the bankers generally received an interest of 20 per cent.

To protect temporarily embarrassed ship-owners from money-lenders who were capable of asking what interest they liked, Venice established its Public Bank. The idea for this was put forward as early as 1346 by Giovanni Dolfin and was supported twenty years later by Michele Morosini, but it was not until the sixteenth century that it was finally realized. If it had existed when poor Antonio laid himself open to the whim of his enemy, the unlucky ship-owner would have been content to ask the State Bank for the sum he needed and pay a reasonable interest. Gino Luzzato tells us in his *Studi di storia economica veneziana* that the Senate offered loans repayable in three years to all shipbuilders who produced craft of 300 to 400 tons; these loans were at the rate of three ducats per ton first of all, but when it became urgent to accelerate building, they were raised to six ducats.

Since the founding of Venice, the fleet had always been the commercial instrument on which the economy of the State depended. The woollen and silk industries, and crafts like glass and bronze work played only a minor role [30]; the main part continued to be played by the transport trade. In the fifteenth century, Marco Antonio Sabellico proudly declared, ' there is no port on the inland sea, from the strait between Africa and Europe right up to Syria and Egypt, or as far as the Bosphorus, no harbour even on the least known shore, that the Venetians do not visit for trade according to the ancient tradition of the City.' A prodigious flow of wealth gradually transformed the habits and customs of the Venetians in this way. Where they had been obliged to subject themselves to a strict civic discipline in the first place in order to acquire it, it was now their object to derive as much pleasure from it as they could.

34. Courtyard of Goldoni's house. The Gothic arches of the staircase and the mediaeval well are particularly interesting.

35. ' Madonna and Child ': detail of altarpiece by Giovanni Bellini; Sacristy of the Frari Church. This work, signed and dated 1488, is regarded as one of the most beautiful and characteristic achievements of a great painter.

This is the Venice described by Commynes in his Memoirs. The historian went there in 1494, and although in France he was well acquainted with the splendours which filled the households of the Dukes of Berry and Burgundy—probably even more lavish than those of the King himself—the amazement which he felt continually increased. As he puts in his own colourful language, ' I was indeed filled with wonder to see the setting of the city, to see so many bell-towers and monasteries, such large dwellings—and all on water. The people have no means of travel other than the boats, which I believe to number some thirty thousand.' Commynes was the first traveller of all to declare that ' the Grand Canal is the most beautiful street in the world.' He was also astonished by the large number of convents and monasteries; ' there are full seventy of them, as many for men as for women, very rich and beautiful, both in architecture and decoration, and with very beautiful gardens... and some seventy-two parishes

The Dogana and Church of la Salute;   Guardi.

and many brotherhoods, and truly wondrous it is to see such fine large churches rising from the sea.'

The new ways of life adopted by the Venetian people—especially the ruling class—called for a new setting. The modest dwellings of old Venice, which were usually made of wood and continued so in some quarters until the beginning of the Renaissance, gave way to stone houses which were more beautiful and less prone to catch fire; Venetian chronicles often report terrible fires, and the one which occurred in 1114 and was never forgotten destroyed the greater part of the quarter near the Rialto Bridge.

By the time of Commynes the tumbledown hovels had disappeared. ' The old houses are very large and tall, of fine stone and all painted; the others, built in the last two hundred years, all have a façade of marble which comes from Istria, one hundred miles away, and in addition, many large pieces of porphyry and serpentine on the front. Within, most of them have at least two bedrooms, with gilt-covered bedsteads, painted and gilded draught-screens, and very well furnished.' Today, the Venetian palace which gives the best idea of what an aristocratic building of the Renaissance was like, in spite of the restoration and additions which transformed it, is the Ca' d'Oro on the Grand Canal. Here we can see the blend of luxury and good taste, of bourgeois comfort and lordly splendour which characterizes Venetian society and distinguishes it from what was to be observed at the same time in other countries in Europe, and even in other Italian states. The almost austere elegance of the Florentine palaces of the Quattrocento is in striking contrast with the Ca' d'Oro, though the Medici, the Strozzi and the Tornabuoni were also bankers and financiers like the Contarini, for whom Matteo Raverti built this enchanting home; it seems as light and delicate as lace or as a shimmering reflection in the water. In contrast with the powerful, heavy

The Lower Reaches of the Grand Canal, facing the bend. Brownish-black/greyish-brown ink over pencil; 8⅝" x 14¾"; Canaletto. In the distance is the unfinished Palazzo Rezzonico, and the Palazzo Querini is in the foreground. The scene is viewed from in front of the Scuola della Carità, now reconstructed, as is the church adjoining it, to form the Accademia di Belle Arti.

immobility of Tuscan palaces, Venetian Renaissance architecture infuses all its creations with an ethereal weightlessness.

It was in honour of his marriage to Sordamore Zeno in 1412 that Maino Contarini, the Procurator of St. Mark's, converted an old house near the church into a magnificent dwelling. He was twenty-one years old and Sordamore sixteen: the young couple wanted a home which was worthy of the high rank of the Contarini and the Zeno families in the Venetian aristocracy, and it was to be built and decorated in the newest and most exquisite taste. He obtained the collaboration of the two most famous architects of the time—Bartolomeo Bon of Padua and Matteo Raverti, a Lombard. Together they accomplished the miracle of grace and delicacy offered by the two storeys of loggias in the façade overlooking the canal. In their elegant colonnades, their slender columns and florid sculpture are reflected the youth of the bridal pair and the splendour of Venetian life.

93

The graceful inner staircase connects the courtyard, decorated with a beautiful well and flowering trees, to the floors above; this was very much admired by Ruskin when he saw it in 1840. A Frenchman while on a visit to Venice, Jean Charlier, covered the ornate Gothic decoration on the walls with lavish, sparkling gold and it was this which earned the house the name given to it by the people: *la Ca' d'Oro*—the House of Gold.

In order to bring these beautiful Venetian dwellings to life again—those converted into museums, like the Ca' d'Oro, the Palazzo Rezzonico and the Palazzo Pesaro, those left derelict and in disrepair, or skilfully restored and still inhabited by the descendants of the old families for whom they were built—we have to turn to the paintings of Gentile Bellini and Giovanni Mansueti; we must look for the true, living face of Venice as it was, in a series of paintings which these artists produced for the Scuola di San Giovanni Evangelista, and which are now in the Accademia.

The Scuola is a typically Venetian institution, so closely bound to the life of the people that, although several of the *scuole* have disappeared, many are still as active as they were in the past. The name 'scuola' was given to a civic society which grouped the inhabitants of a district round a church or a specially revered Saint. It was their communal house, with a chapel where they could hear Mass, and assembly rooms where they could discuss the important problems of the community. Proud of their fellowship and wishing their *scuola* to be the most beautiful in Venice, they would have it decorated by famous artists. For the Scuola of Saint Ursula, Vittore Carpaccio painted the life of the young girl who married the King of Brittany and was slaughtered with her eleven thousand attendants by Attila's Huns on the banks of the Rhine at Cologne. In the Scuola of Saint Roch, Tintoretto produced his most dazzling masterpieces and the 'brothers' of the Carmini entrusted the decoration of their chapel ceiling to Giambattista Tiepolo, who lavished on it a genius which was more sensual than pious.

The organisation of the *scuole* was not directly dependent on the guilds as were the *arti* in Florence, for they brought men of different professions together. The State was tempted on a number of occasions to intervene in the control of these rich and powerful societies, but in the main they were freely and independently administered by a council presided over by the *gastaldo*. The Doge reserved the right to appoint the *gastaldo*, who was responsible for the management of the society's property, the settlement of any disputes which might arise between the members, and giving help to poor *consorti*. Indeed, one of the main objects of the *scuola* was to ensure that its members never went in need, for it was considered immoral that there should be poverty in a town of such great wealth.

Political equality was one of the oldest principles of the Venetian constitution, but in fact it barely existed, for certain citizens enjoyed considerable influence whilst others were scarcely heard. Economic equality was even less of a reality: changing fortunes in trade and the shipping world meant that a man might be renowned for his riches at one moment and ran the risk of being ruined the next. Those who still had credit could obtain money from the bankers of the Rialto, but when they no longer had any ships or money they joined the ranks of the impoverished noblemen; by a curious paradox, there were already many of these in Venice during the fifteenth and sixteenth centuries.

Quoting from a Venetian chronicle of Malipiero, Jacob Burckhardt tells how two senators asked for the sum of sixty thousand ducats to be voted for the assistance of impoverished noblemen. The Grand Council was about to grant their request when the Council of Ten decided that a measure of this kind would create a very bad impression abroad; if the Republic acknowledged that some of its most notable citizens were reduced to pauperdom, general confidence in Venice's

36. 'St. Mary Magdalen': detail from 'Madonna and Child with St. Catherine and St. Mary Magdalen.' Giovanni Bellini; Accademia. Painted at about the same time as the Frari altarpiece, this picture displays all the major elements of Bellini's genius: the grace, the strength, the spiritual and earthly beauty.

37

38

immense prosperity would be shaken. The two men who were responsible for this unfortunate request were hastily sent to Cyprus and the ruined noblemen were forced to rely on private charity to escape dying of hunger. [31]

This happened in 1492; seven years later, a member of the famous Contarini family declared that he had no money or work, and possessed no more than sixteen ducats a year on which to keep nine children. At about the same time, another Contarini was driven to rob one of his neighbours, and a Soranzo was hanged for the same offence.

Social inequalities existed in Venice just as they did elsewhere, and it was to remedy them, as far as this was possible, that the *scuola* performed charitable work among its members. There was also another type of *scuola*, which was distinct from those established on the basis of piety, trade, or community spirit: foreign residents who arrived in Venice and found difficulty in settling down were accommodated by their own national *scuola*. Whilst the *fondachi* were business buildings used as offices, warehouses, shops and inns—the German and Turkish *fondachi*, for example, both of which were on the Grand Canal—the *scuole* of the Albanians, the Greeks, and the Slavs, like those of the Venetians, were centres for prayer, assembly and social gathering for national as well as guild purposes.

The Scuola of St. John the Evangelist possessed a Crucifix with miraculous powers, and the stories of miracles it had achieved were depicted there. Among the finest and most characteristic paintings of the life of the people in the fifteenth century, there is an outstanding work by Carpaccio which represents the cure of a man possessed by the devil as he is touched by the relic; and there is the work of Gentile Bellini depicting the tragedy which occurred one day when the Cross was being carried in procession by colleagues of the Scuola and fell into a canal; it was retrieved by the *gastaldo* himself, Andrea Vendramin.

In both compositions, vivid, evocative detail plays a more important part than the religious element; and apart from the verve, beauty and imagination which the painters have brought to the narration of these events, the most intensely striking feature of their work is the documentary precision with which they reproduce architecture, costume and gesture. The costumes are particularly splendid, for they belong to young men who took pride in squandering their inheritance in this way; they banded themselves in societies with strange titles and were recognizable by complicated emblems embroidered on their jackets and sleeves.

The Miracle of the Holy Cross fallen into the Canal shows the old wooden bridge of the Rialto, the houses with blunderbuss-shaped chimneys, and the terraces or *altane* where women spent hours in order to bleach their hair. In this picture one can also see a host of gondolas, covered with light canopies and propelled by supremely elegant young men. The Miracle of the Cross brought a large number of Venetian dignitaries on to the embankment, and among them, surrounded by ladies of the highest rank, we can distinguish the old Queen of Cyprus, Caterina Cornaro, who played an important part in Venetian politics through her marriage with Lusignan, King of Cyprus and Jerusalem.

Another painting from the same *scuola*, and like the previous two, now belonging to the Accademia, represents a procession on the Piazza San Marco. This masterpiece of Gentile Bellini, dating from 1496, shows the Basilica as it was at the end of the fifteenth century, when it still possessed the old mosaics in the portals, now replaced, with one exception, by work of the eighteenth century. The Doge, the members of the Councils, the *pregadi* and the *procuratori* march in the procession behind the Miraculous Cross flanked by monks bearing huge candlesticks and swinging censers.

These three pictures are valuable for the light they throw on the way in which Venetians dressed during the Renaissance and their behaviour in official cere-

37. ' Madonna del Parto ';
Accademia. The endearing, archaic quality of this anonymous painting is characteristic of late fourteenth century Venetian art.

38. ' St. Antony of Padua.'
Alvise Vivarini; Correr Museum. Vivarini was the last important representative of the Murano School, which played a large part in the development of Venetian painting. This picture, painted in 1480, dates from the latter half of his career.

monies. They show us the 'fair-haired men with slim figures, grave, silent tread and careful speech' described by Burckhardt. In this they differed from the other peoples of Italy; to some extent Nordic in their ways, they were nevertheless apt to dress with all the ostentation of orientals when they were not wearing their uniforms of office—which remained unchanged from the Middle Ages to the eighteenth century.

The normal dress of the solemn, middle-aged patricians of Venice bore no resemblance to the garish and luxurious costume which so delighted the young men of the time. Basically they dressed in a long gown of black cloth, revealing the collar of a white shirt above the neck clasp. This heavy garment with its wide folds was also worn by the men of the professional classes, and as it reached right to the ground, those who wore it were obliged to walk with a slow, solemn, dignified step. This was the characteristic walk of the bourgeoisie and aristocracy at a time when only children and workmen were so indiscreet as to run in the streets. On ceremonial occasions, Senators wore gowns of crimson satin, for this was the distinguishing mark of their office.

If the men's clothing was dull and monotonous, the women of Venice redeemed their husbands' drabness with the colour and grace of their own attire. They even went to such an extreme in the luxury of their array that the magistrates decided it was time to introduce laws regulating private expenditure; they sought to put an end to the rivalry in splendour which was ruining rich households and was an outrage to the needy. Officials bearing the title of *provveditori alle pompe* were entrusted with the task of enforcing these laws. In 1474 the use of pearls and costly Eastern materials was prohibited. These were imported from Asia for re-export at a huge profit to Germany and France, but in Venetian society the practice of retaining a large part of these goods for home use had become widespread. Ladies of fashion frequented the shop of a certain Master Bartolomeo, who, so it was said, 'even made his purchases from the Grand Turk himself, and displayed such beautiful red and green and yellow brocades that no painter's brush could ever do justice to them.' [32] Some years later, in 1514, ladies were requested to be less prodigal with diamond studs, pearls, lace, and damask materials, but it was to no avail; for whenever Venice received the visit of a foreign ruler, it was naturally important for the elegance of the ladies to be a credit to her. On occasions of this kind, the laws relating to luxury were waived, and that is what happened in 1574 when Henry III, the King of France, made his visit to the Most Serene Republic. 'Notwithstanding all decrees to the contrary,' it was proclaimed, 'each of the ladies invited to this festivity will be allowed to wear all clothes and jewels most suitable for the adornment of her person.' [33]

On these occasions, which were frequent, jewel-boxes were ransacked and precious stones were to be seen glistening on the heads and shoulders of the ladies, their hair interwoven with pearls and gold thread. Even their stockings were of golden gauze. Dressed in this way, so Giacomo Franco tells us, they were very goddesses, and foreign visitors, accustomed to the magnificence of their own courts, were astounded by the splendour of the ladies of Venice. In 1490 a Frenchman was amazed to see dresses covered with precious stones worth thirty or forty thousand ducats, and as early as 1433 the Chronicle of Lio estimated that there were as many as 600 ladies who wore silken dresses with gold and jewels. [34]

The present furnishings of the Ca' d'Oro, with its tapestries, and painted and gilded *cassoni*, preserve it as it was in the days of its first splendour. Everywhere there was gold in abundance, both inside and outside. No doubt this show of luxury was ostentatious; the Venetian aristocrats, it should be remembered, were ship-owners and merchants, and they probably felt the urge to dazzle their visitors with a display of their wealth. When the King of Portugal came to Venice in

39. 'Madonna of the Little Trees.' Giovanni Bellini; Accademia. Bellini painted this exquisite, calm picture in 1487. It is so called after the small trees which appear in the background.

98

40

41

1428, as Alazard recalls, he thought that all the men living in such dwellings must be princes. The Florentines, who were accustomed to the discreet simplicity of Medici palaces, were overwhelmed by such glowing colour, though they tended to poke fun at it. There is an ironic tone in Leonardo Frescobaldi's description of the house of Remigio Soranzo, 'which seemed entirely of gold; where even in the bed-chambers, all one saw was gold and fine azure.'

No doubt festive occasions in these palaces were full of magnificence to match the splendour of the setting, though laws were still in force which limited expenditure on furnishing and decoration. Banquets gave chefs and pastry-cooks the opportunity to make the fullest use of their talent; they were very long—so long that the guests of Cardinal Grimani, at a dinner he gave for the nephew of the Pope, Ranuccio Farnese, saw ninety dishes brought before them over a period of four hours. The glassware and the crockery were superb, and forks, still quite exceptional in European courts even in the sixteenth century, were already commonly in use among the Venetians. In 1540 the Senate attempted to bring an end to the wildly lavish expenditure on banquets, and decreed that no meal was to be served at a cost of more than half a ducat per person.

What did the guests eat at these gargantuan feasts? A lot of fish, of course, for there was always an abundance of fine quality fish in Venice, and many recipes were known for serving them; a large amount of poultry and game; a vast quantity of truffles and an endless variety of pies, some of them containing live birds which were released at the end of the meal for the entertainment of the guests. Venetian cooks also exercised their ingenuity in disguising dishes, a fashion already much favoured by the Romans, and table decorations at the banquets were as strange and beautiful as the courses themselves.

In honour of King Henry III of France, who visited the Republic in 1574, someone had the curious idea of making a whole table-service of sugar for the meal which was served to three thousand guests in the Hall of the Maggior Consiglio in the Doge's Palace. 'For this banquet,' says Bailly, [35] 'the Venetian cooks and confectioners, masters in their art, undertook to serve their culinary masterpieces in sugar settings; the plates, dishes, knives, forks, napkins and even the bread were all made of sugar which was melted, moulded, pulled and spun into shape. The table centrepiece which stood in front of the king represented a queen sitting between two tigers. The queen, the animals, and the whole construction in fact were sculptured in sugar. In order to make them, special moulds similar to those used by bronze-workers were fashioned. All the tables were covered with statuettes of Minerva and Justice, Saint Mark and David, popes, kings, doges, all the beasts of Creation, trees, fruits, and flowers. Whether they were human, animal or vegetable, all were made of sugar, to designs by Sansovino.' At the end of the meal, these delicate specimens of the great sculptor's art were distributed among the guests who attended this fairy-tale banquet.

Weddings were also the occasion for a great display of wealth and beauty. When a Badoer married a Nani, binding the friendship and alliance of two of the most powerful families, the procession accompanying the couple to the church included fifty ladies dressed in gold brocade; the livery of the servants was covered with gold, and there was gold shining on the uniforms of the gondoliers. When Andrea Gritti's niece married Paolo Contarini, a hundred young girls wearing sparkling jewels escorted the bride, who was charmingly dressed in pink velvet, and a hundred men-servants carrying torches accompanied them to the ball-room. There was dancing the whole night long: the lively galliard, with its quick light hops, and the sensual dance of the hat, which, to the music of flutes, harps and lutes, seemed to convey all the pert, changing moods in a conversation between lovers. It was in Venice, finally, that ladies conceived the idea of representing

40. 'Dream of St. Ursula': detail. Vittore Carpaccio; Accademia. Between 1490 and 1496, Vittore Carpaccio painted a series of episodes from the life of St. Ursula, for the Scuola di S. Orsola at the church of SS. Giovanni e Paolo.

41. Panel of tapestry, about 10″ across, representing the head of a Doge; Correr Museum. The clever, vital face of the Doge is like that of many Venetians who have been prominent in political and business life. The cap he is wearing always went under the Doge's ceremonial *corno*.

in terms of dance the wiles used by both male and female in the disturbing seduction
scene where the peacock tries to win his mate. This dance, which was called the
pavane or *pavona* was destined to conquer the whole of Europe and remain in
fashion up to the eighteenth century.

Balls were given in convents when a new abbess was appointed, according to
Marino Sanudo the old historian, and even cardinals would deign to put in an
appearance. These festivities were naturally opportunities for the beauties of
Venice, and even those who only thought they were beautiful, to parade their
finest Turkish velvets, their Persian shot silks, and the famous family jewels which
were handed down from generation to generation—the souvenirs and spoils of
foreign conquest.

The courtesans, however, outdid the *donne oneste* in order to attract men. By
law they were compelled to carry yellow handkerchiefs instead of white ones as
a sign of their profession; apart from this they dressed as magnificently as the ladies
of high birth. Their status was determined by very strict precepts but they were

Isola di S. Clemente. Pen and bistre; Antonio Visentini.

not held in contempt for it and there were a number of gentlemen who did not
disdain to marry them. During his travels in Italy, Montaigne was surprised to
see more than a hundred and fifty who were dressed like princesses.

For the convenience of travellers who were anxious to find them, a list was
published in 1547 of all professional courtesans, together with their addresses
and the prices they charged for their favours. These varied considerably; a night
spent with Paolina Canevo, for example, cost thirty crowns, whilst Diana La
Fouina, who lived on the Rio della Fornasa, charged only two crowns. This
is what we learn from the famous Catalogue—intended for foreigners (and no
doubt for the Venetians themselves)—which bore the long and informative title,
' *Questo è si e il catalogo di tutte le principale e più honorate cortigiane di Venetia, il nome
loro, e il nome delle loro pieze, e le stanstetie ove loro habitano, e di più ancora vi narra la con-
trata ove sono le loro stantie, e il numero de li dinari che hanno da pagar quelli gentilhuomini,
e al che desiderano entrar nella sua gratia.*' In the Correr Museum there is an amusing
painting by Carpaccio which shows two courtesans playing with their dogs; they
are waiting patiently on their balconies for the wink from a passer-by who seeks
permission to visit their rooms.

The courtesans of Venice were not common prostitutes; some of them were women
of great talent and culture whose society was sought by scholars and humanists,

for like Aspasia and Lais in ancient times, theirs was a grace of both mind and
body. Veronica Franco, for example, who went into a convent towards the end
of her life, is referred to in the catalogue as living in the Piazza Santa Maria Formosa; she was able, nevertheless, to attract a select gathering of men of letters,
painters and musicians to her house. Music was an even greater gift for the lovely
Lucia Trevisan, a talented singer, who received all the finest instrumentalists
and singers of Venice. Tullia d'Aragon presided over debates on love which
would not have been a discredit to the courts of Provence in the Middle Ages.
They were respected and admired by the humanists themselves, and we know what
an important part the revival of ancient culture played in Venice when Constantinople was taken by the Turks, and the learned Greeks who fled the fury of the
Moslems were driven towards Italy. With them they brought very rare manuscripts, and these they were to reveal to an astonished world.

It was natural enough for humanism to take firm root in Venice before it did
so in other cities, for it was there that the refugees landed with their ancient
treasures. In Venice they found printing houses in full operation: Aldo Manuzzio
was reproducing Latin and Greek texts with complete accuracy, achieving a
perfection rarely known in the art of printing. Even before the fall of Constantinople, Byzantine scholars and men of learning were paying frequent visits to Venice
and the Universities on the mainland—especially the one in Padua. Manuel
Chrysaloras, a Hellenist and famous grammarian, was sent as imperial ambassador.
He was accompanied by George of Trebizond, the Aristotelian scholar, and Gemis-
thus Plethon, the distinguished exponent of Plato.

This contribution from the East gave a new boost to the passion for culture
which affected all classes of society; the Querini and Zeno families organized
literary and philosphical discussions in their palaces which were attended by all
the great minds of the day. In this way they promoted the establishment of many
academies with the greatest variety of titles—the Ornate, the United, the Uranians,
the Seraphic and the Pilgrims—and these encouraged the diffusion of literature
and scientific knowledge. The Pilgrims established two printing houses which
rivalled those of Aldo Manuzzio and his brother Paolo, who printed books for the
Academy of Renown. Without neglecting his important commitments in the
Doge's Palace, a patrician like Ermolao Barbaro was able to translate Aristotle
and taught Greek at the University of Padua. Some made a special study of
the natural sciences: Domenico Zeno in botany, and Francesco Massario in ich-
thyology. Andrea Navagero became the historiographer of Venice. Pellegrino
Brocardi created a new science of Egyptology in the course of many voyages to
Alexandria and Cairo, whilst Gasparo Contarini, in his book on the *Perfection
of Political Life*, laid the foundations of civil law.

Where literature was concerned, it is true that Pietro Aretino acquired an unfortunate notoriety with his licentious works and the insolent letters with which
he extorted pictures from artists by threatening to make them unpopular (he was
also able to use this device to blackmail princes when the occasion presented itself).
At the same time, however, great lustre was brought to Venetian Renaissance
literature by the work of the delightful humanist poet, Pietro Bembo, and Leonardo
Giustiniano, whose songs were loved as much by beautiful ladies as by the gondoliers who sang them at their work. Women were already gaining their freedom
and had no wish to be behind the men; the names of Gaspara Stampa and Cas-
sandra Fedele were as famous as those of Bembo and Giustiniano. Veronica Franco,
the courtesan visited by Montaigne and Henry III during their visits to Venice,
wrote verse which was much admired by connoisseurs.

The feeling for nature and the love of the country which were later to become
so widespread were already common among the men of Renaissance times.

Although there were vast, beautiful gardens in Venice, especially on the island of la Giudecca, and streets like the Merceria, which are so congested today, were planted with trees, poets and philosophers often went to their villas on the mainland, to breathe the fresh air of the woods and fields. Bembo delighted in his little house at Santa Maria del Non, where he loved to wander in the woods, listening to the birds, gathering strawberries and writing poetry. Here, to the heights of Asolo, came Caterina Cornaro, the Queen of Cyprus, when the Republic had used her for its own ends, then proclaimed her downfall and prevailed upon her to return to Italy.

There was close intimacy between the writers and artists of the time, for universality was the great ambition of Renaissance man, and the humanists' aim was to acquire as much knowledge as possible and enjoy, if not practise, all the arts. In many pictures of the fifteenth and sixteenth centuries, we meet the taste for symbols and allegory which was so widespread among learned gentlemen of the time. But there was nothing bookish in the culture which gave artists their inspiration: only a deep feeling for the human, a new concern with the problems of giving expression to space, form and colour, and an extraordinary decorative splendour linked with the most direct and moving representation of human passions.

* *
*

With the encouragement and support of the humanists, Classicism reached the lagoon in the course of the fifteenth century, almost half a century after it came to Tuscany. Venetian taste had remained faithful to the florid Gothic style just as it had held fast for so long to the styles of Byzantium. This was the ' decisive turning-point ' referred to by Jean Alazard, when the ideas and forms of central Italy were introduced into Venice, engendering the evolution which began with Mauro Coducci and was to end with Andrea Palladio. [36]

When we study Coducci's most important achievements, the façade of the Church of S. Zaccaria, that of the Scuola San Marco, and the Palaces of Contarini dal Zoffo and Loredan-Vendramin-Calergi, we are compelled to admire their beautiful and sober simplicity of line, the felicitous balance of their proportions, and the harmony of horizontal planes. In all Coducci's work, these features reflect an impulse tempered with a tranquil power—a power wholly permeated by that spirit of measure and reserve which is justly termed classical. A native of Bergamo, Mauro Coducci spent the last thirty years of his life in Venice, and from the church of S. Michele in Isola, with which he truly began his career, to S. Maria Formosa and S. Giovanni Grisostomo, which are the masterpieces of his maturity, he brought an increasingly distinctive Venetian character to Renaissance architecture.

The same sense of perfection inspires the work of Pietro Lombardo and Tullio, his son. Architects and sculptors, they introduced the styles of their own province of Lombardy, though infusing it with the unique, original character which Venice confers on everything she creates, or on everything created on her soil. The lovely church of S. Maria dei Miracoli, which has all the delicacy and refinement of an ivory and crystal casket, represents the peak of Venice's first stage in Classicism, the Quattrocento. Slower to reach the banks of the Grand Canal than the margins of the River Arno, the Quattrocento assumed a typically Venetian quality when it did arrive, and the disposition of the Piazza San Marco, which virtually received its definitive form in the fifteenth century, is an achievement of the Renaissance.

42. ' Eve '; statue by Antonio Rizzo, in the Doge's Palace. A copy of this statue stands in the Arco Foscari, with Rizzo's 'Adam.'

43. One of the bronze Moors on the Clock Tower which chime the hours by striking a bell with their mallets.

44. There are many Roman sculptures of crouching lions like this one, crushing a man or a demon between their paws. At one time this sculpture stood in a church doorway; now it is imbedded in the base of the S. Polo campanile.

42 43

44

45

46

The square was originally the site of a convent's kitchen garden, but ceased to be used for this purpose when more space became necessary for the gathering of the people at the *arengo*. A number of buildings were subsequently constructed, in the rather disjointed though spirited manner of a city which has no strict town-planning scheme. In the fifteenth century, when large classical squares were everywhere making their appearance, the Piazza San Marco was duly graced with Jacopo Sansovino's Libreria, which Palladio regarded as the richest and most beautifully decorated building to have been erected since ancient times. With the coming of Vincenzo Scamozzi, who had lived for a long time in the city of the Popes, the Nuove Procuratie which was opposite the old Procurator's Palace (known as the Procuratie Vecchie), introduced something of the atmosphere of Rome.

Classicism, which had a proper place in areas where there were ancient monuments in abundance, was completely foreign to Venice, which had never had any. With her outlook to the East, and her sea outlet, she naturally adopted Byzantine forms as they were and transformed the Gothic ones for her own purposes. But Classical forms were too fixed and rigid to unbend completely when they were accepted. When once syncretism had succeeded in bringing Gothic and Renaissance into the same stream for a time—in the architecture and decoration of palaces rather than churches—the 'Classical orders' at length prevailed: the Palazzo Corner della Ca' Grande by Jacopo Sansovino, and the Palazzo Grimani di San Luca of Sanmicheli, both mark the victory of Classicism in their own way. It seems, nonetheless, that Venice had to yield—for such is the law of aesthetic evolution —to the acceptance of a style which was basically foreign to her; its hard, straight, static lines conflicted with the nature of a city born of the sea by which she lived.

It is thus paradoxical to observe the great Classical architects—Sansovino with greater flexibility and grace, Scamozzi with greater weight, and Sanmicheli with his wholly theoretical allegiance to the precepts of the ancient world— accomplishing their great work in Venice. It is an even greater paradox that Andrea Palladio, born at Vicenza, the fanatical theorist of Classicism and the brilliant inventor of new forms, an artist who accepted the dictates of Classicism with the most extreme religious devotion, was also to achieve his most perfect masterpieces in Venice: the church of the Redentore on the island of Giudecca, the church of S. Giorgio Maggiore, that of S. Pietro di Castello, and the façade of S. Pietro della Vigna.

Palladio's Venetian churches, cold, severely majestic, massed with a proud perfection and uncompromising intellectualism, reveal that he was relentlessly determined to impose a Classicism on Venice which was organically foreign to her, and out of place in her atmosphere. Palladio employed almost complete austerity of form; he foreswore all decorative elements and treated volume for its own sake, the mass contained within the stone shell, as a delicate substance which he quickened with surface ripples, and eddies barely perceptible to the uninitiated eye. Emotion is dominated in his churches as it is in a Monteverdi recitative, where the dramatic rhythm is balanced and intensely concentrated. It is here that Classicism achieves its highest expression, with an economy of means which detracts nothing from the eloquence and majesty of perfect proportion.

Venice was not a land of sculptors like Tuscany; yet during the Renaissance, with Pietro Lombardo and his sons, Antonio and Tullio, her plastic art, though very inferior to her painting, achieved the same level of brilliance as her architecture. The finest work of Lombardo and his sons is to be found in two great repositories of Venetian art, the churches of the Frari and San Zanipolo, where they were summoned to design the tombs of Doges and distinguished citizens. The wholly

45. 'Holy Conversation': detail. Giacomo Palma the Elder; Accademia. The beautiful, sensuous, female figure, lost in dreams, represents a type of Venetian womanhood beloved by Palma. The background, already slightly Romantic in tone, is in perfect harmony with the hint of melancholy seen in the faces.

46. 'St. Antony distributing alms': detail. Lorenzo Lotto; SS. Giovanni e Paolo. This unusual, vigorous work was painted in 1542; of special interest, therefore, is the extremely 'modern' look of the women shown in this detail, the brilliance of the colours, and the strong contrasts of light and shade. The St. Antony to whom the title of the picture refers was an archbishop of Florence, who died in 1459.

Florentine perfection of the monuments to Pasquale Malipiero and Niccolo Marcello by Pietro Lombardo; the more developed, more Roman Classicism of the monument to Doge Andrea Vendramin, by his son Tullio; and the tomb of Pietro Mocenigo, a very symphony in stone in the breadth and harmony of its proportions: all of these works rise to the peak of excellence in a Classicism which Venice had made her own. Antonio Rizzo sculpted the tomb of the Tron family in the style of the Lombardos. Riccio and Leopardi began to produce a Venetian statuary which was both more subtle and more florid than that of Florence; its significance was less for the mind than for the senses, and at times it seems to be imbued with the very movement of the sea.

* *
*

Unlike the sculptors, who nearly all came from outside Venice, from Tuscany, Rome or mainland Venetia, the greatest painters of the Venetian Renaissance were Venetian by birth. They were all fired by the spirit which first asserted itself in the school of Murano, producing an essentially Venetian painting, a style which was no longer dependent on Byzantium, and no longer indebted to Verona or Padua for its initial stimulus.

In the eloquent portrayals of Venetian life among the works of Carpaccio, Mansueti, and Gentile Bellini, we have already witnessed the level of perfection to which Venetian painting had risen, the vast field of experiment and discovery it covered, and the new emotions it sought to express. The work of Jacopo Bellini still contains, perhaps, a residue of archaic, mediaeval stiffness, but his sons Gentile and, more especially, Giovanni, were literally possessed by the spirit of the Renaissance in all its triumphal splendour. Giovanni Bellini achieved supremacy in every sphere of painting in his time, and the Franconian Albrecht Dürer, a man of fine judgment, and one who learned a great deal from him, rightly hailed Bellini as ' ever Venice's greatest painter. ' [37]

He can indeed be regarded as the inventor of the modern landscape, in that his paintings do not have a background of more or less formal design, but represent a particular site at a particular time of day. He was the first to reveal a passion for the late hours of the afternoon, and for sunsets, which were later to be so brilliantly realized in the work of Tiepolo. But whilst the life and breath of his landscape is measured by the Panic pulsing of the earth, his figures are radiant with human passions, with a profane and ardent inner life whose light is reflected in the faces of his Madonnas; the rich fullness of their physical beauty is no more than a mirror to the Platonic beauty of the soul. And Alvise Vivarini, the last of the line of Muranese artists who effected the transition between the Middle Ages and the Renaissance, is at one with Giovanni Bellini in this splendid simultaneous apotheosis of the flesh and the spirit.

Whilst, as we have seen, Carpaccio was a chronicler, almost a reporter, of Venetian life, Giovanni Cima da Conegliano portrayed the gentleness, the music and the rich fullness of Venetian landscapes, where each passing hour changes the light over every mountain and every forest. In the serious, meditative faces of his virgins and saints, he reflected the passing moment whose delicate beauty can never be repeated.

In the process of building the State of Venice, this feeling of impermanence, inevitable in a people living by and on the sea, was only surmounted at a cost of increasingly keen and exacting effort. In Venetian painting it has its most moving expression. Constantly changing light, iridescent in fog and mist, varying com-

47. ' St. Ursula and the King':
detail. Vittore Carpaccio;
Accademia. This scene in
Carpaccio's huge series shows
the young Princess Ursula
enumerating to her father
the reasons why she should
accept the foreign prince's
offer of marriage.

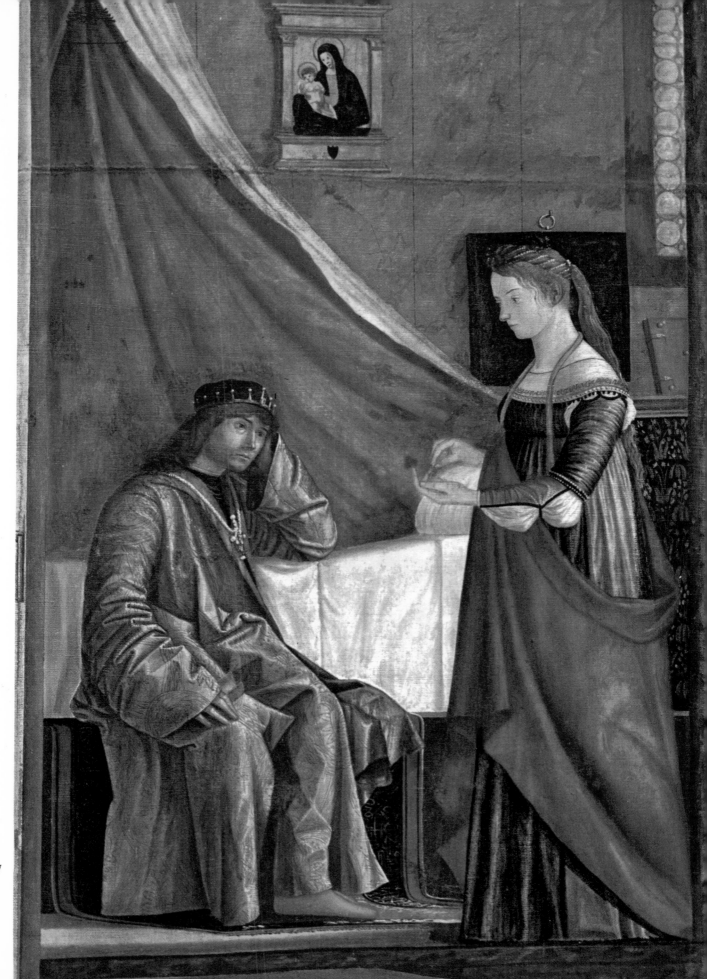

binations of colour over the waves, and the kind of 'philosophy of motion' which
led Turner, during his period in Venice, to the discovery that the most beautiful
forms are those which deny their nature and dissolve in the light—these are the
things which bring man and landscape to a sense of the same sadness at the frailty
of life, at the rapid passage of time, at the ephemeral beneath the cloak of per-
manence. For Giovanni Bellini, anguish at the rapid passing of time is cast out
by the religious feeling which pervades his work—the great polyptych of St. Vincent
Ferrier in the church of San Zanipolo for example, or the Virgin among the saints
in the church of the Frari, or again, the Pala of S. Zaccaria, and the many
Madonnas in the Accademia. For Giorgio da Castelfranco—famous under the
nickname of Giorgione—it became an obsession; his anxiety became the incurable
disease of a man who suffered, perhaps more than any other, from the knowledge
that, like all his fellows, he was the fool of time.

*
* *

Life could not be wholly idyllic in a Venice drawn, in spite of herself, into the
labyrinth of European politics. Well aware that her future lay with the sea, she
avoided entering into the disputes of other Italian states any more than her prestige,
power or prosperity made it necessary to do so. By the great wisdom of her government, she was held remote from conflicts in which her interest was not directly involved, but it is not possible to practise a policy of neutrality and non-intervention
without weakening and allowing rival states to become dangerously stronger. Her
previous clashes with the Papacy, Genoa and the Franks had originated in open
or concealed aggression, of which she was the victim. It had then been sufficient
for her to maintain the balance between states of equal strength; but when one
of these states, the Duchy of Milan as it happened, seemed to be gaining supremacy
in Italy, it was in her interest to curb its excessive growth. From the fifteenth
century onwards, therefore, Venice was obliged to practise a mainland policy
which made her position a dangerous one, because of rival principalities inflated
with an inordinate will for power, and the ambition of one of her greatest Doges,
Francesco Foscari.

Francesco Foscari received the *corno* and 'married the sea' in 1423, and was
to rule till 1457. His reign was thus one of the longest in the history of Venice,
lasting thirty-four years, but even then he only relinquished his power following
a scandal involving his son which had certainly been engineered as a means of
overthrowing him. In 1422, Filippo Maria Visconti, the Duke of Milan, had
led his armies right into mainland Venice and occupied Genoa, the Republic's
old political and commercial rival. Foscari was the man the state needed to check
the advance of a greedy and ambitious enemy.

The balance of power between Italian States, and the relative parity of their
strength was all-important as a guarantee for one medium of Venetian trade which
was closely bound up with her sea trade: the waterways. Exchange with France,
Germany, the Low Countries and England was conducted by the river routes
as well as by road. Venice had a fleet of river craft which carried her produce
to all her main clients. It was therefore imperative to ensure that this network,
and particularly the use of the Po and the Adige, was not jeopardised by a neighbour's
evil intent. If Venice could continue to control the waterways as she controlled
the seas, she would be able to proceed with her trade but it was necessary to ensure
that no one could create a barrier to it.

Having almost expelled the Genoese from the Mediterranean, and at the same

48. ' St. John the Baptist and
Saints ': altarpiece by
Giambattista Cima da
Conegliano on the south
wall of S. Maria dell'Orto.
Perhaps no other Venetian
painter ever succeeded in
conveying with such intensity
the mellow splendour of the
mainland near Venice;
a splendour which is seen
to best advantage at the
end of the afternoon,
as the sun goes down.

time managing to maintain a *modus vivendi* with the peoples of the East which was always precarious though so far to her advantage, she had no reason to fear that she would be driven from the Inland Sea. On land, however, the princes who were envious of her wealth and power could, if they became strong enough, sever her communications with customers in London, as well as with Bruges, Ghent, Nüremberg, Bremen and Paris. Since the reign of Giangaleazzo Visconti, the designs of the Dukes of Milan on certain towns of mainland Venice (Brescia and Bergamo in particular) had seemed to foreshadow a desire to embrace the whole of Italy in the neo-Roman Empire for which the poet Petrarch prayed. Yet Venice could only prosper—indeed, could only exist—in an Italy divided as it was at the beginning of the fifteenth century.

Peacefully inclined—where land was concerned at all events—Venice was thus compelled to involve herself in wars which were contrary to her traditions and to her means of combat. She was forced to enter upon the tortuous by-ways of an obscure and complex diplomacy, and raise an army in whose basic elements, since hers was a seafaring people, she was completely lacking. She thus exposed herself to the greed and dishonesty of the ' captains of adventure ' who were known as *condottieri*, and whose assistance was costly, humiliating and unreliable. Most other Italian states did the same until Machiavelli, a brilliant strategist and a politician of genius, advocated their replacement by national armies. [38]

Venice was very much at an advantage in the sphere of diplomacy, for she had a corps of ambassadors far superior to those of other states at the time, and every Venetian living or travelling abroad on business was traditionally a propagandist and often a spy. The very remarkable work by Orestes Ferrara on the ambassadors of the Republic [39], reveals that most of the reliable information we have on foreign courts is to be found in the reports of Venetian envoys who saw, heard and knew everything. Their abilities, and no doubt the material means they could draw upon in order to buy information, enabled the Grand Council to follow day by day what was being done, what was being said, what was being kept quiet, and in fact, what was brewing in every capital. In this way, Venice was sure of never being taken unawares, unless her enemies had the extraordinary powers of silence and deceit of Julius II and Cesare Borgia. In Byzantium itself she had thousands of informants, and that was why one of the first actions of the Turks, when they took the capital of the Basilei, was to massacre the ' Latins ', who were all suspected of being spies.

When Giangaleazzo Visconti died in 1402, his weak and incompetent brother, Giovanni Maria, took his place. But Giovanni's successor, Filippo Maria, proved to be a formidable opponent and his reign was to last thirty-five years—a year longer than that of his ' intimate enemy ', Foscari. Between these two men there was a veiled animosity, a basic hostility which sprang from their willingness to use any and every means to ensure the triumph of their respective countries. Physically they were alike; as we see them represented on a medal by Pisanello and in a painting by Gentile Bellini in the Correr Museum, they both had short, thick necks, huge heads, set lips, and an air of cunning and ruthlessness. Foscari was well described by Tommaso Mocenigo, a man who himself favoured a policy of peace, being acutely aware of the danger to Venice of a war on land: ' Proud and deceitful, ready to expend a great deal of money and plunge the Republic into conflicts which would place her at the mercy of military men '—a man, indeed, whose vanity and ambition were to involve him in perilous adventure.

In fairness to Foscari, he served Venice with great energy and an unshakable will to win. A war waged over a period of four years produced no definite result, but by the Treaty of Lodi in 1454, Venice was able to retain her mainland possessions. Some years later, the advent of Lodovico Sforza in Milan and the Italian ambitions of Charles VIII and Louis XII of France were to renew the conflict with even greater violence, and when the Emperor Maximilian entered into hostilities, the issue became general and brought about a kind of European war for which Italy served as the battle-field.

Mocenigo had been right when he predicted that war with Milan would lay the Republic at the mercy of military men—the *condottieri* on whose help she had been forced to depend. As Machiavelli wrote in *The Prince*, ' The Venetians have always won their victories with their own weapons, and by this I mean war at sea. The period of their decline began when they sought to make war on land, adopting the ways of the other peoples of Italy.'

The rise of the *condottieri* brought about an upheaval in the relative strength of the various states. The *condottiere*, in fact, was a soldier of fortune who hired

A Group of Seven Men Standing on a Quay. Pen and brown ink; Antonio Maria Zanetti.

his services and those of his army to anyone who paid for them, but his prices were high. He entered into a contract for a specified time, and when the period had elapsed he sometimes took advantage of his liberty to join the enemy he had just been fighting. If sufficiently stimulated by ambition, he carved himself a principality from the possessions of his employers and enemies, and, in his turn, became the ruler of a state. The Baglionis of Perugia, the Malatestas of Rimini, and the Sforzas of Milan all adopted this method.

Among them there were great fighting men, whose courage and energy were incomparable and whose generalship was genuinely inspired. Indeed, some of the faces in this gloomy portrait gallery of adventurers emerge in a remarkably brilliant light. Guidobaldo da Montefeltre, Braccio di Montone, Alberico da Barbiano, Niccolo Piccinino, Gattamelata, Alviano, Giovanni delle Bande Nere, and above all, two captains in the service of Venice: Carmagnola and Colleoni.

No moral ties bound the *condottieri* to the princes they served; these dealers in warfare sold themselves to the highest bidder, showing no sympathy or preference for one side any more than for another. Most of them acted like honest tradesmen in fulfilling a contract they had signed, but there were some who did not scruple to betray their masters and grow rich at their expense. It was to prevent treachery of this kind that those who employed them sometimes took the wives and children of the *condottieri* as hostages, and thus made certain that they were reliable.

The *condottiere*, on the other hand, had every reason to be wary of the employer who jibbed at settling accounts for loyal and faithful service: it was quite as common for princes to be unappreciative as it was for their captains to betray them. The relationship which was thus established between the mercenaries and the cities engaging them was a product of fear and personal interest on both sides, hardly the basis for friendly, confident collaboration. It was quite normal for a prince to punish a *condottiere* where incompetence, negligence, or a secret arrangement with the enemy had brought defeat. Even success was poorly rewarded, for the *condottiere* who became too rich and powerful was a threat to his master. Roberto Malatesta, when he achieved victory, was assassinated at the order of Pope Sixtus IV.

A story told by the Florentine historian, Guicciardini, gives a clear illustration of the curious relationship which bound the mercenary to his master. A Tuscan city, probably Siena, had been so well and loyally served by its *condottiere* that it wondered in what way it could show its gratitude. No reward seemed adequate. The members of the government discussed the matter for a long time, some proposing that he should be offered a large sum of money in addition to his pay, others that he should be given land, castles and villages. Each one held the opinion that it was impossible to do enough for a man who had done so much for the city. One magistrate who showed greater shrewdness than the others restrained their enthusiasm. 'Be careful,' he warned them. 'By showering gifts on this man, you will encourage him to ask for more. What will you do if he becomes threatening? Don't forget that the money and domains you confer on him will give him more strength, more power, and consequently more arrogance and ambition. To give him the reward he is entitled to, and which his outstanding services have earned over so many years—without, however, exposing ourselves to danger on his account—this is what I propose: let us kill him; we can then declare him to be the guardian spirit of our city, we can raise statues to him, honour his name, and in this way everything will be wisely and fairly settled.'

This was the pragmatic and utilitarian moral code of Renaissance Italy; unfortunately it was not peculiar to the country or the period. It explains the mutual distrust between the *condottieri* and the states they served, especially after they ceased employing foreign captains. The period of John Hawkwood, of Albrecht Sterz, of Konrad von Landau and Werner von Urslingen, of their Swiss pikemen and German foot-soldiers, had almost completely passed. The *condottieri* were now Italian but there was no increase in patriotic spirit because of it, and the armies were made up of ill-assorted regiments, under various commanders who were all reluctant to defer to a supreme authority. In the works of Sanudo and Malipiero we find an account of the regiments used in certain wars. In 1495, for example, a critical time for the power of Venice, her cavalry of 15,526 horses was divided into a number of small companies, each of which had its own commander and sometimes numbered no more than 50 or 60 horsemen. The largest regiments, those of Gonzaga of Mantua and Gioffredo Borgia, had 1200 and 740 respectively. There were six others of only 600 horses each, ten of 400, twelve of 200, and fourteen of 100. With the mercenaries totally lacking in unity of heart or spirit, the outcome of a battle in these circumstances was altogether dubious.

The Republic feared her captains and suspected their treachery; on more than one occasion she executed some who had served her well but of whom she could not feel certain. Prato claims that the Venetians poisoned Alviano in 1516 for his suspicious behaviour at the battle of San Donato. The Venetians managed to find an ingenious method for ensuring the good faith of their *condottieri*; they compelled them to leave the money they earned in Venice, so that it could be easily appropriated if they were treacherous, or even thought to be inclined to treachery.

Historians have never succeeded in discovering the truth about the grim Carmagnola affair, which is a stain on the history of Renaissance Venice and illustrates only too clearly the troubled relationship existing between the Republic and her

The Piazza San Marco looking south-east. Brown ink over pencil; 10¹/₂″ x 15¹/₈″; Canaletto (or possibly Bellotto).

condottieri. Was Carmagnola really guilty of treachery or was he denounced by rivals who stood to benefit by his fall? Was the Senate over-hasty in seeing a traitor in an adventurer whose endowment of honesty was probably much like that of other men of his condition? Today we find it impossible to decide because contemporary documents seldom agree, but Carmagnola's story is too characteristic of Venetian policy towards mercenaries for us to leave it untold.

Carmagnola was a peasant whose real name was Francesco Bussone. His nickname was taken from the village where he was born and was applied to the type of red cap which it was customary for him to wear. Entering the service of Facino Cane, a *condottiere*, he soon distinguished himself with his exceptional talents as a fighting man and earned the favour of Filippo Maria Visconti, the Duke of Milan.

Having awarded him many honours, including the governorship of Genoa, Visconti was persuaded by bad counsellors to show his disfavour to this brave soldier, who was justly incensed. Enraged to see that he was now disregarded, that Milan now favoured men of lesser talents, and possibly fearing that he would be arrested or assassinated, Carmagnola fled and offered his services to Visconti's sworn enemy—Doge Foscari. The latter promptly conferred the title of captain-general of the Republic on him, together with a large payment and the highest honours.

Carmagnola achieved some brilliant victories over the Milanese under the Standard of St. Mark: conquering Brescia, Bergamo and Cremona; three months later peace brought an end to the war which had cost two and a half million ducats but had still proved very profitable to the Republic. Carmagnola was generously rewarded, but in January 1429, when his contract binding him to Venice expired, he asked to be released. The Senate prevailed upon him to renew the contract, and Carmagnola, after a good deal of hesitation, accepted; his pay was increased and he was given the county of Chiari. After hearing solemn mass in the Basilica, a magnificent ceremony was held in the Piazza San Marco, and amid the clamour of the crowd, Carmagnola received the commander's baton.

But Visconti had been in touch with his old captain and asked him to return to the service of Milan. All the decrees passed against him since his defection had been revoked; his confiscated fortune, his domains and his titles would be restored to him, and new ones would be added. Whether he had allowed himself to be tempted by this request or whether he was just unlucky and events did not go his way, it became evident from this time onward that Carmagnola no longer gave his old enthusiasm to the business of making war and that his ardour in the service of Venice had cooled considerably. His slowness in proceeding with military operations, his lack of vigour, and his apparent responsibility for the defeat of the fleet commanded by Trevisan at the mouth of the Adda, aroused the suspicion of the Senate. Possibly accusations were lodged with the Council of Ten, who would be bound to examine them very carefully. Certainly, Carmagnola's attitude could be well calculated to render him suspect, but there was no evidence to support the contention that he was maintaining secret contact with the enemy and intending to betray the Republic to Milan.

In similar situations where there was no more than a suspicion, it was the custom of the Council of Ten to act very quickly. First the suspect was seized: it was then up to him to prove his innocence. Carmagnola was accordingly arrested by a trick: he was summoned to the Doge's Palace—apparently to take part in a council of war—and was thrown into prison. The tough soldier proved to be unable to withstand torture; he confessed everything wanted of him and was duly condemned to death. Not unanimously, however: nine members of the tribunal asked for a further enquiry and more definite proof, but the majority of twenty-six prevailed. Only one of his judges believed him innocent.

When sentence had been pronounced, the Doge and three councillors, Luca Mocenigo, Francesco Barbarigo and Daniele Vitturi, proposed prison for life rather than the death penalty, but the majority had their way. On the 5th May, 1432, dressed in red from head to foot and wearing the famous red velvet carmagnola which had been quickly adopted by his troops, accompanied by the priests of S. Maria Formosa, he kneeled at the place where it was the custom to execute criminals. Between the two marble columns in the Piazzetta, one bearing a statue of St. Theodore with his crocodile, the other the Lion of St. Mark, he was beheaded. A gag had been placed in his mouth, perhaps so that he would be prevented from shouting his innocence to the people.

Bartolomeo Colleoni, the most famous *condottiere* of the Republic, immortalized

by Verrocchio's splendid bronze equestrian statue in front of the church of
SS. Giovanni e Paolo, had rather better fortune than his predecessor. Freed
from a Milanese prison by Venetian troops, he entered the service of the Republic
in 1448, and served it faithfully for nearly thirty years. Colleoni died peacefully
in his castle of Malpaga, which he had received as a reward. In the will of
this noble captain, apart from the large sums he intended for the erection of a

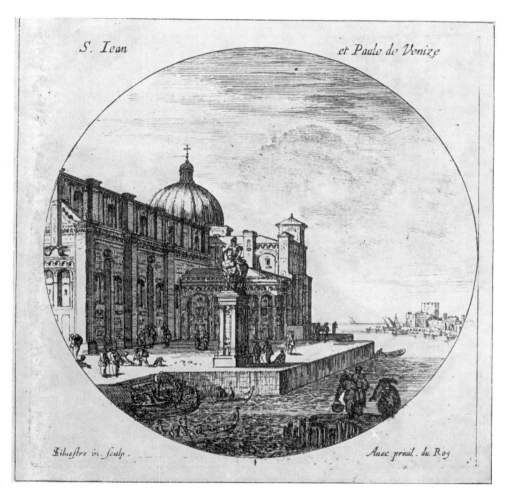

S. Iean et Paule de Venize

Siluestre in sculp. Auec priuil. du Roy

The Church of SS. Giovanni e Paolo.

splendid funerary chapel for his family in his native city of Bergamo, he left a
bequest of a hundred thousand ducats to help Venice proceed with the war
against the Turks. In return for this magnificent gift, the *condottiere* asked for
only one thing: that a statue be raised to him in the Piazza San Marco.

The money was worth having, but the condition was an embarrassment to
the Senate; a statue had never previously been erected in the Piazza. Probably
this was for aesthetic reasons, but also the number of great servants of the State
to be rewarded in this way would have been too large. The terms of the will
were strict, however, and since Colleoni was too good a soldier to be denied this
concession to his memory, the Senate found itself in an awkward situation when

it met on the 30th July, 1479. After an attempt to find a solution, a compromise was reached; it was proclaimed that the terms of the will were not clear and that instead of Piazza San Marco, he really meant the square containing the Scuola di San Marco.

Four years passed between the *condottiere's* death and the commissioning of the statue. The most distinguished Italian sculptor of the day was chosen for the monument, but its fate was still far from settled. Verrocchio brought the model of the statue to Venice and began working on it. The horse was ready to be cast in bronze when certain senators sought to replace Verrocchio by Bellano, a sculptor of lesser repute. Verrocchio, enraged by this, destroyed the head and legs of the horse and left for Florence once more.

The Senate, angered by his insolence, notified Verrocchio that if he ever set foot in Venice again, he would lose his head. The sculptor waggishly replied that he would take good care not to go there again. for if he lost his head, no one would be able to give him another one as good; but if required he could make another for the horse, and that this would be even more beautiful.

This answer pleased the Venetians, who had a sense of humour. Verrocchio was told to come back to Venice at once in order that the statue could be finished, and this he did. Unfortunately he fell ill in 1488 and died. In his will, he directed that the work was to be completed by his pupil, Lorenzo di Credi, but the Council of Ten preferred Alessandro Leopardi, who was exiled from Venice at the time for using false documents and forging signatures. Leopardi was pardoned for the sake of his talents, and it was he who completed the *condottiere's* statue. On the 21st March 1496, it was placed on the pedestal where it still stands today, looking proudly and menacingly towards the enemies of the Republic on the mainland. It had taken twenty years since the death of the *condottiere* for his statue to be offered to the admiring gaze of the people of Venice.

*
* *

Whilst occupied with European adventures in which she stood to lose more than she gained, Venice found herself exposed to another terrible danger. Since the taking of Constantinople by the Turks, the Ottomans were established on the Bosphorus, and from there were threatening Venetian possessions in the eastern Mediterranean—possessions very necessary to the security of sea communication and the trade which was its object. Less than twenty years after the fall of Byzantium, the Turks laid siege to two islands which were all-important to free traffic—Crete and Negroponte. Negroponte fell in 1470, the seventy Venetian ships being no match for the three hundred vessels of the Turks. The blame for this defeat was laid at the door of Niccolo Canale, who commanded the fleet, but the inferior strength of the Republic, not his alleged incompetence, was an adequate explanation for his failure, though he was always accused by his enemies of ' wasting his time reading.'

The consequences of this defeat were morally and physically terrible ones for Venice: apart from Negroponte, she lost Lemnos, Scutari and part of the Peloponnese. The Turks were masters of the Aegean Sea and compelled Venice to pay an annual tribute of ten thousand ducats for the possessions it pleased them to leave her. This humiliation and the obvious fact that the Republic was no longer proud mistress of the sea were big blows to her confidence, both in herself and her reputation for invincibility in sea warfare.

49. Rowlock of a gondola. The functional curves of the rowlock, varying in shape to correspond with the movement of the oar, have a strange beauty of their own.

The Turks, encouraged by their successes, decided that it was no longer enough to attack Venetian ports and fleets; they now proposed to carry the war on to Italian soil and accordingly landed huge forces in Friuli and Istria. After some daring and successful raids, they penetrated as far as the Isonzo and the Tagliamento, and only halted their advance when the rivers barred their way.

It was then that the Republic, alive to its new peril, sought to avail itself of new weapons in its defence and called on Leonardo da Vinci, whose reputation as an inventive genius was known in all the courts of Italy and even in France. In March 1500, he presented the Grand Council with plans for making the Isonzo valley impassable by means of canals and locks which would flood the country and drown the invaders. He showed them his designs for fortifications and weapons of war, quick-firing cannons and machine-guns; he also boasted that he knew how to produce incendiary-bombs that nothing could put out. What interested the Venetians more were his sketches for submarine craft which could surprise and sink an enemy fleet, and flying machines from which the enemy could be bombarded with missiles.

Unfortunately Leonardo refused to use his weapons for naval warfare. It was degrading, he maintained, to take an unarmed enemy by surprise; water, further-more, was a sacred element which should not be sullied or profaned. His under-water craft were the 'gratuitous' creations of his inventive genius and were to remain within the realm of theory. Since he was the only man at the time who was capable of putting into practice ideas which the Venetians, as men of good sense, thought too fanciful anyway, the plan for collaboration between da Vinci and the Republic fell through for lack of mutual understanding. The defence arrangements for the Isonzo were the only ones which could be used. Venice was accordingly forced to be content to use her own strength and tradi-tional methods of war in her struggle with the Turks, and in the following year the great artist entered the service of Cesare Borgia.

But the Republic found consolation in a diplomatic victory in default of a military one, when the skilful handling of her policy enabled her to place the daughter of a Venetian patrician on the throne of Cyprus by marrying Caterina Cornaro to King Jacques II of Lusignan.

From ancient times onwards, the Isle of Aphrodite had always been one of the strategic key-points in the Mediterranean, and whoever sought to control the inland sea also had to make certain that Cyprus was one of his possessions. In the fifteenth century it was very important for Venice to be there and perhaps even more important to ensure that her enemies were not; this applied to her old rivals, the Genoese, to the Spaniards, who aspired to a dominant position in European maritime politics, and finally to the Turks, for whom Cyprus repre-sented an advance bastion for their military positions. For a long time, further-more, the Knights of Rhodes had asserted rights for the possession of the island which the Republic refused to recognise.

The choice of Caterina Cornaro as wife of Jacques II of Lusignan was a master-stroke of Venetian diplomacy; the Cornaro family, indeed, had large domains in Cyprus, and it was in its own interest as well as the Republic's to keep the Lion of St. Mark in Nicosia and Famagusta. The marriage of the young girl to a man she had never seen was negotiated by the ambassadors of the two states in the same way that they would have arranged a treaty of alliance or a trade agreement. Once Caterina had become queen she gained considerable influence over her husband, and used it zealously for the benefit of her native city. Jacques was weak-natured, lacking in will-power and ready to accept the view of those who protested loudly enough or spoke last. By her efforts, he agreed to remain

50. 'The Feast in the House of Levi': detail. Veronese; Accademia. When this monumental, and truthful, work first appeared, accusa-tions of impiety and heresy were heaped on Veronese, and he was hailed before the Inquisition. Fortunately, however, he was absolved.

51. 'The Rich Epulum': detail. Bonifacio de' Pitati; Accademia. The work of this painter, a native of Verona who worked in Venice and died there in 1553, embodies both the splendour and the sadness so typical of the period of transi-tion from the Renaissance to the Baroque era.

in a state of dependence on Venice, a situation which was humiliating to his personal pride and damaging to his interests.

When the King died, however, Caterina sought to safeguard the inheritance of her son, who was destined to die young. She forgot her duty to her motherland, and out of loyalty to the memory of her husband and to her people, she became an ardent Cypriot patriot. In the teeth of the encroachments of the Republic, which planned to subject Cyprus to its authority, she encouraged and stimulated the national feelings of her subjects. The Senate, expecting to make use of her as a convenient instrument, was confronted instead by an adversary who was not to be bent by her parents' entreaties or official warnings. A show of strength was necessary before the Venetian who had become more Cypriot than her subjects could be removed and the Republic was able to impose its direct authority over the island. Caterina Cornaro had to return to Venice, where she was received with great honour and was still addressed as Queen, though the title no longer had any meaning since the kingdom had been seized from her.

Venice thus consolidated her hold on this bone of contention in the eastern Mediterranean and remained mistress of it until an attack launched by Sultan Selim II against Nicosia. After a long and difficult siege, it fell into the hands of the Moslems on the 9th September, 1570. Famagusta resisted six months longer; its inhabitants were alarmed by the massacres which followed the surrender of Nicosia, and they awaited the arrival of a fleet which Venice had promised to send to their help. Tragically, the Republic was unable to come to the aid of its remote possessions at that time, and on the 18th August, the Crescent flew over the remains of the demolished strongholds, fire consumed the cities, and their inhabitants were ruthlessly put to the sword.[40]

Venice's empire was too widespread, scattered over too many different countries, for her to protect it effectively when a number of enemies attacked at the same time. Her efforts to defend herself against the growing might of the Turks since 1453 would have been enough in themselves to keep her busy and consume her entire military budget. But when the states of Europe joined forces against her in the early years of the sixteenth century, she was obliged to meet them on a number of fronts at the same time, and fight on land as well as water.

Her attackers found a pretext for their aggression in the belief (repeated by Machiavelli) that she sought to assert her power over the whole of Italy: this idea of a kingdom of Italy which would be capable of confronting the kingdoms of France and Naples or the Empire, certainly inspired the great statesmen of the day, especially Cesare Borgia and Pope Julius II. It was becoming apparent to everyone that Italy, divided as she was into little principalities, presented an easy prey to her greedy neighbours. Yet in all probability Venice, of all the states in the Peninsula, was the one least moved by the dream of Italian unity or the desire to accomplish it. Having no great liking for war, she could only bring herself to wage it when absolutely compelled. In the midst of all the quarrelsome states of the Renaissance, Venice seems to have been remarkably gifted with good sense, and well worthy of the eulogy accorded to her by Muratori when he praised her 'happily conceived system of government, the laws which bring the people peace and justice, her unhampered trade, and the clearsighted guardianship of a wise Republic.'

Venice kept her wisdom and sense of proportion even in the expansion of her trade. In the century when the Spaniards and Portuguese were venturing into unknown continents, and the French, Dutch and English were vying with one another in the New World, she was untouched by the fever for discovery and conquest. Content with the acquisitions she had made in the Middle Ages, she

52. 'The Tempest': detail. Giorgione; Accademia. The meaning of this picture, Giorgione's greatest work, has always remained a mystery. A compromise can be clearly seen, however, between the exuberance of Venetian art and the inner restlessness of an unhappy soul.

was more concerned with the strengthening of her influence than the extension of it. She was Queen of the Inland Sea, and was distrustful of the oceans and their hazards. The daring times when Marco Polo penetrated to Cathay were past, and Venice showed a tendency to retire within herself, to live once again within the limits imposed on her by her insular nature; it was always with reluctance that she put her prosperity and prestige to the test.

It could almost be said that, since the Middle Ages, the wars she had waged had only been defensive ones, and neutrality, which is so valuable for trade, had been the object of her foreign policy. Her balanced, pragmatic outlook even led her to buy peace when she could get it by no other means. It was for this reason that she agreed to pay tribute to the Turks as long as this satisfied them; when a breach occurred it was through no fault of hers. The irony of the Republic's destiny was that when she tried to obtain peace at any price, she was drawn into a succession of disastrous wars which gradually sapped her strength and brought about her decline.

* * *

It was a coalition between Venice's most formidable enemies, the Spaniards and the Papacy, which laid the foundations of the so-called League of Cambrai, joined by France and the Empire in 1508. These allies intended to divide Venice's mainland possessions among themselves. The agreement they signed on the 10th December, 1508, was the gravest threat encountered by the Republic throughout her history. She had barely succeeded in buying her shaky neutrality from the Ottomans when she found the whole of Europe bearing down in a plot to destroy her.

What saved Venice during this period was that in the mainland towns attacked by her enemies, there was a kind of 'resistance' movement which developed for the most part among the common people; the nobility was more sympathetic to the coalition. Whilst the troops of the Holy Roman Empire were laying siege to Vicenza, Padua, Treviso and Verona, for example, the *popolani* of these cities took up arms against the invaders and proved a great help to the Venetian armies in containing them and driving them back.

Lack of co-ordination between the allies and, most important of all, the defection of the Emperor Maximilian, brought about a change in the trend of events. One after another, Venice was able to recapture the cities which had been taken from her in September 1509. Pope Julius II, in his turn, proved willing to negotiate some months later. The League was practically dissolved and Venice was saved—as much, it should be observed, by her diplomacy as by her armies. It looked as if she had lost control of the Adriatic, but in fact she had kept it, and that was the main point of the struggle.

Three years later, the shifting tide of alliances, which plays such an active part in international politics, produced the situation in which France, formerly Venice's enemy in the League of Cambrai, was now her friend and even her ally. King Louis XII of France, who was interested in gaining help in Italy in his campaigns against Lombardy and the Spaniards in Naples, promised in an agreement signed at Blois on the 12th March 1513, that he would support the Republic in the reconquest of all her former mainland possessions.

Unhappily, the Italian adventure which was begun by Charles VIII, continued by Louis XII, and brought to such a disastrous conclusion by Francis I, exposed Venice to the anger and revenge of the French King's greatest rival, the

53. These sixteenth and seventeenth century pikes are among the most beautiful pieces in the armoury of the Correr Museum. They are from Venice and from the East, and clearly demonstrate that a civilised society will turn even an instrument of murder into a work of art.

Emperor Charles V. Charles made the Republic pay dearly for her mistake in siding with the French. At the Congress of Bologna, where the victors shared the spoils, Venice lost control of the southern Adriatic and Apulia, which went to the Pope, as well as the Romagna. Her treasury, which had already been grievously weakened by war, was now compelled to meet a heavy indemnity. Frustrated in her territorial hopes, she was driven, for good and all, to rest her future on her power at sea; but even there, terrible perils lay in wait for her.

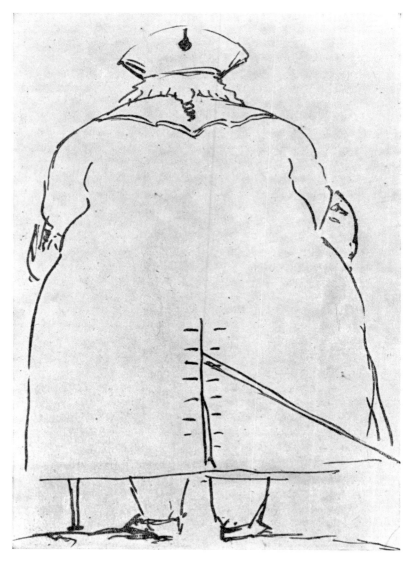

A Stout Elderly Man, probably Sebastiano Ricci. Brown ink; Marco Ricci.

THE BAROQUE PERIOD

AT THE VERY time when Venice's power on the mainland was suffering severe onslaughts, her supremacy at sea was simultaneously threatened by two equally dangerous enemies: the Turks and the Spaniards. Emboldened by the capture of Constantinople and the establishment of Islam on the Golden Horn, the Turks, as we have seen, felt strong enough to brave the Venetians in Italy itself, whilst their galleys set to the task of driving the standard of Saint Mark from the Mediterranean. The Spaniards also aspired to mastery of the sea, and their possession of a European and colonial empire ' on which the sun never set ' justified their highest ambitions.

The new sea routes, as we said, created serious competition for Venice's trade; the spices and other merchandise originating from the Near East, Central Asia and the Far East, were re-routed, making her trade-posts virtually useless. Her fortunes were determined in such a way that she relied on political power to establish her economic prosperity, and the wealth derived from her trade to maintain her authority and prestige. From the way things were going since the Turks and Spaniards had been profiting from the Republic's growing weakness, it seemed possible to predict that the speed of her decline, both politically and economically, would lead to her complete collapse. Fortunately, the enmity which prevailed between the Cross and the Crescent ensured a balance of power, and Venice was able to take advantage of this.

The qualities inherent in the people of the lagoon remained intact, despite the aristocracy's fondness for luxury and extravagance. The devotion of the common people and the traditional heroism of the patricians belied this decline. The story of Marcantonio Bragadin, who fought bravely at Famagusta in 1571, was captured by the Turks and flayed alive, is eloquent proof of this. So is the daring of the two Venetian sailors who retrieved the gallant captain's skin from the very heart of the Arsenal, the Moslem stronghold in Constantinople, when they heard that it was being held there as a trophy. The monument built to the hero's memory in the church of San Zanipolo, and the urn containing his remains, are clear evidence of the way in which the essential qualities of the Venetians endured.

The heroism of Tommaso Morosini, who in 1647 held a Turkish fleet at bay, the magnificent stubbornness of the defenders of Candia, who resisted the Moslems in a siege lasting twenty-two years, the feats of arms of Giuseppe Delfino outside Constantinople in 1654, and the senseless engagements in the Dardanelles under Jacopo Riva in 1649, are proof that if the Republic was compelled to defend herself against her enemies, she did so valiantly. Morosini's ten years of campaigning in Greece even seemed reminiscent of the brilliant adventures of the Dandolos and Contarinis in the Middle Ages, though this was no more than a final upsurge of Venetian pride and the desire for conquest.

Little by little, Venice lost all her possessions in the Mediterranean: Cyprus, Crete, and all the island bastions commanding the sea routes, fell one after the other, and the loss of Morea in 1714 marked the end of her foothold in Greece. At the battle of Lepanto, which was really won by the Venetian fleet, there is clear evidence of Spanish duplicity. Admittedly Philip II instructed his admiral to defeat the Turks, but he made it plain that Venice—his ally—was to derive no advantage from the victory. [41] During a battle which seemed to everyone like a miraculous triumph and the crowning achievement in a holy war against Islam, it became clear that Spain's major preoccupation was to conduct her affairs in such a way that her ally suffered almost as much as her enemy. If Philip II had been able to bring about the simultaneous defeat of the Turks and Venice, his joy would have been complete. For the Venetians, who did not have much faith in their ally, Lepanto stood out as a striking instance of divine intervention on their behalf. The paintings of the battle in the chapel of the Rosary in San Zanipolo and the Sala del Collegio in the Doge's Palace, bear witness to the splendid part played by the galleys of Sebastiano Venier; on this unforgettable day in October, 1571, he fought, at the age of seventy-five, like a young hero.

But the walls of the Republic, once perfectly intact, were beginning to show clear signs of cracking. The institution of State Inquisitors in 1539 was something quite new, for their task—to watch those in a position to give away state secrets—had never been previously thought of as necessary. When Romanin declared that the Inquisitors had saved the Republic by extending their duties so that they embraced the Council of Ten itself—the very source of their origin—he was admitting that the Republic in the sixteenth century really had been in need.

Venice still continued trying to ward off the danger represented by the new routes which the Portuguese had discovered and were using so profitably. It was a Venetian who had the ingenious idea of building a canal through the Suez Isthmus so that the Red Sea and the route to India could be made to communicate directly with the Mediterranean. [42] The plan was never elaborated beyond this, probably for fear of angering the Sultan; the idea had taken root, for all that, and Suleiman the Magnificent began considering it on his own account, though he did not get any further than the Venetians. Another, completely new, idea occurred to the Venetians at this point. Hitherto their way of life had always been dependent on the sea; Doge Alvise Cornaro now showed a new interest in agriculture—'holy agriculture' as he called it. He contended that since revenues from the sea were diminishing, it was important to make up for them by rational exploitation of the land's natural wealth. [43] It was unfortunate that this remarkable initiative for a new agricultural policy came at the very time when Venice was losing the mainland possessions which she could have used for intensive cultivation.

The fact that Venice tried to right her affairs by establishing committees, commissions, and offices, is evidence that she was now reduced to desperate emergency measures; in the days when trade was prosperous and her financial resources at their height, committees had been unnecessary. Yet neither the *Giunta delle Spezerie*, which supervised the spice trade, nor the *savi alla mercanzia*, which organized shipping, proved able to check the decline. The most useful achievement of the *savi* was to recognize the disastrous state of affairs at the beginning of the seventeenth century. They say quite explicitly in their report

54. Bronze door knocker from the Palazzo Grimani, now the Court of Appeal. About 16″ × 12″.

55. Detail of a bas-relief, from an arch in the south entrance of St. Mark's Cathedral. Here the mediaeval sculptor seems to have been inspired by an Oriental style.

56. Detail of a bas-relief at the base of a pilaster in the church of S. Maria dei Miracoli. The siren theme, a favourite subject in ancient times, has here been adopted by an Italian sculptor. He has associated it with the figure of an angel, apparently Christian, in accordance with the religious syncretism which was a Renaissance ideal.

54   55

56

of the 5th July, 1610, as quoted by Bailly [44]: 'We have lost all our trade and sea-routes in the western Mediterranean. Those we have in the Levant are only sustained by a few companies which have been crippled by losses, lack shipping, and are daily growing weaker'.

Certain sea-routes disappeared from the map completely, especially those serving England via Southampton; this had once been one of Venice's richest sources of revenue. Trade with Germany was falling just as rapidly. Old-established banks with the soundest reputations were failing, and the dockyards were threatened with unemployment [45]. The devotion of the patricians to the common good was no longer to be taken for granted—in peace-time at all events—and those who had been proud of commanding their own ships now left the task to their sub-ordinates. It would seem that the upper classes of Venice, discouraged perhaps by the declining state of affairs, were more interested in enjoying their diminishing fortunes than in putting their ingenuity to work to increase them. On the surface, the great magistrates of the Republic kept their grave dignity, and the paintings of the Doges and senators by Tintoretto, Veronese, Palma, Bassano or Paris Bordone, continued to show the same serious, meditative faces with all the nobility and quiet authority which were the characteristic mark of Venetian aristocracy.

It would be unfair to attribute all the responsibility for the decline to Venetian society; it was a product of circumstances, of the shifting balance of power, both in European and Eastern politics, and of the inevitable development of commerce and the sciences. It was the outcome of the relentless fate which takes both peoples and individuals from childhood to maturity, and from there to old age and death. Venice in the seventeenth century was passing through a period comparable to the last hours before sunset; and just as those are the hours when the sun achieves its greatest colour and brilliance, so Venice's primacy shifted from the sphere of trade and politics to that of art.

Venetian painting, which had possibly been somewhat behind that of other Italian cities, was now to show that Florentine genius was dying, and artistic supremacy had passed from the mainland to the lagoon. Venice's Baroque art was unequalled, and neither Rome, Naples nor Bologna could challenge her in her splendid superiority.

By all but a few years, Giorgione was the contemporary of the great Renaissance painters we mentioned earlier. He died before Bellini, before Carpaccio, and could have known Dürer during the period that the Franconian artist spent in Venice; in terms of time, and because he died very young, he is almost exclusively a man of the fifteenth century, yet by the nature of his genius and his work, he belonged to the seventeenth century.

Venetian Baroque painting, linked as it was with the Renaissance, began very early and very mysteriously with him. His date of birth is a matter for conjecture and the stages of his artistic development are also shrouded in obscurity. Tradition holds that he died of the plague before he was forty, but this is only a theory. Scholars argue unendingly about the paintings to be attributed to him: the *pala* of the Virgin, which he painted for the Cathedral of his native city, Castelfranco, is one of the few works definitely accepted as his.

The subjects of most of his paintings are as much a riddle as the character of the painter himself: they are called by names such as *The Three Philosophers*, or *The Tempest* (the latter is in the Accademia of Venice), according to a tradition on which time has conferred authority. We can only attempt to imagine what he thought through the mysterious atmosphere of his landscapes and the dreamy expressions on the faces he represented. We are as mystified by his work as we are by his character, and it is in this respect that the strength, the secrecy and the baroque in his nature, conflict with the clarity of the Renaissance. It is suggested

57. 'Portrait of a Man.' Titian; National Gallery. This magnificent picture is enriched by the 'grand manner' which Titian always displayed in his portraits, and which allowed the character of his sitters to shine through their outward appearance.

131

that he had ties with the neo-Platonist philosophers, with hermetics and occultists; that they communicated some of their tenets to him and that he embodied them in his work. But how did he himself interpret the equivocal content of his paintings? We shall never know.

He is unique in Venetian painting, and indeed, in the painting of the world. Few artists have been so surrounded by secrecy, and this is only heightened by the discussion his work has aroused. The virtually inexplicable nature of Baroque painting, an intense dramatic quality which defies explanation, these are the elements which bathe Giorgione's work in a half-light of dream and vision. It would have been impossible for him to develop anywhere but in the watery, sparkling, transparent atmosphere of Venice. Castelfranco is not far from the Dolomites, and from them Giorgione brought a taste for the forest, for horizons blue-tinted by the clouds or rosy with snow. The Venetian humanists were delighted by the riddles they found in his work, and they expended a great deal of knowledge and ingenuity in trying to solve them.

The deep unrest which pervades a painting famous for its enigma as for the splendour of its art—like the Mona Lisa—is characteristic of the Baroque style. It was inevitable that it should make its appearance, even in an ardently pragmatist city—a positive, dynamic city, whose constant stimulus was an instinctive and unremitting will for power. The physical climate of Venice, with its air of unreality so typical of all maritime cities—and especially an island-city—encouraged the rise of an individual Baroque style. This now reached a magnificent flowering, but perhaps more in music and architecture than in painting. There were, in fact not very many great Venetian Baroque painters apart from Lorenzo Lotto, Francesco Maffei, Tintoretto—from a certain standpoint—and above all Giorgione. It seemed that the Republic had obtained all the glory and prosperity it was possible to achieve and now could only lose them again. A foreboding of this decline was given its earliest and most disturbing expression in the melancholy ever present in Giorgione's work.

In the melodious sadness which pervades the landscape of *The Tempest*, the group of musicians in the *Country Concert* in the Louvre, and the troubled faces in his portraits, we are confronted with a supreme example of the subtle, insidious Baroque melancholy which could well lead to despair and death if it were not vigorously counterbalanced by practical activity. Baroque gloom could not eat very deeply into the soul of Venice or its vital force, for the city was immunized against it in advance. The Baroque painters were to remain splendid but rare exceptions within a general trend. [46]

This becomes more apparent when we compare the paintings of Giorgione to those of Titian. With Titian we enter a world in which everything is wonderfully clear, a world unknown to Giorgione, for whom nothing was clear or determinate among the metaphysical and aesthetic problems which engrossed him. Even so, with some compositions, it is still possible to be uncertain whether to ascribe them to one or the other of these two very different painters.

Titian belonged to the great family of sensualist painters who flourished so magnificently during the Venetian sixteenth century—their golden age: Palma il Vecchio, Paris Bordone, and Bonifazio dei Pitati. Of these three artists, Pitati, in some respects, is the one who comes closest to Giorgione, much closer than Titian, whose early work, for all that, had a strong Giorgionesque tinge. His painting of *The Feast of Epulum* in the Venice Accademia is one of the finest examples of Venetian Baroque; it earns this description through the important part played in it by music—the whole picture seems to throb to the sound of the lute and singing—and through the melancholy which is present in the dark-tinged sensuality of the Dives and his female companions.

58. Interior of the Scuola San Rocco; view from the Room of the Crucifixion. It is in the Scuola San Rocco that the fiery and manifold genius of Tintoretto is seen to greatest advantage. The composition on the right of this picture shows Christ summoned before Pilate.

59

Venetian sensualism, which was already asserting itself with the Renaissance and was to do so to excess in the eighteenth century, was the favourite element of the Baroque style in this city which was so fond of enjoyment. It would seem that Palma the Elder was afraid of mingling pleasure with the ' poisons of the soul ' which were capable of destroying it; he restrained himself completely to the ' flesh without the soul ', knowing that it would offer no nagging problems. His *St. Barbara* in the church of S. Maria Formosa is representative of the ideal of beauty which was generally accepted by sixteenth and seventeenth century Venice: generous, healthy bodies, full luminous flesh on which the sun shed reddish-gold rays, and the luxuriant ' Venetian blonde ' hair which the women of the town acquired by exposing their locks to the sunlight through holes in the crowns of the huge straw hats they wore to protect their complexions.

Titian also represents a wonderful renewal of aesthetic sensibility in Venetian painting. Although we do not know the exact date of his birth at Cadore, he was probably at least twenty-six when Bellini died, and had by this time already produced a number of works in which there was clear evidence of his originality and maturity. Dates have their significance in matters of this kind, and it is worth recalling that Giovanni Bellini had been dead for no more than two years when Titian painted his superb *Assumption* in the church of the Frari.

He must have escaped quite soon from Giorgione's ruling influence and from the fascination which this extraordinary master must have exerted; or perhaps he only borrowed certain technical elements which would be important to him as an artist but not affect his inner being. Again, his dominant sensuality may have given him full protection from the peril of spiritual worries. Until quite late in his career he seemed unshakably composed, his mind as free of anguish as his hand was of hesitation. Between 1540 and 1545 a crisis occurred in his artistic life which plunged him completely into the Baroque style; it did not, however, affect the essential part of his personality or genius. It has been said that it was ' more than just a halt dictated by weariness, it was a courageously aggressive act which Titian accomplished in defiance of himself, in defiance of the serene, contented vision which was born of the Renaissance '. [47] Yet in actual fact, before going to Rome and coming face to face with Michelangelo during his period at the Vatican (Michelangelo, indeed, had just completed the *Last Judgment* in the Sistine Chapel and the frescoes in the Pauline Chapel) he had felt the coming of the Baroque and had heard its call.

But the real and most important crisis, the crisis which proved most productive because it was not restricted to the formal world of painting, was the spiritual one which disturbed his old age. The finest example of his achievement in this period is *La Pietà* in the Accademia, an unfinished work which in some ways may be regarded as his testament. Here matter is dissolved in light; the voluptuous beauty he loved yields to the inrush of the spirit. Hedonism and the careful balance of heart, senses and intelligence, on which he built his life and work, are battered by a metaphysical storm—caught in it, shaken and thrown into confusion. His creatures become ethereal phantoms, moving restlessly in a dramatic chiaroscuro which anticipates Rembrandt. Titian came late to the Baroque, but when once it had entered his being, it took possession of him—perhaps all the more completely because his resistance had been so strong and unyielding.

Beside Titian, and perhaps in opposition to him in the panorama of Venetian Baroque, stands Lorenzo Lotto; restless, disquieting, the most ' baroque ' figure of the century, the most surprising and the most inexplicable. His use of space created problems for which he found bold and unexpected solutions. He broke ruthlessly with the Renaissance. His new approach was more radical than that of Sebastiano Mazzoni, who belongs completely to the seventeenth century, or

59. ' The Crucifixion ': detail. Tintoretto; Scuola San Rocco. Every detail in this huge, animated composition is in itself a perfect example of flowing beauty and unsurpassed technical mastery.

that of his contemporary, Francesco Maffei, in whose work the Baroque is more external, more theatrical, and in some ways more formal.

Mazzoni and Maffei were extrovert painters; the dramatic quality of their work seems somewhat conventional, despite the great beauty which we are compelled to admire in their painting, but in them the Baroque is as one would expect to find it. In Lotto, on the other hand, it is stranger, more secret, and unforeseen.

In his *Glory of St. Nicholas* in the Carmini Church, we see what could well be considered the first 'romantic' landscape in a period when the Baroque was already paving the way for Romanticism; his *St. Antony distributing alms* in the church of the Frari shows quite a striking taste for oddity, and an artistic enterprise which was in every way in advance of the art of his century. Lotto was a native of the Romagna but Venetian by temperament and choice, and in the melancholy and unrest of his paintings he portrays one of the most curious aspects of seventeenth century Venice, where an awareness of her declining splendour and prosperity cast an aura of sadness over her life and art.

The Bassano family originated from the mainland. In their work, by contrast, we recognise the robust quality of an art inspired by the themes of country life. Jacopo da Ponte (called Bassano after his native city) and his father Francesco were both luminists, following in the wake of Caravaggio, and forerunners at the same time of the eighteenth century *tenebrosi*. Like them, they were fascinated by the wealth of mystery in chiaroscuro, the contrasts of light and shade. Jacopo's three sons, the third generation in a dynasty of painters, carried this contrast to an extreme of theatrical artifice which was really foreign to the Venetian mind, and more in keeping with the aesthetic of Naples, Bologna or Genoa.

Because his work embraced all the very special features of the Queen of the Adriatic, the most Venetian of the seventeenth century painters was Paolo Cagliari, called Veronese because he was born and served his apprenticeship in Verona. He became known so quickly that he was not yet twenty-five when he began work in the Doge's Palace on the vast, joyous, shining magnificence of the decorations which made him famous. His name is inseparable from the *Glory of Venice* which he painted on the ceiling of the Maggior Consiglio, and from the *Rape of Europa* in the Sala dell'Anticollegio. If to this we add the astonishing collection of paintings covering almost the entire interior of the Church of S. Sebastiano, and the frescoes in the Villa Maser near Asolo, we gain some idea of the splendour, the harmonic breadth, and the feeling of ease and contentment which are present in his works.

There was no better interpreter of Venetian life during the period, for he gave even his sacred scenes the sensual magnificence of profane ceremonies. His paintings were a mirror which he offered to the Republic that she might look on herself in her most splendid finery. It has been said that his work does not come from the heart; if this is so, it is because the painter preferred to represent the surface of things and generally showed little concern for the hidden depths. [48]

By contrast, Tintoretto, as described by his contemporaries, was 'the most terrible mind ever known to painting'. There was a stormy violence in the lightning speed with which he worked; in his genius, which shows such great subtlety despite his superhuman strength, there was always something elemental: and these were the qualities through which the work of this bewildering painter stirred a whole mysterious universe—probably inaccessible to the elegant, magnificent Veronese. He showed, in some respects, a kinship with Michelangelo, who was also violently impulsive and at home in the visionary world. In Tintoretto's painting of the *Last Supper*, the room we look on seems to be filled with a supernatural storm, resounding to the sonorous wings of countless angels.

It is enough to have examined the huge cycle of his paintings in the Scuola

San Rocco to understand what Zanetti calls his *furioso entusiasmo*; its violent, tempestuous atmosphere engulfs his figures in their ecstasy and torture, transcending them and giving them titanic proportions.[49] Tintoretto treated the fantastic and the everyday, the familiar and the miraculous on one and the same plane. He overwhelmed Venice with the sudden violence of his fire and imagination, revealing a little known and not easily discerned aspect of the Venetian character: the gift for expressing the supernatural world. This was to emerge fully during the following century in the engravings of Tiepolo, which show us a frightening world of wizards, sorcerers, witches and executioners.

Tintoretto represents the other face of Venice—grim, tormented, uncertain of itself—which was gradually unmasked with the growth of Baroque art. However un-Venetian he may have seemed, Tintoretto, as much as Veronese but on another plane, represented the essential reality of Baroque Venice, which manifested itself in her music as well as her painting. Where architecture is concerned, it is to be observed that once Venice had freed herself from the radiant but frigid perfection of Palladio, she gave place to the fitful genius of Longhena and the dizzy splendour of his masterpiece, the Church of La Salute.

The church was built in gratitude to the Madonna for help she gave the city during a terrible plague epidemic. It is here indeed that we are best able to study the features of Baroque religious architecture, and to note how it contrasts with that of the Renaissance in that it is dynamic, not static. Everything is in motion, even in the very structure of the architecture; wherever the eye settles, it is inevitably forced to move both horizontally and vertically—as in the paintings of Tintoretto. This is pre-eminently emotional art; it appeals to the heart more than to the head, to impulse and enthusiasm rather than to intellect. In the basic structure, this supremacy of dynamic over static is demonstrated for the most part in two ways: in the interior of the church, with a return to a circular plan, and externally by using undulating façades which enliven the stone with the free movement of waves, and the lightness and mobility of water.

Baldassare Longhena, whose art seems rather too solid in his palaces, the Palazzo Rezzonico and the Palazzo Pesaro, first conceived the Church of La Salute as a gigantic votive offering, with the central structure surmounted by a magnificent cupola. In its majesty and splendour, the building was to represent the love of the city as a whole for the Madonna, and its deeply felt gratitude. The site of the church, on a headland between the Grand Canal and the Giudecca Canal, dictated its circular form, chosen by Longhena for its artistic value as well as its symbolic meaning. The circular form also helped to lighten the effect of this huge mass; it would have loomed oppressively against the surrounding country had it not been heightened by a series of spirals which lend a strong, sustained, rotary movement to its outer forms. In this there is no denial of the real weight of matter, nor is it handled as though it did not exist; far from it, Longhena lays stress on the weight and majesty of the mass but he contrives a subtle play of light and shadow in the outer projections of the chapels, in the lavish volutes supporting the tambour—from which the cupolas rise in their turn, and in the many animated statues. And this engenders a buoyancy, a constant displacement of mass which, depending on lighting, can make the Salute seem almost weightless. In Venice, then, where the memory of the classical architects, Sansovino, Scamozzi and Palladio, could have been crushing, paralysing in its effect, Longhena found a stimulus, the incentive to emulate them. His major concern, however, was to achieve harmony between S. Maria della Salute and the nearby Byzantine Basilica of St. Mark, where the same method for lightening the appearance of huge architectonic masses could have been applied once again and adapted to the individual needs of Venetian Baroque. [50]

Longhena had many splendid successors—among them Giuseppe Sardi. He desinged the ornate façade for the 'family' church of the Barbaro Doges—S. Maria Zobenigo (also known as S. Maria del Giglio) and the extraordinary decorations in the church of the Gesuiti, where polychrome ceramics give the illusion of solid matter converted into soft, silky fabric.

In the Church of S. Moisè, which contains a remarkable *Moses on Sinai* behind the high altar, the dazzling virtuosity of Arrigo Meyring the sculptor and the genius of Tremignon the architect produced a wealth of extravagant paradox. With the curious baroque altars in the Church of S. Marciliano, the campanili of S. Maria Formosa and S. Bartolomeo, and the resplendent marmoreal wealth of the church of the Scalzi, Venetian Baroque demonstrates its variety of form and imagination. It reached its peak, however—and after that there was nothing more than caprice, absurdity and extravagance—in the tomb of Giovanni Pesaro in the Church of the Frari. The collaboration between Longhena, who provided the overall plan in 1669, and two sculptors, Falcone of Lugano, and Melchior Barthel, a German, resulted in this strange accumulation of monsters, skeletons and negro slaves supporting the entablature on their enormous shoulders and wearing breeches and slashed tunics, the black marble of their flesh shining through the holes.

There are still two further names which immediately call Venetian Baroque to mind: that of Francesco Pianta, the sculptor of obscure allegories, strangely comic or terrifying figures, and the woodwork in the Scuola San Rocco, and Brustolon, who devised extravagant furniture, twisted in a thousand different ways and supported by dragons and lifelike negroes rolling onyx eyes in faces of ebony and whose masterpieces are now to be seen in the Settecento Museum and the Palazzo Rezzonico. It was Brustolon, out of pure defiance and to show that daring could achieve anything, who set a portait of Benedict III, encircled in enamel and precious stones, in a cherry stone. Was this the end of an art? Perhaps the twilight of a civilisation, the setting of the sun in the sea...

CITY OF CARNIVAL

In the eighteenth century, Venice became the city of carnival. Everyone, Doge and beggar alike, paraded in *bauta* and *tabarro* [51], and in a city once determined to dominate the seas and extend its power and trade into every corner of the globe, there was no longer thought for anything save amusement, perhaps to hide the memory of the faded glory and the lost prosperity. But the amusements themselves were so gay, so charming, so tasteful, that pleasure-seekers from all over Europe—gentlemen of leisure, financiers, noblemen and adventurers—flocked to Venice to take part.

One of these visitors was a clever mischief-maker called Ange Goudar, half-satirist, half secret agent, who frequented Venice in order to pick up useful information. He left a thinly-disguised self-portrait in the six volumes of his book *Chinese Spy*, and in 1774 he wrote that ' entering this town, one breathes an atmosphere of voluptuousness that is scarcely conducive to morality. Nothing is to be found there but spectacle, pleasure and frivolous diversions. In other European countries, the madness of carnival lasts but a few days; here it continues for six months in the year.' [52]

The carnival opened, in fact, on the first Sunday in October and went on until Lent, with a short interval from Christmas Day till Epiphany. In other words, for six months every year the people of Venice abandoned their regular avocations, and, protected by the anonymity of the mask, threw themselves into the lighthearted pastimes which immediately became their main preoccupation. It was a charming, unreal way of life which the Venetians led during these six months when everyone did as he pleased, forgetting age and rank, but in time it grew to seem their only way of life. In other countries and earlier times, the carnival, like the Saturnalia of antiquity, represented a brief moment of licence and indulgence to every whim in defiance of customs and laws. It was, in other words, an orgy, and probably a useful safety valve; after a few days of mad debauch, people would return to their work in a decent and orderly manner.

In Venice, however, the carnival did not have the orgiastic elements which were found elsewhere—and which are still found today in places such as Basle, Cologne and Nice. It retained an air of elegance and discretion, even in its excesses, and filled one half of the year so pleasantly that the other half was taken up with waiting for it to come round again. Then, as if touched by a magic wand, the town became a kind of fairy world, where all tasks were forgotten, all obligations neglected, and everyone enjoyed himself with unflagging zeal. If a piece of business was absolutely unavoidable, then only the minimum of time was expended on it. A solemn Senator would not wait even to leave the precincts of the Doge's Palace before donning his Pulcinella cloak, pulling its huge sleeves over his ceremonial attire and running down the broad staircase four at a time towards the gondola where a beautiful girl awaited him.

Behind the shelter of the mask, everyone did as he liked, mocking social con-

The Torre dell'Orologio and Piazzetta dei Leoncini. Black/dark brownish-grey ink over pencil; 10⁵/₈″ x 14⁷/₈″; Canaletto.

vention but remaining nonetheless within the bounds of taste and discretion. These required, for instance, that no one should ever be recognised, even if his mask did not completely conceal his identity. 'Signor Maschera' was the correct form of address, admitting no distinctions of age or profession.

The mask most usually worn by ladies and gentlemen of rank was an extraordinary white face, adorned with a huge nose shaped like the beak of a bird of prey, through which the wearer breathed. When we come across this mask today in museums or collections of old costumes, there seems to be something disconcerting, frightening, almost ghostly about it. For the eighteenth century Venetians, however, it had the advantage of covering the face completely. Furthermore, it was always worn with a long black cloak which hid the entire body.

A crowd dressed uniformly in black and masked in chalky white would have looked doleful and funereal, but fortunately gayer disguises were also to be found, in fantastic shapes and gaudy colours. One of the most popular was Pulcinella, who wore a tall white conical hat, a wide tunic, huge trousers, and a colossal nose. This mask had a long history; it existed in Roman times, and it may even have been worn by the Etruscans. Pulcinella is a clown, but a grotesque and sinister clown, strangely bound up with legends of death and sexuality; his tremendous nose is a phallic symbol. Usually Pulcinellas went about in groups, indulging in all kinds of pranks. By tradition they were gluttonous, stuffing themselves whenever possible at other people's expense. They shouted obscene jokes, and, all dressed in white as they were, they seemed like noisy, lewd ghosts.

After Pulcinella, the favourite masks were those of the *commedia dell'arte*. There was Arlecchino, with his tight-fitting costume made of multicoloured pieces of material, his wooden stick, and his black leather mask made in the shape of a permanent, infectious grin. Tartaglia, his companion and victim, was a great stammering booby, foolish and awkward in everything he did. Brighella was the traditional comic valet, sly and stupid by turns. Pantalone was a finicky old man, always the target for humiliating tricks, as was Doctor Balanzon, a gesticulating, ridiculous windbag, with the glib tongue of a charlatan and the stubbornness of the simple-minded. The young girls and waiting-maids of the *commedia dell'arte*, Isabella, Colombina, and Smeraldina, were the most popular costumes for pretty women.

Apart from these, there was a limitless profusion of designs and colours at the disposal of the *signori maschere*. They could seek inspiration in the exotic garbs of Africa and China, Turkey and the Caucasus. The various regions of Italy could also provide traditional dress charming enough to satisfy the most exacting wearer. Famous personages of history and mythology were an excellent source for those who prided themselves on their learning.

At carnival time, then, a Venetian's main concern was to show off his costume and observe other people's. The great rectangular, marble-carpeted drawing-room of St. Mark's Square, set between the Courts and the Basilica, was turned into a vast ballroom for twenty-four hours out of twenty-four. It was cluttered with fortune-tellers and acrobats, quacks and puppet-shows, theatres and animals. Trained monkeys, lions in cages, giraffes and rhinoceroses brought from overseas, attracted hordes of curious onlookers. During the carnival of 1751 a rhinoceros became so popular that, pandering to the general excitement, Pietro Longhi painted its portrait and medallions were engraved with its likeness.

The entire city might therefore be compared to a theatre where all the inhabitants were both actors and audience. For those, however, who sought an entertainment more subtle and varied than that to be found in the streets, seven theatres opened the doors of their magnificently decorated auditoriums, blazing with lights reflected in an infinity of mirrors. Administered by famous impresarios and subsidised by noblemen for love of acting—or actresses—these theatres offered a tempting diversity of pleasures, from tragedy and *opera seria* to farce, fantasy and the comedy of manners.

Farce and fantasy were the prerogative of the *commedia dell'arte*. Their conventions were rooted in the far distant past, and their particular feature was that they acted impromptu—*a soggetto*, as the Italians say. Traditional characters, wearing masks, portrayed the comic or grotesque personages whom we have already met in the carnival: Arlecchino, Brighella, Pantalone, Colombina, and so on. These actors, accustomed to improvisation and gifted with astonishing vitality, had no need of a text. The producer would hang up in the wings an outline of the evening's play, and the actors would read this before making their entrances. After that they relied on their native wit, inventing jokes and dialogue as they went along. Some of the actors identified themselves so completely with the characters they played that they even adopted their names; thus the famous Sacchi, Carlo Gozzi's favourite actor, was known as Arlecchino Sacchi.

In certain pieces, only the roles of the four chief masked characters were played impromptu. The rest of the cast would use a script, only occasionally adding some dialogue when enthusiasm or special circumstances inspired it. Current events were used to lend topicality; for instance, on the day when the first newspaper appeared in Venice, Arlecchino Sacchi made his entrance on the stage dressed as a newsvendor.

The finest works of the *commedia dell'arte* were the fantasies staged by Carlo Gozzi. They were full of Oriental potentates and sorcerers and princesses and heroes, while the four masks mingled with the action, removing any semblance of probability from the plot and providing the element of buffoonery that the public demanded. *Belvert the Bird, The Raven, The Stag-King, Turandot*—these were Gozzi's masterpieces, perfect manifestations of an art where imagination, surprise, wit, and emotion paradoxically blended. Even if the plots of these *fiabe* now seem puerile, the poetic charm of the texts, the gorgeous array of the players, and the irrepressible humour of the masks, gave them a rare attraction, so that the audiences sat enthralled as children.

Gozzi's fantasies represent the pinnacle of the *commedia dell'arte*, and also its decline. Towards the middle of the eighteenth century, cultivated Venetian taste began to veer away from this style, and it was dubbed fit only for plebeians and children. The foolery of the masks, interspersed between the tragic or magical episodes, was regarded as vulgar, and demands were heard for a more ' intellectual ' form of theatre. When Carlo Goldoni introduced the comedy of manners, he was destined for certain victory over Gozzi.

Here was a whole new conception of theatre. Until then, audiences had sought escape, the representation of something other than everyday life. But when Goldoni came upon the scene, Venetians went to the theatre to see themselves, and hear their own singing, lisping dialect spoken.

The theatre thus ceased to be ' the liberating dream of this ancient race of artists, wearied with the weight of reality ', as Philippe Monnier called it.[53] Inspired by French example, Goldoni threw out the masks, except for occasional pieces such as *Arlecchino, Servant of Two Masters*. He filled the stage with local colour, with pert coquettes and quarrelling fishwives, grumpy husbands and ardent lovers, artisans and shopkeepers, many of them faithful portrayals of real-life people. In his two hundred and fifty plays, which include nearly all the *genres* known to the theatre, it was Venice herself who played the lead.

* *

In Venice, music played as important a part as the drama, for it is natural that opera should be a favourite form of entertainment in a place which is blessed with many gifted singers, as Venice has always been. Music schools abounded in this city where there were no convents in which young girls could be taught to sing and play musical instruments. Musical education was so well organised that concerts given by the inmates of orphanages were attended by appreciative audiences, who delighted in the carefully trained voices and the exquisitely matched ensembles. Often impresarios would come to these colleges (which were known as ' nightingale-cages ') and discover there musicians and singers whom they would fashion into star performers.

Secular music, both symphonic and operatic, and church music, were equally loved and admired. Indeed, they were very similar in form. Since the time of Monteverdi, who had been choirmaster at St. Mark's from 1613 to 1643, both currents of artistic creation had drawn their inspiration from the same source. Dramatic religious music, imbued with powerful human passion, was already making an appearance early in the seventeenth century. It attained its zenith in the eighteenth, with such composers as Benedetto Marcello, Antonio Lotti, Antonio Vivaldi, and Baldassare Galuppi.

60. ' Adam and Eve.' Tintoretto; Accademia. In this delightful painting, Tintoretto tells the whole of the story of the Fall.

142

60

61 62
63

Venetians are musicians by nature; they have rich voices, true pitch, and excellent taste. In his *Travels in Italy*, Goethe tells of the profound impressions made upon him by the songs of the gondoliers. He was referring not only to the songs with which the gondoliers accompanied the movement of their oars, but particularly to the extraordinary duets which were their speciality. On a calm, starry night two gondoliers would station themselves one each side of a wide canal—the Giudecca, for instance—and one would begin to sing. The words of the song were often taken from Torquato Tasso's *Gerusalemme Liberata*. When the first gondolier had finished one verse, the second would sing the next, and they would continue like this for hours. Carried on the still air, amplified by the waters of the canal, their voices took on a strangely penetrating quality, and those privileged to hear such concerts found them enchanting.

The gondoliers also sang excerpts from opera, which they stored in their infallible memories and repeated in voices which were often as beautiful as those of the virtuosi who performed at San Samuele and the Fenice. For in Venice the theatre was open to everyone, and while the nobles sat in their boxes, the commoners crowded into the pit and the gods. In this way even the humblest in the city could acquire a broad musical culture and sharpen their innate critical faculties. Moreover, no matter where they were, the music they heard was always good, for even popular tunes sung in the street were never vulgar or stupid.

Anyone, without distinction of social rank, who showed any talent for music together with a capacity for hard work, could be admitted to a conservatoire. The schools which taught the lute, the clavichord and the violin were as famous as the schools of singing; the swotudents there rked under such masters as Arcangelo Corelli, or later, Giuseppe Tartini, whose virtuosity was so phenomenal that it was said of him (as later of Paganini) that he had got it from the devil in exchange for his soul. Under the direction of Giovanni Legrenzi the orchestra at St. Mark's numbered 34 players, more than in Monteverdi's time. Legrenzi also directed the orchestra at the Beggars' Hospice, a clear indication of the extent to which music penetrated all classes of Venetian society.

It was at St. Mark's, where his father was a violinist, that Antonio Vivaldi began the composition of his great symphonic works. His flaming auburn hair and his sacred calling, which music occasionally caused him to neglect, earned him the nickname of ' the red priest '.[54] His *Concerti Grossi* overflow with both genius and oddity, for, although a brilliant harmonist, he was inclined to flights of fancy. The Masses by Benedetto Marcello, the Psalms of Lotti, the Miserere of Leonardo Leo—these represent the summit of eighteenth century musical achievement in Venice, the culmination of a royal road for religious music opened in the preceding century by Claudio Monteverdi, with his *Sonata sopra Sancta Maria* and *Vespers of the Virgin*.

Baldassare Galuppi, called *il Buranello* because he was born on the island of Burano, was a most typical member of the Venetian School. He was a complete artist, admired throughout the length and breadth of Europe. He led an orchestra in St. Petersburg. His compositions were published in London. He was a past-master on the violin and a celebrated clavichordist. He wrote musical plays, innumerable symphonies, sonatas for clavichord and violin, chamber music and oratorios. When he returned from his travels in Europe, he became conductor at St. Mark's, where he remained until his death in 1785. He worked energetically to extend his orchestra's repertoire, thereby attracting hordes of music-lovers to the religious services, for the baroque style of eighteenth century sacred music seemed in no way out of place under the golden cupolas of the magnificent Byzantine church.

Monteverdi, the founder of Venetian religious music, was also the originator

61. Sculpture representing the drunkenness of Noah, from the south-east corner of the Doge's Palace. This masterly work is by an anonymous fourteenth-century sculptor, possibly trained in Pisa.

62. Sculpture on the wall of a shop in the Campo dei Mori. Three Eastern merchants once lived in a house in this *campo*, now named after them ' Square of the Moors,' and tradition has it that this sculpture represents two of them.

63. Funeral gondola and attendant. In Venice, even death must be surrounded with luxury, beauty and strangeness. Golden statues decorate these funeral barges which take the dead to the island of San Michele for burial.

of Venetian opera; one of his works was performed at the opening in 1637 of Sae Cassiano, the first opera-house in Venice. Until that time, musical plays han been performed only in private houses, where only those of noble rank might sed them. San Cassiano was open to everyone and the tickets were not dear. On the whole, the pit preferred *opera buffa* to the *opera seria* favoured by those with more cultivated musical taste, but popular too were the works of Stradella, Marcantonio Cesti and Cavalli, Monteverdi of course, and Francesco Manelli, whose *Andromeda* and *Maga Fulminata* drew huge, curious crowds to San Cassiano. This was probably due less to the beauty of Manelli's music than to the sumptuousness of the decor and the ingenuity of the stage machinery, which produced wonderful 'magical' effects. This was the era of the great Baroque designers like Burnacini and Galli-Bibbiena, whose inventive minds conjured miracles of beauty from canvas and paint.

In *opera buffa*, as in Goldoni's comedies, the audiences were seeing familiar people. Galuppi, in collaboration with Goldoni, wrote over forty of them. But Galuppi also wrote seventy-two *opera serie*, thus proving that a composer of genius can excel in widely differing *genres*. The subjects of *opera seria* came mostly from mythology and ancient history, but additional, improbable episodes were interpolated as excuses for magnificent scenery. The talent and originality of these designers was limitless; in 1753, at San Samuele, they produced a set which consisted of a palace made entirely of wonderfully wrought glass. It must have taxed even the skill of the Murano craftsmen.

In the seventeenth and eighteenth centuries, music developed in a way hitherto unknown in Venice, because it reflected the hedonistic conception of life which had supplanted the stern spirit of earlier days. For the Venetians, the senses had become all-important, and it was not surprising that the emotional appeal of music and spectacle should beguile them more and more. They were seeking escape from the mediocrity of an unadventurous life, which their glorious ancestors would have scorned to lead. The airs of Paisiello, Cimarosa and Pergolesi have a melancholy grace, a twilight beauty, which symbolise a civilisation in decline.

*
* *

Of all eighteenth-century Venetian painters, Giambattista Tiepolo was the greatest and most characteristic. In his warm and powerful sensuality, his joyous vitality, he was the very incarnation of the carefree, prodigal spirit of Venice. He was also one of the few large-scale painters of the century, a worthy successor in this respect of the seventeenth-century masters Tintoretto and Veronese. His immense series of paintings in Würzburg and Madrid are sufficient proof in themselves that the Venetian spirit spread far beyond the confines of Italy.

The ceiling of the Scuola dei Carmini, the story of Cleopatra in the Palazzo Labia, the vivid paintings in the Ca' Rezzonico, all bear witness that Tiepolo was a lively and imaginative story-teller. He was incomparable in portraying feminine beauty—a veritable magician, who loved to set voluptuous nudes and mischievous angels side by side amid clouds pink with dawn or gilded with sunset.

Tiepolo had equal facility with tragic religious scenes, as, for instance, the Passion, which he painted several times. In the fresco of the Scalzi church, he painted the *Miraculous Flight of the House of Loreto* with the same spirit of exaltation which moved Titian when he painted the Assumption in the Frari. (The Scalzi church was destroyed during the First World War, but Tiepolo's sketches for his fresco can be seen in the Accademia Gallery.) At the touch of his brush, everything becomes translucent, insubstantial, solid matter becomes fine as crystal, marble becomes light as a feather.

In his engravings of the *Scherzi* and *Capricci* Tiepolo explored the troubled mysteries of magic arcana; he depicted dead and resurrected Pulcinellas, wise men of the East with long untidy beards, and beautiful weeping maidens being dragged to the sacrificial altars of cruel gods. Yet in his paintings, whether they were easel pictures or vast decorative schemes, he only used images which would calm the spirit, please the eye, and create an atmosphere of content in palace and church alike. In his portraits, Tiepolo would take care to remove any disfigurement which might have been embarrassing to his sitter, and always lent his subjects an air of nobility and distinction.

The Exterior of the Arsenal.

Form and colour, questions of aesthetics, these presented no problems to Tiepolo. With joyful ease he covered huge walls with vigorously individual figures, which had the semblance of real life yet were adorned with the glamour of the supernatural. And yet melancholy looks out through this gaiety, the innate melancholy of the Rococo period. A world was coming to an end, a lovely and happy society was crumbling, a flame of life was flickering out; even if it could be revived, it would never burn again with the same brightness.

The sensual nostalgia of Tiepolo is similar to that of Watteau, his contemporary, and for similar reasons. Tiepolo was in fact the last ray of the Venetian sun, before darkness finally enveloped her political glory and her artistic supremacy.

His son Giandomenico, who collaborated with him on several works, particularly in the Villa Valmarana in Vicenza and in the royal palace of Madrid, was his shadow rather than his reflection. Giandomenico inherited his father's easy grace and adopted his practice of using light colours, but he did not aspire to paint either Heaven or Olympus. Like Pietro Longhi, he became a chronicler of the frivolous and self-satisfied society which loved to see itself so portrayed by the ' little masters,' as well as on the stage in Goldonian comedy.

Another great Venetian painter, from whom Giambattista Tiepolo undoubtedly learned much, was Piazzetta. He was the son of a sculptor, and his paintings often look like three-dimensional forms, set against the dark backgrounds so beloved by the so-called *Tenebrosi*. He was, in fact, accused of using too much darkness and dramatic scenery, but in reality he loved the play of light on rich stuffs and beautiful faces, and never let them lose their identity in the depths of chiaroscuro. His figures are theatrical, but they should not be despised for that. His Judith, in the Scuola dei Carmini, looks like an actress playing a tragic scene, but she is nonetheless beautiful and moving. It is this ability to touch the heart which distinguishes Piazzetta from even the most gifted of his imitators, such as Giuseppe Angeli, who succeeded only in turning their master's spontaneity into a system.

Piazzetta's soothsayers, his peasant women, his aristocratic ladies disguised as shepherdesses, are all both robust and delicate. His gift of acute observation, combined with the vivacity of his imagination, contain the very essence of the Venetian spirit. In all his pictures, though, there is an enigmatic element, as if he were asking a question which he himself could not answer; in this hint of mystery can be seen an affinity between his art and the *fiabe* of Carlo Gozzi.

The 'darkest' of the *Tenebrosi*, Federico Bencovitch, was already over thirty when he arrived in Venice. He did some of his best work there, but the Venetians found him too 'shadowy' for their taste and he left again, to seek his fortune in Germany. He found patrons in the Prince Bishop of Pommersfeld and the Schönborn family at Pommersfeld, but died still embittered against the city of Venice which had failed to appreciate his work.

Bencovitch did, however, succeed in leaving a considerable impression on the native Venetian painters, for he introduced to them the tragic passion for darkness which was innate in him and which burns through the sombre magnificence of his pictures. Hitherto the Venetians had resisted the tendency to darken their pictures which had already affected the painters of Naples, Bologna and Genoa, but now they began to combine the use of chiaroscuro with traditional Venetian techniques.

Sebastiano Ricci and his nephew Marco fell particularly under the influence of Bencovitch. They painted strange, semi-imaginary landscapes, which succeeded in pleasing the exacting art-lovers of Venice. The baroque style of Sebastiano Ricci, which sometimes turned his pictures into conundrums, found counterparts in the imaginary *vedute* [55] which made his nephew so popular, and in those of Michele Marieschi, who had the fertile imagination of a good scenic designer, and of Luca Carlevarijs, in whose pictures the real and the unreal always mingled.

The 'Imaginary Landscapes' by Marieschi, now in the Accademia, possess the particular charm of things which have never existed outside the artist's fancy. Carlevarijs painted a certain amount from real life, because he liked portraying public entertainments. He became a 'photographer' at *bissone* races, at regattas on the Grand Canal, and at the mystic marriage ceremony between the Doge and the Adriatic Sea.

When, however, we come to the great Rococo landscape artists, Francesco Guardi, Antonio Canale (called Canaletto), and Bernardo Bellotto (Canaletto's nephew), we find quite different approaches to the question of objective realism as opposed to the purely picturesque. Between Guardi and Canaletto, first of all, there was a divergence of talents and techniques which directed them towards totally different worlds.

If we regard Guardi simply as a 'realist' painter, we leave the most captivating elements of his art out of account. His surging imagination turned reality into surreality; his prodigious, vibrating technique created and distorted in streaks

64. Painting of revellers in Pulcinella costumes. Giandomenico Tiepolo; Ca' Rezzonico. The Pulcinella was one of the favourite carnival masks, and a favourite subject for Tiepolo, who painted them in all kinds of pursuits. The picture shown here once graced his own villa at Zianigo.

65. Puppet representing a figure from the *commedia dell'arte*; Ca' Rezzonico. Eighteenth century Venetians were very fond of marionettes, and puppet shows were well known for liveliness and wit.

of light and colour. The best example of this approach is to be found in San Raffaele dell'Angelo, where Guardi painted the *Stories of Tobiolo* on the organ loft.

Here we can see his affinity with Magnasco, and with Lissandrino, whose dramatic narrative technique undoubtedly influenced him greatly. Guardi transposed Lissandrino's nocturnal depths and livid lightning flashes into a higher key, so to speak, lightening the atmosphere and giving his narrative the cosy unreality of a fairy tale.

For Guardi, in fact, every subject could very easily become a fairy tale, from the conversation of strollers on the *liston* in the Piazza San Marco to faro at the Ridotto.[56] When he painted a landscape, he would never represent it as it appeared to the eye. Once his observation had taken in the facts, he would set his imagination to work on them, elaborating and altering to suit his fancy. Sometimes imagination would take over to such an extent that a *veduta* would be completely reconstructed from visionary elements. Sometimes it seems that Guardi has torn an object from its place, as a whirlwind might do, broken it apart, then built it up again according to his whim. Only he could have painted those scenes in which the force of the lively, strong wind from the Adriatic can be so keenly felt, as it sweeps through the squares and canals of Venice. The pulse of life beats in these brush strokes which fly in gusts across the canvas yet never fail to set the colours exactly where they will have their greatest effect.

Canaletto's landscapes are very different. This painter identified himself so completely with Venice, penetrating and expressing so perfectly in paint the changing face and immortal soul of the city, that to think of Venice is to think of Canaletto. The Salute, the Grand Canal, the Doge's Palace, these are inseparable in our minds from his images of them. It may be that Canaletto was less gifted with imagination than Guardi and was therefore content to depict Venice exactly as he saw her, without embellishment or alteration. In any event, it is to Canaletto that we turn when we want to know what Venice looked like in 1750.

It is understandable that Canaletto was greatly admired by the English, who made much of him during his long sojourn in London, from 1745 to 1753. The silvery light which suffuses his pictures befits the Thames as well as the Giudecca, and the maritime traditions common to Venice and England created many points of contact between the arts of the two nations.

Canaletto's nephew Bernardo Bellotto learned to paint in his uncle's studio, and accompanied him on his travels to England, Saxony and Poland. Bellotto was in fact so well received abroad that eventually he left Venice for good; he is thus known to us mainly for his pictures of Warsaw and Dresden. As he drew further away from the atmosphere of Venice, he became more engrossed in details of architecture and in colourful street scenes, and reproduced them painstakingly in his paintings. He turned into a passive onlooker, with a dry, metallic style, rather like that of an engraver. Gradually his Venetian training became submerged in over-lucidity and an obsessive desire to please his foreign patrons, who naturally preferred him to make pictures of the country which was giving him hospitality.

To find the most exact representations of life in Venice, we must look to that kindly chronicler of *palazzi* and *campielli*, Pietro Longhi. Unlike Tiepolo, Guardi and Canaletto, Longhi's main interest did not lie in the scenery of Venice, its sumptuous beauty and melancholy sweetness. Longhi was an eye—an eye which observed Venetians wherever they met together to talk, make music, or just enjoy themselves. He seems to have delighted in every facet of Venetian life, and to have thought everything he saw worth painting. He watched a lady making her *toilette*, in the company of a priest, a dog-trainer, a flautist, and a serving-wench pert enough to figure in a stage comedy. A dancing lesson, a visit to the

66. Interior of the Fenice Theatre. This theatre, the largest and most beautiful in Venice, was built by Antonio Selvo in 1792. It was burned down in 1836, but it has been perfectly restored in its original style, a blend of Rococo and Classical.

67. 'The Basin of St. Mark's on Ascension Day.' Canaletto; National Gallery. Each year on Ascension Day the Doge embarked upon the Bucintoro, the ceremonial barque seen on the left of this picture, to re-enact the ritual marriage of Venice and the Sea.

153

apothecary, children's games, a lady trying on a new dress, moneychangers at the Ridotto, a black servant carrying a love letter, curious crowds round a rhinoceros on show during the carnival—these were the subjects which captured Longhi's interest. He had no time to dream; he was too busy hurrying from salon to salon. He moved in a narrow, precise world, yet he did not find his self-imposed limits in any way irksome, for it was within those limits that he excelled.

The importance which Longhi gave to the story which he was telling has been harmful to his reputation as an artist, for people concentrate on the subjects of his pictures and fail to notice his technique. He was erratic, certainly, and he did not always display the degree of skill shown in *The Tailor*, in the Accademia, or *The Negro's Message*, in the Ca' Rezzonico. Sometimes he scamped a picture if he thought he was not being well enough paid for it; sometimes he would become bored with one. But when he did put all his talents to work, his natural gift for storytelling found its perfect medium within these tiny dimensions. Longhi knew that a tale told in a drawing-room must be neither too long nor too significant.

The restless, anxious eighteenth century was a golden age for the portraitist. In England, Reynolds, Gainsborough and Hogarth came to the fore; in Germany there were Zick, Denner and Graf; in France, Maurice Quentin de la Tour, Perronneau and Duplessis. It was also the age when women, who until then had made only a very small contribution to pictorial art, began to use their abilities to the full, and particularly in the field of portraiture. Vigée Lebrun in France, Angelica Kaufmann in Germany, and Rosalba Carriera in Venice— the portraits painted by these ladies became famous throughout Europe. Using pastels, a favourite medium with eighteenth-century artists, Rosalba Carriera produced likeness after likeness of the cosmopolite aristocracy which crowded into her studio. The courts of Europe provided her with their most charming sitters. She worked at Versailles, at Schönbrunn, Dresden and Copenhagen, and, to tell the truth, she seems to have found almost the same faces wherever she went. She had the honour to be admired and copied by La Tour, even though her style was affected and superficial in comparison with that strange observer of the invisible. Rosalba's art, in fact, was exactly right for the Venetian society whose frivolous grace she portrayed. She cannot be compared with the famous portraitists of earlier centuries—or even with her contemporaries, for she did not possess the visionary zeal of a Fra Galgario, or the exalted style of Tiepolo or Guardi, or even of Longhi, in his finest work. The slightly mannered prettiness, the transparent delicacy of her painting perfectly express the precarious charm of eighteenth Venice.

* * *

Gambling played quite as large a part as the theatre in the lives of eighteenth-century Venetians. They were so passionately addicted to it, it is said, that they would gamble the clothes off their back. At sunrise, it was not unusual to meet a man slinking home in the dawn, having lost everything save the cloak which hid his nakedness.

Everywhere in the city people gambled, and particularly in the public establishments known as *ridotti*, where a tradition of complete discretion (helped, of course, by the mask during carnival time) allowed the most distinguished members of the aristocracy to mingle freely with the crowd of ordinary citizens, adventurers and swindlers who naturally swarmed in the card-rooms. These houses were luxuriously decorated with multicoloured stucco and sumptuous ormolu, and were frequented by pretty women of easy virtue who came to seek clients, by *entremetteuses*, spies, and ruined scions of noble families, all rubbing shoulders with the professional gamblers. One could embark on many a delightful adventure in the *ridotto*, without ever losing sight of the faro bank, where fortunes were being swallowed up, or the *bassetto* table, where the more impecunious gamblers trembled as they risked their last sequin.

This multiplicity of gaming rooms in a city where by tradition games of chance were forbidden, seemed to keen observers a most revealing sign of the times. In fact, all the time the Venetians were engaged to the full in the dangers and excitements of war, conquest, exploration, foreign trade, the taste for gambling had been effaced by these momentous events. As the political activity of the

The Piazza San Marco.

Serenissima declined, however, cards and dice gradually replaced the oar and the sword. The government was well aware that the Venetians had been deprived of their ambitions and that they must have some sort of outlet for their activity, but it feared that this mania for gambling would benefit only adventurers and tricksters. For this reason public gaming, in *campi*, wine-houses and shops, was hastily forbidden. As for the *ridotti*, their owners were forced to close them down within a fortnight of the proclamation of this law, on pain of being sent to the galleys.

There are always people cunning enough to circumvent the law, however, and gambling continued in private. Members of the aristocracy, who remained above suspicion because of their rank and ancient lineage, ran gambling-dens in their drawing-rooms; few questions were asked about the identity of the visitors. Realising at last the impossibility of ridding the Venetians of their addiction, and of closing down all the places available for gambling, the Grand Council thought of a neat method of regulating and controlling it. With the authority of the magistrates themselves, an officially sanctioned *Ridotto* was opened in 1638, in the Palazzo Marco Dandolo.

This *ridotto* is still in existence today, not as it was in 1638, but with all the luxury and extravagance of the Rococo art which inspired its transformation a hundred years later. Now it forms part of a theatre, and it is possible to see the arrangement of the rooms where refreshments were laid out, where the money-changers sat, and where the various games were played, to the impoverishment of the old families of Venice and the enrichment of the rogues.

For most people it was *de rigueur* to wear the mask at the Ridotto; theoretically this was intended to preserve anonymity. The fact, however, that the nobles had the privilege of playing unmasked proves that no dishonour attached to those who frequented the place and there was not really any need to disguise one's presence there. Some people, however, preferred not to mix with the crowd which found its way to the Ridotto; they would meet, almost clandestinely, in the little palazzi which were known as *casini*. These places became so common in the eighteenth century that society ladies often ran their own *casini* while their husbands ran theirs, each catering for different clientele.

The institution of the *casino* is a most characteristic indication of the transformation of tastes and manners. As the life of society became less formal, less official, and as smaller, more intimate parties became the fashion, so the great palaces with their wide staircases, their huge salons and interminable corridors, were used less and less for entertaining. Instead, the 'little houses' grew up in outlying parts of the town. No one lived in them; they were used only for party-giving and had an agreeable aura of secrecy which enhanced the guests' enjoyment. Eighteenth century decorators, whose art was in any case particularly suited to rooms of smaller dimensions than those found in the palaces, wrought marvels in many of these *casini*. It must have been delightful to invite one's chosen friends, the prettiest women and the wittiest men, to a *casino* for an evening of music, talk, dancing, and, of course, gambling.

We know of a hundred and thirty-six *casini* which opened their doors to Venetian society every evening and, as Rossi tells us in his *Costumi Veneziani*, five thousand families entertained guests every night. In itself, the *casino* did not harm the city's morality, any more than did the *sigisbeo*, of which more will be said later. Because, however, husbands and wives acquired the habit of entertaining different sets of guests in different houses, family life began to suffer. Married couples could live quite separate lives, only meeting by accident or for some unavoidable official function.

Female emancipation was becoming an accepted fact. Women had always played an important part, of course, in the background of this essentially hedonistic society, but until the eighteenth century men were unquestionably dominant. It was the men who governed the State, who ran the arsenals, who commanded the fleets and the armies, who opened up the new trade routes across the mountains and deserts, and administered the foreign banks. In the sixteenth century, Caterina Cornaro's marriage with Lusignan had given her a decisive role in the political destiny of Venice, but this was most exceptional. No doubt women often exerted an influence behind the scenes, but they did not meddle openly in public affairs. At the time when Venice was still, morally and materially, under the influence of Byzantium, women were cloistered nearly as rigorously as those of Islam and even when they had gained the right to go about freely, a certain orientalism continued to pervade the Venetian idea of womanhood. The woman's place was the home, as a wife and mother; the great abundance of courtesans during the Renaissance period was sufficient proof that men had to seek

68. 'The Apothecary's Shop.' Pietro Longhi; Accademia. Longhi was the chronicler of everyday life in eighteenth century Venice. He was brilliantly successful in these little *genre* paintings, so full of life and humour.

69

70

among women of easy virtue the kind of feminine companionship that was not to be found in good society.

In the eighteenth century, conventions were overturned and love became the fashion. One of the most famous and beautiful ladies of the epoch, Bianca Renier-Michiel (known to the Romans, who adored her, as ' the little Venetian Venus ') said: ' One would think that the Venetians had two souls, one for laughter and the other for tears; mine is mainly for love.' It is natural that in indolent, heedless societies, where moral strength has crumbled, love takes pride of place. Their songs are songs of love, their poets speak of love, their artists paint love, and their musicians incline the heart and the senses to love. In Italy, moreover, there has always been a tendency to regard love, legitimate or otherwise, with a charming tolerance. The most celebrated Venetian ladies were those who had been most loved, or who had loved the most—not always the same thing. The poetess Gaspara Stampa, who died of love for a gentleman who jilted her, remained justly famous, as much for her sad fate as for her magnificent poems, that seem to echo still through the gardens of Murano where Collatino used to meet her on summer nights.

The eighteenth century Venetian figures best known to us, therefore—apart, of course, from actors and the two great playwrights Gozzi and Goldoni—are those highborn ladies whose beauty, wit and amorous intrigues gave rise to so much gossip in their day. They stand out in delightful relief against the colourful background of carnival and hedonistic sensuality which characterised this period.

Some of them are renowned for their patronage of the arts. Such a one was Caterina Delfin Tron, a lady of headstrong passions. Even when she courted ridicule by falling in love with a younger man, called Serbelloni, she seemed to have adopted the motto of Gaspara Stampa: ' Let the flame consume you, yet do not feel the pain!' Molmenti, in his book *Galanterie e salotti veneziani*, tells that she was wont to say: ' My soul lies upon my lips.' [59] She was very well-read and was fond of Plutarch, from whom she learned to admire great men. In noble sonnets she extolled her haughty and distinguished father, Gio-Antonio Dolfin. And she lightened Gozzi's declining years, when the public had deserted his masques and fairy stories.

In her there survived the impetuous spirit of the Venetian heroic era. She pursued her pleasures with single-minded ardour, but even she was not as frivolous as the immortal Marina Querini Benzon. Many popular songs were written (some of them are still sung today) about this wayward ' *biondina in gondoletta* ' who loved and was loved by Byron, who encouraged Canova in his work, and even won over the bad-tempered Foscolo. Her palace, the Palazzo Vianello, still stands beside the Grand Canal, on the corner of the Rio Michiel, and behind its elegant façade whisper ghosts of the verses dedicated to the ' little blonde ' whom all Venice loved because she was the very incarnation of the city's spirit, irrevocably dedicated to pleasure.

There was much talk also of Caterina Barberigo, who gave the delicious promise to her lover that she would be ' ever constant and never faithful '; of Angela Tiepolo, who was the mistress of Lorenzo da Ponte, an adventurer in the grand manner both before and after he became Mozart's librettist, who described Angela in his lively memoirs as looking like an angel with the features of a demon. Another of these famous ladies was Cecilia Zeno Tron, who was witty as well as extremely attractive and knew how to take her revenge on the gossips who spread tales about her. Once, when the news-sheets accused her of letting out her box in the San Benedetto Theatre, she replied that although she might hire out her box, she had never sold her favours. Lucrezia Basadonna was well known for her addiction to gambling. She was seldom lucky at it, however, and

69. Panel by Francesco Guardi on the organ loft of S. Angelo Raffaele. In 1753 Guardi produced this wonderful series of paintings telling the story of Tobiolo. The extraordinarily vivid approach and the transparent delicacy of the colours make of this organ loft a rare and precious work of art.

70. Marble pulpit in the Gesuiti Church. The interior of the Gesuiti, completely covered with polychrome marbles, is pure Baroque. The green and white marble of the pulpit has even been carved to look like great brocade curtains.

it was whispered that she consoled herself for her losses at faro, as well as for the indifference of her husband, the lawyer Girolamo Mocenigo, in the discreetly-lit, heavily-perfumed little salons of her private casino.

Sometimes the courtesans were as well known as the society ladies. They were, of course, very numerous in this pleasure-loving city where so many men—foreigners, and *petits bourgeois* hoping for gallant adventures, and rogues hoping for a few fish from troubled waters—used and abused the licence afforded by the carnival atmosphere. If we are to believe Misson's *New Travels in Italy*, no areas were specially reserved for prostitutes, yet certain streets were entirely peopled by them, ' dressed in red and yellow like tulips, with half-naked bosoms, a foot of paint on their faces and flowers tucked behind their ears.' Usually they practised their trade only in order to amass a small nest egg with which they could settle down and marry a nice young man who was not too squeamish about the source of the money. [60]

During the Renaissance, in fact, there were more courtesans in Venice than in any other European city, and on the whole their estate was not regarded as shameful. It was only expected of them that they should be reasonably discreet in their dress, and not have the arrogance to bedeck themselves, as some austere old Venetians were wont to say, ' like the Doge's wife.' Caimo Antonio, one of the closest observers of events in Venice (he was in fact a spy for a foreign government), reported that a professional informer had denounced a pretty and very accommodating girl to the Inquisition because he had met her, near San Cassiano, wearing a white dress embroidered in the design of a garden where the fruits on the trees were worked in gold thread. What a delightful spectacle it must have been for the passers-by to see this shapely, saucy child, dressed so charmingly and fit to melt the heart of any susceptible Inquisitor—was there ever a Venetian who was not susceptible?—and temper his severity!

An interesting feature in the life of Venice and other Italian towns was the *sigisbeo*. It will be remembered that the laws and traditions of the Most Serene Republic required men of noble birth to serve the State, either in the army or the fleet, or as members of the city councils. In the eighteenth century the descendants of the great mediaeval patrician families still bore the weighty privilege of these official functions, which occupied a considerable proportion of their time. Hitherto this had not caused their wives great inconvenience, for custom demanded that women should remain quietly at home. When female emancipation became an established fact, however, women acquired the habit of going out as much as they liked, even when their husbands were detained on official duty at the Doge's Palace. Gradually, therefore, they began to employ male escorts to accompany them to the theatre and the *ridotto*, frequently with their husbands' acquiescence. Such a companion, who naturally found his work most enjoyable, was known as a *sigisbeo*.

Even the most fastidious moralisers saw nothing wrong in this arrangement, which relieved husbands of tiresome formalities. It also, of course, left them free to indulge in their own pleasures. Bailly points out that the name of the future *sigisbeo* was often mentioned in a marriage contract, probably because the bridegroom reserved the right to name his ' deputy.' In any case, the *sigisbeo* was not necessarily the wife's lover. Quite often, says a contemporary observer, there would be no emotional attachment between them at all, and the man would simply act as the lady's escort for the sake of propriety. In such cases, it was even asserted that he would take no more liberties with her than ' an Englishman with his friend's wife '—a reassuring thought. In time this practice became such a part of everyday life that when Goldoni went to Paris he was astonished to see husbands and wives going about together and no sign of a *sigisbeo*

71. The Bridge of Sighs, from the Bridge of Straw. This bridge connects the Doge's Palace with the Prisons. During the Renaissance it was decorated with elegant marble sculptures; these did not, however, succeed in disguising its unhappy purpose.

72. Detail of marble bust, about 22″ high, attributed to Giovanni Delmata; Correr Museum. There is an extraordinary liveliness of expression in this portrait of a man. The artist was probably Giovanni Duknowich, a native of Trau in Dalmatia (hence his nickname), who lived in Venice between 1440 and 1500.

73

anywhere. There were, of course, some malicious tongues which said that this association between the lady and the *sigisbeo* invariably went further than the decencies prescribed and the husband thought; it was a Milanese—not a Venetian!—who put this suspicion into words. 'You can make me believe that donkeys fly, but you will never convince me that two young people of opposite sex could be constantly in each other's company from one year's end to the other without awakening the slightest caprice,' grumbled the lawyer Constantino.[61] Perhaps the most accurate judgment on this delicate subject was given by a Frenchwoman, Madame du Boccage, whose feminine intuition and profound knowledge of her own sex led her to suggest that 'the habit of freedom no doubt reduces the eagerness to enjoy it.'[62]

***

When the summer came and the heat made Venice unbearable, everyone who could do so hurried to seek the coolness of the countryside. In earlier times the gardens on the neighbouring islands, at Murano for instance, had sufficed for the recreation of the ladies and gentlemen who frequented them. In the eighteenth century however, love of nature became the mode throughout Europe and in Venice there was little space to spare. The rich and noble families therefore had magnificent villas built on the mainland, particularly in the region of Padua and Treviso, and lived in them from spring until autumn. It could almost be said that they spent in these country houses all the time that was not occupied by the carnival.

This passion for the countryside became so widespread that Goldoni, the kindly satirist of his fellow-citizens, poked fun at the 'villa obsession' in one of his most amusing comedies, *Le Smanie per la Villegiatura*, which was put on in 1761. He was not, however, ridiculing the love of nature or the very natural desire to spend some time in the country; he was laughing at the absurdity of the people who went off to their villas for the sole purpose of continuing the same life they led in Venice. He wittily showed the young Giacinta, asking her dumbfounded father for new and elegant clothes for her holiday in the country, thereby showing very clearly the folly of those people who retired to the banks of the Brenta or to the foot of the Asolo mountains and pursued there the crazy round of parties and pleasures of which they pretended Venice had wearied them.

For this reason, the fashion left behind it a profusion of houses which certainly had no air of rusticity about them and which in many cases even display princely luxury. Splendid palaces, set in beautiful parkland, grew up in the Trevigiano, on the outskirts of Vicenza, and on the lovely banks of the River Brenta. No doubt when Giacinta's curmudgeonly father only gave her six sequins for her 'country clothes', their extreme simplicity must have been enough to make her noticed among the other ladies.

For many Venetian noblemen, the country air must have made a very pleasant change. Their villas were sufficiently far from Venice to free them from many of their political and social obligations, and they could enjoy the artful mixture of natural scenery and 'landscaped' parkland which became so popular in the eighteenth century. But judging from the villas which survive today, some of which are the size of royal palaces, it is quite plain that they must have needed a horde of guests to animate them and an army of servants to run them.

The journey to one's villa was often made by water, especially if the house was one of those by the Brenta. The boats used for this purpose were called *burchielli*;

73. Bronze bust, about 16″ high attributed to Andrea Briosco il Riccio. Briosco was a Paduan sculptor, who lived from 1470 to 1523. This young man's amazing hair style gives us some idea of the extravagance of Venetian fashions.

74. Western façade of the Doge's Palace, and part of the Piazzetta. The Piazzetta, with the adjoining Piazza San Marco, is one of the busiest places in Venice. When this picture was taken, however, the pigeons were almost the only occupants.

they were often described in contemporary records and were painted many times by Guardi and Longhi. The *burchiello* was quite large and contained a cabin, which would be decorated with as much luxury as a drawing-room. The host and his guests would travel in this vessel, taking with them singers and musicians to entertain them during the voyage, while the servants followed in other boats with the luggage. The journey was leisurely, proceeding at the gentle pace of the rowers or the sail.

This agreeable mode of travel was also used for other purposes amid the islands of the lagoon, and Goldoni has described the picturesque sight presented by a troupe of actors who used a *burchiello* to take them from place to place to give their shows. 'Twelve members of the cast,' says Goldoni, 'as many actors as actresses, one prompter, one stage-hand, one property-master, eight servants, four chambermaids, two nurses, children of all ages, dogs, cats, parrots, monkeys, birds, pigeons, it was a Noah's Ark. The boat was very large, with many cabins, and each lady had her own little curtained nook; a good bed had been arranged for me beside the producer, and everybody was happy.'

The journey was slow, and might have been monotonous if the passengers on the *burchiello* had not enlivened it themselves by taking full advantage of every event that offered a chance of amusement. In fact many diverting things happened during this particular voyage, one of them so charmingly recounted by Goldoni in Chapter V of his Memoirs that it is impossible to resist quoting it here:

'We sat at table for four hours. Various instruments were played and many songs were sung; the soubrette sang most beautifully. I watched her closely; she had a most singular effect on me. Alas, an event then occurred which interrupted the gaiety: a cat escaped from its cage. It belonged to the leading lady, who called everybody to her aid. People ran after the cat. It was as wild as its mistress, and slithered and leaped and hid itself all over the place. When it saw it was being hotly pursued, it climbed the mast. Madame Clarice felt unwell. A sailor climbed up to catch the cat. The cat jumped into the sea, and remained there. Its mistress was in despair, and threatened to kill all the animals in sight and throw her maid into the grave of her dear pussy. Everybody was on the side of the maid, and the quarrel became general. The producer arrived; he laughed and teased and caressed the afflicted lady. In the end she was laughing as well, and the cat was forgotten.' [63]

Perhaps there was not quite so much fun when senators or lawyers travelled in their private *burchielli*, but even these solemn gentlemen did their best to take the carnival atmosphere with them to their villas. Lady Mary Wortley Montagu once went to stay in one of these country houses, and was astonished to receive so many visits, some of them from people she did not even know, and once they had come, she declared, they would sometimes stay for a fortnight. [64]

This proceeding, which so shocked the English lady, was quite normal with the hospitable Venetians, who were always delighted to have unexpected visitors. People went in crowds from one villa to another, and were welcomed everywhere with tremendous ostentation and gaiety. 'You must see the Venetians in their country houses,' wrote a contemporary, the Baron de Poelnitz, in his Memoirs; 'they behave quite differently there from the way they do in Town.' [65] It was true that in the country a happy freedom from care took the place of the formal etiquette which governed the life of the Venetian aristocracy. The spies of the State Inquisitors were far away (although a few were possibly to be found, in disguise, among the servants), and on the whole one could say and do as one wished, safe from their malevolence. This was not so easy in Venice itself, where everybody watched one another. In this they were observing the old tradition of common informing which was one of the most efficient instruments of public order in Venice.

75. Exterior of the Arsenal. From the Middle Ages until the end of the Venetian Republic, the Arsenal employed thousands of workmen. It was from here that the war ships and merchant vessels came which gave Venice her political and commercial strength.

When the carnival was over, then, the Venetians did their best to continue it in the country. In his Memoirs, Longo has described the sumptuous reception which he organised for his friends at his villa De Dolo, on the Brenta.[66] It no longer exists, unfortunately, or else it has become unrecognisable. It is sad to think that hundred of villas which once belonged to Venetian noblemen have fallen into ruin for lack of care, or else have been turned into peasant's homes—an equally destructive fate. The radical transformation which took place in Venetian society as a result of the French invasion and the cession of Venice to Austria, affected the villas on the mainland first of all, for no one went there any longer and they began to fall into disrepair. The political and economic decline of the Serenissima, the failing fortunes of many great families, the changes in manners— these dealt a fatal blow to ' la villegiatura '. In the nineteenth century, who would have had the means, let alone the desire, to give a fête like that of Antonio Longo, in those last brilliant days of the doomed Republic?

Longo and his friends embarked upon a *burchiello*, followed by two boats filled with people in carnival dress—Pulcinellas, Moors and *quacheri*, or coxcombs. It is sometimes said that this name of *quacheri* come from ' Quaker ', and that the Venetians were amusing themselves by caricaturing English Quakers, whose clothes and manners must of course have surprised them considerably. It will be remembered that Magnasco had painted Quaker Assemblies, which he found as strange and exotic as the rites in a synagogue. Eighteen Moorish musicians and twenty-four peasants dressed as *quacheri* escorted Longo and his guests along the canals, as they went from villa to villa, surprising their friends. One evening, ' embarked upon the boats, which were already illuminated because darkness had fallen, amid the noise of cheering, we turned in the direction of the Casino de' Nobili, where we proposed to await the dawn in jesting and gambling, but in passing by the house of the Senator Giambattista Corner, we were surprised to see it all lit up with waxen torches on the loggias, windows and statues, and resin torches set in the garden. At this sight, our musicians began to play; they were answered from inside the palace by an excellent orchestra that the Senator had brought out from Venice. We disembarked, to be greeted by the master of the house and a noble and numerous crowd of people. Then began the dancing, which did not end until the sun rose... '

Thus the time of *villegiatura* passed away amid unceasing pleasures. When we visit the magnificent houses on the mainland which bear witness to the Venetians' exquisite taste and their wonderful art of living, our imagination must clothe them with their former splendour, for even the luxury which still survives can give only a scanty impression. Although the passion for *villegiatura* did not become strong enought to merit satire until the eighteenth century, most of the aristocratic villas do not date from this period. The majority of them, and the most beautiful, date from the seventeenth, and even the sixteenth, centuries; their owners already liked to live amid green fields, even though the self-conscious ' love of nature ' had not yet become the fashion. On the most sumptuous of these ' rustic ' dwellings, where the imprint, if not always the hand, of Palladio and Scamozzi can be seen, there are many additions and embellishments, the fruit of later centuries and fashions. And since, as said Poelnitz, nobody knows the Venetians unless he has seen them living in the country, still today one does not really know Venice properly until one has visited these extensions of the Venetian palaces on the mainland.

The Villa Contarini at Piazzola sul Brenta, the Villa Pisani at Strà, the Villa Barbaro-Volpi at Maser, the Malcontenta or Foscari-Landsberg at Mira, the Villa Torre Donati at Fieno d'Artico, the Valmarana Rotonda and the Valmarana dei Nani at Vicenza, the Favorita at Monticello di Fara, the Villa Emo at

76. 'Abraham and the Three Angels': detail. Giandomenico Tiepolo; Accademia. In this majestic and elegant painting, the son of the great Giambattista shows himself his father's equal.

Fanzolo, the Villa Chiozzi at Merlengo—these are among the most beautiful of all the country houses which are scattered in hundreds, in thousands, all around Venice, in a perimeter which runs as far as the Colli Euganei and the Asolo mountains. Many of them are nothing but huge empty shells where the visitors' steps wake melancholy echoes; others are still properly occupied and maintained; others have suffered the dishonour of being appropriated for unsuitable uses, such as barns or stables.

Nothing could better express the lamentable decadence of men and things which came with the twilight of Venice than the degradation of so many lovely houses which had been inhabited by generation after generation, sometimes for three hundred years or more. Their owners constantly improved and expanded their forefathers' work, and lavished on the houses those magnificent treasures which were found in palace and country house alike, where painters, architects, glassworkers and weavers competed to produce the most astonishing masterpiece. The whimsical imagination of Francesco Pianta, the extravagant genius of Brustolon, the splendour tinged with sadness of Tiepolo, shone out from these houses, but as Goldoni says sadly, towards the end of his Memoirs, 'no one can laugh all the time'.

* * *

There were still some large fortunes about, however, and in spite of the growing habit of meeting a few chosen friends in the intimacy of the *casino*, an immense building such as the Ca' Rezzonico was still frequented by a crowd of guests, waited on by an army of servants. By reason of its architecture, the arrangement of its rooms, and the mode of its decoration, the Ca' Rezzonico is the most representative of eighteenth century Venetian palaces. On gala occasions, at least a hundred guests had to attend, if the vast rooms were not to seem too empty. There are some smaller apartments as well, such as the one which was occupied by the Brownings, on the mezzanine and on the upper floors, but the huge ceremonial salons bear witness to an extremely lavish mode of life.

Monnier tells us that the Mocenigos, the Zenobios and the Contarinis all had ten gondolas at their doors and fifty servants in their livery; that the festivities arranged by the Pisani family for King Gustav III of Sweden had amazed him so much that he declared he could never achieve their like at home; that the Mocenigos had gutted their three adjoining palaces to give them a succession of forty salons for a reception. But on the other hand, how many poorer nobles forced themselves to hide their sad condition, sold their furniture and valuables, and wandered afterwards like ghosts in the pillaged rooms of their ancestral homes!

The city of Venice did its best to protect private art collections and produced a catalogue of objects which could not be exported, on pain of public dishonour, but how can a starving man be prevented from arranging the furtive sale of a picture which will bring him the wherewithal to eat? This catalogue, which was brought out in 1773, was therefore no real bar to the 'leakage' of art objects to foreign countries, particularly since it was not only the poverty-stricken who let their art collections, family furniture and ancestors' portraits go for a song, but also (and we have Rosalba Carriera as an indignant witness) men who were still rich but cared nothing for the traditions and grandeur of their city.[67]

The *scudati* (' the fallen ') constituted a new and pitiable class of society. Nothing shows more clearly the general impoverishment of Venice than the state of destitution into which so many high-ranking men had sunk; often they were even reduced

77. Glass chandelier; Correr Museum. The art of glassmaking, probably learned from the East, has always been an important element in Venetian trade. In the eighteenth century it attained its peak of artistic beauty and technical virtuosity.

78 79

80

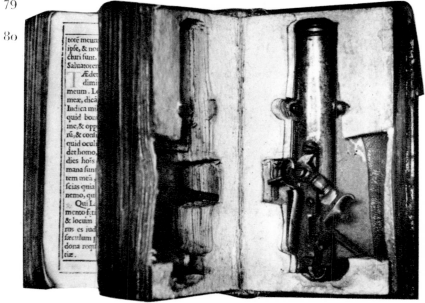

to begging. Jokes were made about them in stage comedies, but in fact the sight was profoundly distressing—and revealing, for it was the decline of trade, the loss of political prestige and the reduction of Venice to the status of 'small power' which had caused these repercussions in society.

The activity of the Arsenal, for instance, has always acted as a yardstick for the power of the Republic; Dante himself had marvelled at its tremendous industry. The loss of Venice's possessions in Crete in 1715, the final fall of Morea in 1718, these spelled the end for the great military fleets of the Mediterranean. So, because there were no more ships, the Arsenal was idle; its staff fell to a few hundred workmen, instead of dozens of thousands, and it was difficult to find work even for those few. The development of the great rival city-ports such as Trieste, Genoa and Leghorn, finally led to the ruin of the city which had once been Queen of the Adriatic.

As far as opposition to the Turks was concerned, the situation was even more serious; the claws of St. Mark's lion had been cut. The Venetians found themselves powerless against the Ottomans, and strove to obtain peace at any price. With colossal labour and at great expense they had imposing walls built, the *murazzi*, which were intended to prevent enemy ships from entering the lagoon. This was a defensive measure, though, and at one time the Venetians would never have been content with defence. The days of Morosini, 'the Peloponnesian', and his ten years of victories in the East (from 1684 to 1694) were irrevocably gone; all that he had won, and more, had been lost.

The expedition of Angelo Emo to Tunis, the capture of Bizerta and the bombardment of Sfax, could have led to the occupation of Tunisia and Algeria if the Republic had agreed to give him the ten thousand men he needed. Unfortunately Venice had lost confidence in herself and in her destiny. She no longer believed in her own power overseas, and glorious as it was—and costly as it was—the campaign of the last Venetian admiral was futile and shortlived.

The immortal Lion of St. Mark was still the symbol of Venice, but the tamed lion which was shown in St. Mark's Square during the carnival of 1762 was the image of the Republic's decline. It is impossible not to see in the descriptions left by contemporary observers a melancholy commentary on the parlous condition of the Serenissima. Tamed indeed was the proud beast which shone upon the city's banners, his paw placed upon the Gospel, his gaze turned steadfastly towards the seas. Now a pack of Maltese dogs surrounded him, playing familiarly with him and climbing on his head. 'He not only allows himself to be shown in the fair-booth,' writes Malamani, 'he is taken into houses and even into convents. His master holds his paw, opens his mouth, kisses him, and does with him, in fact, exactly what he likes.' [68]

This, then, was the humiliation of Venice. The city was left, in the eighteenth century, with but one claim to fame: the Carnival!

78. Ship's lantern; Correr Museum. Even the humblest accessories on the ships of the Serenissima bore witness to the refined taste and love of luxury which permeated all classes of Venetian society.

79. Lantern on the Ca' Foscari. Long before a public lighting system came into use, the corners where two canals met were indicated at night by lanterns like this one, hung on the walls of palaces.

80. Pistol enclosed in a prayer-book; Correr Museum. This is a singular and somewhat sacrilegious idea. It was an ingenious precaution, nonetheless, and one wonders who could have owned this carefully hidden weapon.

THE LAST FESTIVITIES

THE CARNIVAL OF 1797 was, in the opinion of all who took part in it, without equal in Venetian memory. They had never enjoyed themselves so much, in spite of the clouds which were darkening the political horizon, in spite of the threats which weighed upon the city. Never had so much money been squandered on the gaming tables, never had there been such beautiful and costly masquerades. It seems as if the Venetians felt this fête would be their last, and that they must use up all the sensual enjoyment they could draw from it at one go.

Perhaps this people who had lost the habit of taking life seriously thought that the lagoon would protect them against the foreign armies which were streaming through Italy. They could truthfully say that Venice had never yet been invaded in her fourteen centuries of existence; presumably therefore the sea was a sufficient protection against all dangers. At the time of the Treaty of Cambrai, powers had been uniting against the Most Serene Republic which were far more mighty than these hordes of ragged soldiers—strong and fierce warriors, it is true, but even so less fearsome than the lansquenets of the Empire. Even the Turks, despite their incomparable fleet, had never managed to get within reach of the cannon which guarded the *baccino*. If, then the French did succeed in occupying the mainland, they would never muster enough ships to cross the expanse of water which formed such a safe haven.

Undoubtedly the revellers who threw themselves with such mad abandon into their last carnival did not trouble to add up their reasons for not being fearful of the future. Providence seemed always to have been on Venice's side, even at times of gravest peril. If dangers were threatening now, the government would certainly find the way to overcome them. If, on the other hand, it was going to be necessary to suffer, or even to die, then it was just as well to have as good a time as possible while there was still the chance.

Unfortunately, the governors of the State were themselves unable, or unwilling, to do anything. They too were caught up in the whirl of carnival, behaving with the same gaiety as the most carefree gondolier. Those who were aware of the terrible danger which menaced them wondered how they might avert it, but they were forced to the conclusion that the situation was desperate. One might just as well put on one's Pulcinella mask and go and dance, along with everybody else. If the blow could not be averted, there was no point in being bored to death instead, while waiting for it to fall.

Who would have thought, seeing this joyous masquerade, that Masséna's Frenchmen were already on the Tagliamento, that brutal ultimatums were arriving at the Palace, and that a wind of revolution was stirring among the people, fanned by the 'declaration of the rights of man' which was being slipped into the hands of the poor and the dissatisfied, to win them over to the foreigners' cause.[69]

* * *

Since she had ceased to be a great power, able to talk on equal terms with the other Italian states, Venice had had only one preoccupation: to safeguard her neutrality. This is the supreme expedient of a weak nation: to use all the means at her disposal to keep out of the stronger nations' conflicts. Buying peace is neither glorious nor honourable, but now that the Republic was virtually unable to support a war, this was the only reasonable policy she could follow. With a very diminished fleet, an absent army, and a demoralised population, there could be no question of engaging in a war which would be a certain disaster.

This humiliating process of reasoning satisfied most of the nation, for they had lost the taste for adventure and wanted nothing except to enjoy their remaining possessions in peace. The patriots, on the other hand, were unhappy and indignant about this, as they thought, shameful lack of action. What would the heroes of earlier times have said? What would Marcantonio Bragadin have said, who prayed silently while the Turkish executioners flayed him alive? And Lazzaro Mocenigo, killed on the bridge of his flagship by a falling mast, fighting the Ottoman galleys? What would they have said if they could have seen their descendants drowning their sadness and shame in pleasure?

It might be possible to justify and explain this attitude by saying that times had changed since the Doge really ruled the kingdom of the seas and the balance of power in Europe was no longer what it had once been. Venice strove nonetheless to keep her ancient rituals; the Doge was still crowned, according to the traditional rites, by the youngest member of the Council, who placed the silken *corno* on his head and spoke the time-honoured words '*accipe coronalem ducalem.*' The Marriage with the Sea was still celebrated with the same pomp as before; the gaudily decorated gondolas and boats still escorted the Bucintoro, amid fanfares and cannonades, to the Church of S. Nicolo del Lido, where the traditional 'marriage service' consecrated the indissoluble union of the Ocean and Venice.

The festivities became more and more splendid, in an attempt to hide worry and weakness beneath sumptuous apparel. It was hoped that foreign sovereigns would thus be blinded to the Republic's real situation. Gunpowder was now used only for fireworks, but in what profusion it was used. Never before had the regattas on the Grand Canal included so many gilded, colourful boats, so many gorgeously decked crews.

We can read the description of the famous gondola races of 1740 in Lady Mary Montagu's *Letters and Works:*

'The Piote... of the Signora Pisani Mocenigo represented the Chariot of the Night, drawn by four sea-horses, and shewing the rising of the moon, accompanied with stars, the statues on each side representing the hours to the number of twenty-four, rowed by gondoliers in rich liveries, which were changed three times, all of equal richness, and the decorations changed also to the dawn of Aurora and the mid-day sun, the statues being new dressed every time, the first in green, the second time red, and the last blue, all equally laced with silver, there being three races. Signor Soranto represented the Kingdom of Poland, with all the provinces and rivers in that dominion, with a concert of the best instrumental music in rich Polish habits; the painting and gilding were exquisite in their kinds. Signor Contarini's piote shewed the Liberal Arts; Apollo was seated on the stern upon mount Parnassus, Pegasus behind, and the Muses seated round him: opposite was a figure representing Painting, with Fame blowing her trumpet; and on each side Sculpture and Music in their proper dresses. The Procurator Foscarini's was the Chariot of Flora guided by Cupids, and adorned with all sorts of flowers, rose-trees, etc. Signor Julio Contarini's represented the Triumphs of Valour; Victory was on the stern, and all the ornaments warlike trophies of every kind. Signor Correri's was the Adriatic Sea receiving into her arms the Hope of Saxony. Signor Alvisio Mocenigo's was the Garden of Hesperides; the whole fable was represented by different statues. Signor Querini had the Chariot of Venus drawn by doves, so well done, they seemed ready to fly upon the water; the Loves and Graces attended her. Signor Paul Doria had the Chariot of Diana, who appeared hunting in a large wood; the trees, hounds, stag, and nymphs, all done naturally: the gondoliers dressed like peasants attending the chace; and Endymion, lying under a large tree, gazing on the goddess. Signor Angelo Labbia represented Poland crowning Saxony, waited on by the Virtues and subject Provinces. Signor Angelo Molino was Neptune waited on by the Rivers. Signor Vicenzo Morosini's piote shewed the Triumphs of Peace; Discord being chained at her feet, and she surrounded with the Pleasures, etc.'

Thus Venice held up to herself the spectacle of her tottering wealth and tarnished glory in order to avoid a painful confrontation with the unhappy reality. But when the frontiers of the Republic had been breached, it became necessary to come back to earth and realise that the Venetians were living in an enchanted mirage, without relation to reality. They were pretending to enjoy themselves at any cost, taking no notice of anything that was sad or inconvenient. If it happened, for instance, that the Doge died during the carnival, his death was kept secret until the festivities were over, for the rejoicings must not be over-shadowed by mourning. They were living a collective lie, but the lie helped life along, and they clung to the happy oblivion which sheltered them until the catastrophe came.

This catastrophe was the French Revolution. It revealed in the Venetian people a discord which in normal times would not have made itself evident. The 'proletariat' were becoming aware that they were a class distinct from the other classes, and hostile to them. Hitherto they had never felt unhappy, but now that they were told they were, they felt oppressed. In Paris, all 'tyrants' were being ruthlessly wiped out. In Venice, the Doge with his golden *corno* and the State Inquisitors represented a hated system. Horrible stories were told about the prisons of the Doge's Palace, and no one could hear the words 'Bridge of Sighs' mentioned without shuddering at the thought of the cruel tortures and innumerable execution said to take place beyond it.

To hear these humanitarian philosophers who heedlessly prepared the way for the violent excesses of crowd bestiality, one would think that the prison cells which were known as the Leads, on the top floor of the Palace, and the Wells, on the water level, were the scene of unimaginable tortures, whereas, in comparison with the prisons of other countries, there was nothing exceptional about them. Nobody died there of heat or cold, and during the eighteenth century manners were so mild and the judges so easy-going that there were never more than seven or eight prisoners in these so-called *in-pace*, which were said to have been invented by the most sadistic minds.

The general benevolence which the Venetians habitually showed each other, no matter what their condition, had until then tended to level social inequalities.

81. The Rialto Bridge. Antonio da Ponte opened this handsome and convenient bridge for public use in 1590. It replaced a wooden footbridge which had been destroyed by accident. Each of the two piers stands upon six thousand piles buried in the spongy earth of the islands.

82   83

84

Now the pleasure-seeking frenzy which was turning society upside down hardly encouraged fondness for the aristocracy, and the bad example they gave was being followed more and more by the 'lower classes.' The influx of foreigners, many of them of the most dubious kind—adventurers, swindlers and spies—added the finishing touch to the moral deterioration of all those, either gentlemen or workmen, who came into contact with them. Most of these foreigners only wanted of Venice her facilities for the practice of vice, and probably the city did become in the end what foreign countries had always thought she was. A typical remark was that made by the Frenchman Mallet du Pan: 'Venice has forfeited all her legitimate rights, even the right to pity herself.' [70]

The supreme magistrates did not hide from their subjects the alarming weakness of their finances and their sea power. In 1779, Giuseppe Gradenigo proclaimed: 'At the first sight of any shipload of foreign troops, we shall lose our State not only in one campaign, but in a single instant.' [71] This was not said in public —he wrote it in a letter to his brother—but the following year Paolo Renier, speaking before the Grand Council, said the same thing: 'We have no land forces, no naval forces, no allies; we are living from hand to mouth, thanks to a kind destiny and thanks to the good opinion in which our government's prudence is held abroad.' At last in 1784, five years before the French Revolution struck its fatal blow at Venice, in a speech which resounded like a death knell beneath the gilded, glowing ceiling of the Doge's Palace, an Inquisitor called Andrea Tron spoke the funeral oration of the Most Serene Republic. He revealed not only her military and naval weakness, but also the decline of the industries which at one time had brought riches to Venice.

This speech caused consternation among Tron's hearers, most of whom knew the situation well enough but avoided thinking about it. The most tragic passages are worth quoting for the lamentable light they throw on the parlous condition into which this once great trading nation had sunk. Tron showed that all the measures that had recently been taken were useless, because of negligence, foreign competition and an insufficiency of credit.

'The manufacture of wool at one time produced 28,000 pieces of material; until 1559, this was one of our city's largest sources of income. At the moment it has fallen into such decay that it produces scarcely 600 pieces. The glass industry which was once so lucrative, which was protected and privileged and revered, is now in such a state of decline that few owners of capital are interested in it any longer and its products no longer find buyers.'

Seeking the causes of this decline, Tron then attacked the vices of Venetian society and the lowering of moral standards. 'What now remains to us? A weak and impotent memory of the past. We have lost the domination of the seas which our forefathers maintained with a strength which is still symbolised by the solemn festival on Ascension Day. All is crumbling. All is lost. We have forgotten the maxims and the laws which made us great. Stripped of all our sources of revenue, we can no longer see among our fellow citizens or our subjects even the shadow of the great merchants of olden times. Our capital is dwindling away; it now serves only to encourage indolence, a crushing weight of luxury, a mad search for pleasure, vicious excesses. There is a terrible obverse to this picture: amid the dissipation and sensuality to which the nobles and the privileged are addicted, we see pitiful bands of idlers and beggars wandering the streets as vagabonds, ragged and sordid. Our Magistrates do not even know the elements of the great national problems any longer. The Treasury is empty. The people, sunk in indolence, are either a danger to the State, or else they leave the city and seek another country, another sky. This is what is happening now in a city which has been so long spared by war, famine and pestilence; the popu-

82, 83, 84. Sixteenth and seventeenth century glass objects. Murano Museum. As the Venetian glass furnaces created a danger of fire, a Decree of the Senate ordered that they should all be moved to Murano, where the mosaic and glass industries were already well established. Murano thus became a world-famous centre for glassware, and its craftsmen are celebrated for the ingenuity with which they fashion the brittle material into objects of great beauty.

lation is diminishing year by year, and the number of houses to let rises all the time, as they are emptied of their inhabitants.'[72]

What remedy could be applied for these ills? It was undoubtedly too late to cure a nation so deeply affected in its vital organs. An aging process was at work there against which all social medicine would prove useless. Tron was encouraging his fellow-citizens to try to survive, but he made no pretence that they could become again what they had once been. The time machine does not run backwards. The Revolution imposed on the Republic a choice which she would not, even could not make: it was just as impossible to join the league of States ranged against the Revolution as it was to accept the 'friendship' offered by France. It was no longer any use to beat about the bush and refuse to take sides. If Venice hoped to avoid making an enemy by passive procrastination, she would make two. And when the 'little tiger' came upon the scene, the time for choice had passed and the hour of expiation had struck.[73]

* * *

The 'little tiger' (Mocenigo's picturesque expression) was Bonaparte, who was overrunning Italy, setting up new institutions, overturning all the old laws and traditions. It was important for France that Venice should not join the league of her adversaries; not that the French feared a strength which Venice, in any case, no longer possessed, but for vital strategic reasons. It was essential that the French army's occupation of Italy should not be hindered by a Venice secretly or openly favourable to Austria.

Bonaparte had not troubled to disguise his ferocious intentions towards anyone who might attempt to bar his route, even passively. 'I shall be an Attila to Venice,' he exclaimed brutally to the Republican ambassadors who had come to Graz at his invitation, and he made no secret of his determination to reduce the most beautiful city in the world to ashes, if she presumed to oppose him.[74]

It could only be vain to hope to remain neutral, while the French and the Austrians were fighting on Italian soil. To want peace at any price is only any use if the enemy shares your point of view; for the French, the Italian campaign was viewed as a superb revenge by the poor on the rich, of the 'have-nots' on the 'haves.' When Napoleon Bonaparte showed his soldiers the 'magnificent plains of Lombardy' towards which he was sending them, he was exciting their greed as well as their warlike ardour. In comparing their poverty with the overflowing abundance of Italy, he was injecting them with that strong driving force which has so often compelled men to make war: envy, greed, and an obscure desire to plunder.

They were described by observers such as Barzoni as ragged infantrymen, barefoot, half-naked, equipped with any arms they could get hold of, or even just with sticks—in other words, a horde of vagabonds.[75] But these vagabonds had imperious, insolent officers, and above all they had the 'little tiger' of Corsica. Contarini painted a true picture of him when he wrote to the Supreme Court: 'The commander-in-chief, Bonaparte, a young man of 28, is spurred to the uttermost limit by pride; he is resolute in his decisions and believes there is nothing he cannot achieve. If he suspects some opposition to his plans, in a flash he becomes fierce and threatening.'[76]

This, then, was the Attila who proposed to destroy Venice if he could not subdue her as he wished. In fact, his plans were less extreme; he simply wanted to extract money from a State which was believed by everybody to be rich.

85. Exterior of the Scuola San Marco, now a hospital. Built by Mauro Coducci in 1500, this Scuola is a masterpiece of Venetian Renaissance architecture. Particularly interesting are the marble panels on each side of the door, which give the illusion of long galleries.

85

86

He was hardly interested in obtaining the alliance of a city whose military value was, he knew, almost nil. In order to achieve his aims, he would heap on them the coarsest of insults and the most terrifying threats. He pretended that some of his troops had been 'assassinated' by the Italians, and used this to extort huge indemnities from the terrorised towns. On the 15th April 1797, as the Carnival was drawing to a close, General Junot arrived to proclaim Bonaparte's shameful demands, and five days later French warships appeared off the Lido, awaiting the reply which would give them the signal to bombard the town. 'This government is too old, it will have to fall,' announced the conqueror, and he enumerated his complaints against it—the tyranny of the High Council, the horrors of the Leads... 'There will be no more Inquisitors, no more Senate.'

There was panic now, on the slightest provocation; the smallest stirring in a working-class district presaged the revolution, so thought the timorously inclined. Nonetheless, the civil militia organised themselves with great enthusiasm and—this had never happened before in Venice—cannons were dragged into St. Mark's Square. On the 11th May 1797, Lippomano saw the Square, where a few weeks earlier a gay carnival had been in full swing, transformed into an entrenched camp.[77] Dalmatian mercenaries and workmen from the Arsenal mounted guard beside the cannons, matches in hand.

Probably Venice had enough ships to repel the French, but her fighting spirit had died. There was fear, too, of the mass of the people, who were restless and inclined towards revolution. The magistrates confirmed all the surrender terms. Venice opened her coffers and said goodbye to her glory. Practical jokers placed on the sculptures of the Lion of St. Mark the Declaration of the Rights of Man, in the place of the Saint's Gospel. On the 15th May 1797, all the key points in Venice were occupied by the enemy; there were even soldiers posted in St. Mark's Square. The General entrusted with the conquest of Venice, Baraguey d'Hilliers, sent this reassuring message to Napoleon: 'At sunrise today I occupied the city of Venice and the adjacent islands and forts.' Baron Daru, a friend of Stendhal, noticed how the cheerful noise of the soldiers contrasted with the 'cheerless aspect of the city.' The festivities were over.

* * *

Venice is an immortal city, but at that moment something in her died, never to come life again. With Lodovico Manin, who reigned during those last eight years, ended that long line of 120 princes who had administered the Republic, strongly and wisely on the whole, ever since the far-off days of the first of their number, Paolo Lucio Anafesto, who received the *corno* in 697. Exactly eleven hundred years had gone by, and the splendour of Venice had been obliterated.

This tragic ending, more in the spirit of the old Dominante than the city of Carnival, seems to have had a most dramatic effect on all the famous Venetians of those last years. 'Rosalba, who had given such enjoyment to the eye, died blind,' says Monnier.[78] 'Goldoni fell a victim to illness and destitution in Paris, under the Terror. At Dux, Casanova was a laughing-stock for the servants, who put his portrait in the latrines... We shall never know whether, when he fell into the Brenta, Gaspara Gozzi was deliberately putting an end to his life or not. Carlo Gozzi died of chagrin. Gratarol was killed in exile. His inveterate enemy, the powerful Caterina Tron, died a lonely death. The actor Sacchi was drowned in a shipwreck. Antonio Longo, whose life had been one long peal of laughter, lay ruined and dying in a hideous slum, among filth and fleas.'

86. Marble stairway in the garden of the Ca' d'Oro. Every detail of this luxurious house, now a museum created by the cultivated taste of a great collector, indicates the style of a nobleman's dwelling at the beginning of the Renaissance.

The great painters had deserted a city where they were no longer appreciated as they had once been. Bellotto, the nephew of Canaletto, had gone to Warsaw and settled down with his Polish patrons. Giambattista Tiepolo had been working for the King of Spain since 1762, and died twenty years later in Madrid. Canaletto had already returned to his native land to die, although Rome had tried to keep him. Pietro Longhi and Francesco Guardi had done the same, the first in 1785, the other in 1793. Neither of them saw the disaster and the humiliation of the Most Serene Republic. Before the darkness fell on Venice, they had vanished from the scene, taking with them the radiant and fascinating image of the city they had loved and painted.

***

Venice did not, however, suffer so greatly from the French occupation. The Treaty of Vienna returned to her the bronze quadriga of St. Mark, and the pictures which had been taken away by Napoleon. The Austrian domination weakened her spirit of independence, but did not disfigure her face or soul. Conquered and forced to submit to the foreigner, then given back her freedom by the Risorgimento, Venice remained the city of dreams, the enchantment of poets, painters and musicians.

87. Exterior of S. Maria dei Miracoli. This church, encrusted with precious marbles, was built in 1489 by Pietro Lombardo to house a miraculous image of the Virgin Mary (hence its name) which belonged to a rich merchant, Francesco Amadi, and which was held in great veneration by the people of Venice.

88. View of the Campo S. Polo, one of the largest and busiest squares in Venice.

89. Cats in the Calle del Forno. He who kills a cat dies within the year; he who hurts a cat will meet with a bad accident. This is the popular superstition which protects these useful and elegant animals. They swarm in the streets of Venice, and live on the charity of passers-by who take pity on their thinness.

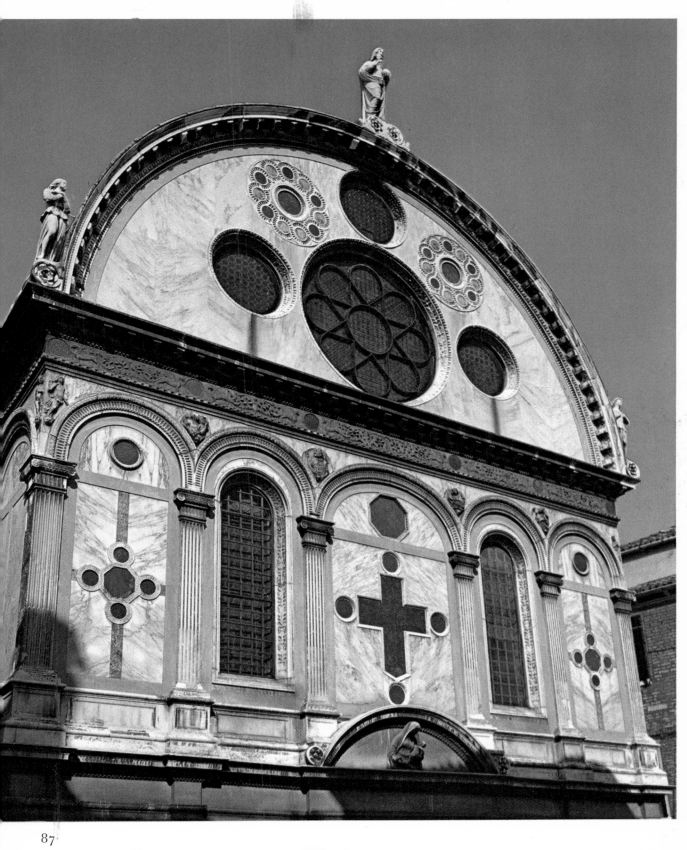

88

89

VENICE SURVIVES
THE VENETIAN REPUBLIC

UNLESS A nation looks specifically to artistic creation for the pride and gladness which can console it in its loss of wealth or liberty, periods of political decadence are rarely conducive to vigorous aesthetic growth. The great statesmen-popes were the creators of Baroque Rome; Florence was the product of the wealth and prestige of the Medicis, and kings without crowns though they were, they dealt on equal terms with the Emperor and the King of France. 'The Age of Pericles,' 'The Age of Louis XIV,' these were not empty titles invented by courtiers, but the straightforward statement of palpable facts.

Even in Venice, artistic flowering began with the consolidation of the Republic's prestige and its rising commercial prosperity. It should also be observed that every period has its own distinctive form of aesthetic expression, directly related to the dominant element in its social life. During the Middle Ages, for example, painting was almost exclusively religious because piety and religion were the prevailing forces in society. With the Renaissance, Man had replaced God at the centre of the Universe; growing importance was attached to the representation of the human form, of man's activities in everyday life, and of his life against the background of the city. And as Venice took increasing pride in her political power and prosperity, she glorified herself in the portraits of her leaders and in ceremonial or informal public demonstrations.

However independent individual stylistic features may be of the factors which shape or determine social change, architecture is still deeply marked by them— if only by virtue of its functional role. Thus we see that style in palaces varies with trends of fashion much more quickly than it does in churches, and it took the Great Plague for Longhena to realize his masterpieces S. Maria della Salute and S. Maria del Pianto (the latter is less well known because it stands within the precincts of a convent), the structure of which is also a symbolic form of the sentiments which inspired their erection.

Contrasting with the strong aesthetic dynamism of the preceding centuries, the early nineteenth century, following the trend started in the latter years of the eighteenth century through to its conclusion, is marked by its basically static quality. Neo-classicism, which succeeded the Baroque or Rococo throughout Europe, was as ill-starred for Venice as occupation by the French or Austrians. In the first place, the great Classical periods corresponded with the supremacy of sculpture; through all the previous centuries, as we have seen, Venice, unlike Florence, was never a home of sculptors. Painting always prevailed over sculpture

90. Caryatid in the entrance to the Library of St. Mark's. The Libreria Vecchia di San Marco, which stands on the Piazzetta opposite the Doge's Palace, was built by Jacopo Sansovino and continued by Scamozzi from 1582 onwards. The statues are in a deliberately ancient style, to harmonise with the classical appearance of the architecture.

91. View of the Piazzetta, from the Clock Tower, showing the façade of St. Mark's Cathedral, the Doge's Palace, and S. Giorgio Maggiore.

because the landscape was lacking in the vast geological masses which so inspire the Florentine sculptor's imagination. In Florence, indeed, even the great painters—Giotto, Masaccio, Paolo Uccello and Michelangelo—were sculptors by temperament, sensibility and aesthetic approach.

The only benefit that Neo-Classicism brought the Queen of the Adriatic came in the person of Antonio Canova, a mainland Venetian (born at Possagno near Treviso) who began his career in Venice, and retained the Venetian tendency towards realism right until his arbitrary and artificial entry into the Greek school. Winckelmann's aesthetic theories left a strong impression on him; they determined his conversion to Classicism, restricting his fresh natural talent within a stiff and often frigid dignity which was foreign to his nature. His *Cupid and Psyche* and the reclining statue of Paolina Borghese in Rome reflect the sensuality, the thrill of life, the kind of tenderness he felt for emotions of the heart and flesh before his work was stiffened into a purely formal Classicism which verged upon academism and prompted a contemporary to declare, ' Canova is a Venetian sculptor translated into Greek.' When he saw the Greek marbles which Lord Elgin brought back from Athens and exhibited in London in 1815, Canova took much greater pleasure in observing how faithfully they reflected the ' loveliness of nature,' as he put it, than in their Classicism; yet he had not enough strength or originality to equal them by renewing the Classical ideal. Like Thorwaldsen, and for the same reasons, he sank his passion and individuality in precise imitations of the Ancients.

Venetian sculpture, therefore, did not gain very much from the phase of artistic evolution from the end of the eighteenth century to the beginning of the nineteenth, and architecture did not derive any great advantage either. By its very geographical setting, against a shifting background of sea and sky, Venice was temperamentally baroque. Classicism was therefore prevented from taking deep root there or producing any rich growth. It could do no more than produce forms which were artificially grafted to a stem ill-prepared to receive them. It soon becomes obvious that a Classical church in imitation of the Pantheon in Rome is out of place here: S. Simeone Piccolo, built by Giovanni Scalfarotto in 1718, does not fit into the surrounding landscape. It is an excrescence in Roman style, and by virtue of this fact alone, wholly incompatible with the character of Venice.

The excuse generally put forward on behalf of this copy of a Roman temple is that Scalfarotto was continuing the tradition of round churches established by Longhena with S. Maria della Salute, but there is, in fact, no resemblance at all between the two churches. The church of la Salute is certainly circular in shape, to symbolize the Resurrection and to inspire a sense of its spiral ascent to the heavens. Contrasting it with the cold, static tambour of S. Simeone Piccolo and the stillness of its cupola, we see that they are worlds apart: the world of passion actuating matter, and the world of matter possessing its own harmony but devoid of any spiritual quality and empty of all human emotion. We can see in this just how impossible it was for Classicism to contribute to the progress of Venetian art, or indeed to reinvigorate it with new blood. There is no more resemblance between the Salute and S. Simeone Piccolo than there is between Tintoretto and Canova. This pinpoints just how naturally the Baroque belonged in Venice and was spiritually in tune with it, whilst the imposition of Classicism could only be damaging.

The harm it did becomes tragically apparent in an alteration carried out in the Piazza San Marco at the beginning of the nineteenth century. Up to that time there was no west wing closing the square. Opposite the Basilica of San Marco there was the church of S. Geminiano, one of the oldest in Venice, going back to the days of Rivoalto and said to have been built by Narses in the sixth century.

92. Courtyard of the Doge's Palace. The four sides of this courtyard reflect the changes of style which took place from the fourteenth to the seventeenth centuries, while the Palace was being built. The south side is the simplest, with its plain archways and its great expanse of pink brickwork, warm in the sunlight.

When Sansovino extended the Procuratie (so-called because the residence of the Procurator stood there on the west side of the square) to meet S. Geminiano, he rebuilt the church in the 'modern' Renaissance style, showing a lack of concern for its great antiquity which was quite typical of the time.

What was the effect of the Renaissance Classicism of the new S. Geminiano, with its brilliant white marble and its statues, as it stood facing the shimmering blaze of colour which was San Marco... Today we can only guess, for the new Geminiano shared the sorry fate of its predecessor; it was demolished in 1807. Giuseppe Soli da Vignola, wishing to extend the Doge's Palace to fill the whole width of the Square, had the church taken away. On its site he built a new wing for the Procuratie, and this is known as the Fabbrica Nuovissima or Ala Napoleonica. This act of vandalism was thus attributed to the French Emperor.

Not knowing what the Piazza San Marco looked like in the days when its west side was still open, we cannot say whether this would be preferable to the closed four sides we know now. The uninterrupted continuity of the arcades and the Procuratie makes the square seem like a reception-hall in which strollers have the illusion of being guests. They can move about or sit on the café terraces in a completely enclosed space which, for all its size, imparts a remarkable feeling of intimacy. The few streets running into the square seem to steal their way beneath the buildings and between the arcades, to pass unnoticed and leave the sense of intimacy undisturbed. When we look at the academic severity of the Fabbrica Nuovissima and the little interest to be derived from the Roman statues on top of the Ala Napoleonica, it cannot be said that Venice gained much from the architecture of Soli da Vignola or the sculpture of Bosa and Banti. There is little of truly Venetian character in their work, and it would be better suited to Turin, Milan or Rome.

The arts of Venice had clearly breathed their last in the declining years of the eighteenth century, and no contribution from the outside world could bring them back to life. It was from within herself, by her own energy and genius that Venice had created her architecture and painting throughout seven hundred years of astonishing aesthetic fertility. Splendid as it was, the eighteenth century was still moving forward under the unchecked momentum begun in the Middle Ages; even when she was no longer a great political and economic power, Venice remained one of the major centres of Italian art. Yet the source of her art was exhausted by the impoverishment she suffered when her trade declined, and the humiliation which followed her loss of sovereign independence. It was only after the Risorgimento that her painting gained a new but short-lived glory.

*
* *

It was not so much in Venice as in Florence and especially Naples that Romantic painting was most active, most original and most brilliant, but one of its chief exponents Francesco Hayez, was born there. When quite young, he worked in Rome among the Neo-Classicists, then settled in Milan, which has always stood for the cosmopolitan tendencies in Italian art. He too was cosmopolitan, for his Romanticism shows French as well as German elements. Hayez belonged only by birth to the great Venetian tradition, derived little from it in his development and nothing in his work. The tradition itself seems to have faded when once the brilliant flame of the eighteenth century had died.

Why was there a break of this kind in an artistic tradition which had flourished continuously since the eleventh century? How was it that Tiepolo had no heir to

93. Capital of a column on the south side of the Doge's Palace. On these capitals the sculptor depicted symbolic figures of the Virtues, but his symbols have a charmingly human, lifelike appearance.

succeed him in Venice—that his line seems to have been continued by the Frenchman, Fragonard, and the Spaniard, Goya? This is one of the mysteries often to be encountered in the history of art and which can never be wholly explained by historical, economic, or even aesthetic considerations. The magnificent revival of painting technique in Italian art during the nineteenth century was achieved by the Tuscan *macchiaioli* with the sensitive vibrant touch which they applied in seeking to perfect it. The Venetian heritage contributed more to this tachiste art than did the Florentine heritage, but it was not the Venetians who developed it.

It redounds to her credit, on the other hand, that in the wake of Romanticism, and possibly inspired by it, a style which could be called 'poetic realism' found a profusion of colourful, evocative themes in Venice which artists were never to tire of developing. Mostly these painters were Venetian in origin, like Giacomo Favretto; he was at home with every feature of the poorer districts ever since the days when, as a child, he had wandered through the streets and strolled through the sunlit *campi*. In his paintings, it was not only the people of the eighteenth century, with their mannered grace and outmoded elegance that Favretto restored to life; to paint their satin, lace and velvet, he rediscovered the art of Guardi and Longhi. The lagoon's constantly changing colours at different hours of the day are reproduced in Favretto's work with incomparable subtlety and a sadness which tragically reminds us of passing time. The nostalgia for the past which prompts Favretto to imagine encounters between the lovely ladies and the gentlemen of another age in the Piazza San Marco becomes a kind of ghosts' ballet; for though he too loved the cheerful clamour of the crowds thronging past the shops and cafés, Favretto resembles the writers of the nineteenth century who looked on Venice as a 'dead city,' finding in it a pleasure tinged with sorrow, the smell of decay which pleased the fancy of the decadents.

Venice has never really been a dead city; there are few cities in Europe where the people are so fast-moving, so sharp, so young and so alive in everything they do. For all that, it has become a literary convention to bewail the lost glory of the Most Serene Republic, to look on modern Venice as a 'beautiful embalmed corpse' in a coffin of silk and glass. And when Favretto paints the Venetians of another day, he suggests the dance of kindly yet tragic spirits.

Ettore Tito, on the other hand, seems very much less sensitive to evocation of the past. He was a native of Castellamare Adriatico, but came to Venice when very young. He too is an exponent of poetic realism, but for him the accent is on realism. A more robust figure than Favretto, less inclined towards the amusing anecdote, he takes his characters from the Venice of his own period and not that of Goldoni. He does not waste time in trying to bring back the charms of a bygone age; he is content to observe the fishmongers' and greengrocers' stalls, surrounded by sturdy, laughing housewives, to bring out the true poetry of realism which Favretto often concealed behind theatrical artifice. To Ettore Tito, at all events, fell the perilous privilege of succeeding Tiepolo—of painting a ceiling in the church of the Scalzi to replace the *Transport of the Virgin's Household*, which was destroyed by an Austrian bomb during the first world war.

There can be no question of a comparison between the merits of the eighteenth century master and those of his successors; suffice it to say that of all the Venetian painters of the second half of the nineteenth century, Ettore Tito was the only one fit to take such a risk and acquit himself worthily. Tito, indeed, had a feeling for large-scale composition and a strength in using masses which preeminently suited him for the task. The other Venetian artists of the period were more at home at their easels, painting in the grand, heroic style or reproducing the 'slice of life' so dear to realist painters and novelists. The most pleasing elements in

94. The Senate in the Doge's Palace. Beside the magnificent clock, in its frame of carved and gilded wood, is a painting by Giacomo Palma the Younger. It is an allegorical representation of the victory of the Doge Leonardo Loredan over the enemies of Venice, united in the League of Cambrai.

95. A prison window. Many romantic exaggerations have been made about the sufferings of prisoners confined in the Leads or the Wells. Undoubtedly, however, it was necessary that enemies of the Republic and common malefactors should be securely locked up; hence these enormous bars, too thick for any file to tackle.

95

the work of Luigi Nono, for example, are the familiar moments in the life of the fishermen of Chioggia, with their baskets spread over the pink and russet quays, and their brightly-coloured *bragozzi* with their brown or yellow sails covered with stars. Nono, like Ettore Tito, applied himself to the task of faithfully reproducing the extraordinary play of light over the shifting waters of the canals, the constantly changing colour which one can never tire of watching.

Guglielmo Ciardi turns his eye more to the vast, luminous spaces, to the dazzling light which shimmers across the lagoon in the afternoon, and the sadness of the setting sun as it casts a blaze of purple flame over the clouds. If it was not their signal honour to be Venetian by birth, other Italian artists, soon at home in Venice, became her adopted sons and dedicated themselves to extolling her infinite splendour. Mario di Maria of Bologna, Pietro Fragiacomo of Trieste, Cesare Laurenti from the strong and rugged Romagna, and Italico Brass of Gorizia complete the picture of Venice's part within the larger canvas of the history of nineteenth century Italian painting.

But what of today? With its Biennale of Modern Art, Venice has taken pride of place among the cities in which contemporary painting is exhibited. Every two years, pavilions for all the different countries participating are erected within the gardens, and a host of artists, critics, amateurs and others drawn by idle curiosity are brought together. Many of the painters taking part are either natives of Venice or settled there, but the language of modern art increasingly tends to rid itself of regional idiosyncrasies; its vocabulary is international, becoming generally accepted in all countries and making distinction between schools increasingly difficult. There are painters *from* Venice or who *live in* Venice, but what makes them specifically *Venetian?*

* *
*

Political and artistic development in Venice follows a smooth uninterrupted curve until the declining years of the eighteenth century, but it was at this period that all the forces which had worked for Venice's progress and well-being suddenly turned violently against her, striving to destroy everything she had built. Whenever the Republic had been threatened by some dangerous situation, she had been able to ward it off and even turn it to her advantage. Yet a time comes in the life of a state when the strength of its active—if not passive—resistance and the ability to meet all situations prove of no avail. When Venice became embroiled with the 'Great States', France and Austria, she was no longer a great power but a mere ally they could use as they pleased and crush as soon as she offered opposition. This humiliating state of affairs struck Venice in her life, her soul and her arts.

Without a Doge, noblemen or a rich middle class to give them patronage, artists lacked the means for their life and work. As early as the eighteenth century, many great Venetians had been emigrating. Tintoretto had hardly ever left Venice, but Tiepolo went to Madrid and Würzburg, and Bellotto to London and Warsaw. The interest other nations showed in Venetian art was certainly flattering but also harmful to Venice, who saw her best sons leaving her. A time came at last when, as a pleasure city for foreigners, she was content to supply what they wanted —and this was by no means new and original art forms.

Venice survived the death of the Republic, but in one sense she was now nothing more than a shadow of herself; what her visitors valued in her most often was not always the best of what she had to offer. Her architecture and painting still

96. West wall of courtyard in the Doge's Palace. The work of Antonio Rizzo and Pietro Lombardo, this wall epitomizes the exquisite delicacy of Renaissance art; the intricate detail does not detract from the imposing strength of the whole.

97. The Grand Canal, from the Traghetto of Ca' Garzoni. There are only three bridges over the Grand Canal: the Accademia, the Rialto and the footbridge at the Station, and these are at some considerable distance from each other. In between, '*traghetti*' carry passengers across the Canal, plying to and fro between their small wooden quays.

won the admiration of artists, but in the eighteenth century, when the Grand Tour was a necessary part of the education of young people and the artist's development, it was to Rome they went—drawn very largely by the remaining fragments of her early history. Piranesi, himself a Venetian, applied his energies almost exclusively to the study and representation of Roman monuments.

Tourists would devote several days to visiting the churches and palaces, now largely shorn of their collections, which had been sold abroad by their needy if not poverty-stricken owners. But once they had paid tribute to Venice's reputation as a city of art, most tourists turned their attentions to the cafés, theatres, gaming-houses and all the places of amusement where they could enjoy to their heart's content what their own respectability and local cant would have condemned at

A Race of Gondolas on the Grand Canal. Pen and bistre wash over black chalk; Guardi. This is approximately the view from the Palazzo Foscari. On the left is the Palazzo Balbi, behind the floating pavilion or *Macchina*, still erected on Regatta days in the same place, to seat the guests of honour and to mark the winning post.

home. But an ancient capital converted into a kind of watering-place or pleasure resort during the season can hardly be expected to remain an active source of inspiration for the arts. When the foreigners left and the winter months brought their squalls, rain from the Dolomites, and icy winds over the Adriatic, Venice in the late eighteenth century was more like a *ridotto* with its doors closed at dawn, or a café whose last customers drift away in the early hours of the morning.

The new French and Austrian masters whom the changing fortunes of European politics had given to Venice did nothing to raise her from the physical and moral depths to which she had fallen, for humiliation is not a favourable state of mind for insurrection. As time passed, however, Venice's reputation changed, and this change was largely due to Romanticism. Whilst the eighteenth century had seen nothing but an artistic curiosity in the work of the Gothic, Byzantine and Baroque periods, conflicting as they did with the demands of 'good taste', the Romantic mind marvelled at them. The stirring events in the early history of

the Republic enthralled poets and novelists; these events and the places where
they occurred stimulated painters, who saw a Venice which differed from that
of Lady Montagu, de Brosses or Casanova. The decline of Classicism led also
to a decline in the absolute supremacy of Rome, and the Romantics found in
Venice a source of passion and emotion which fulfilled all their desires and
expectations. 'Pilgrims of Beauty' succeeded the tourists who had merely come
to amuse themselves, and when Venice was seen as a centre of art rather than
of pleasure, her patrons changed also—and to her advantage.

An emotional element was, however, blended with the aesthetic. Lovers found
a new happiness with one another in the ancient palaces, lulled by serenades;
gondolas, moonlight over the lagoon, the mystery of the little canals, the night,

A noble lady stepping into a gondola.

the romantic atmosphere kept alive by old Venetian tales—all these were an
attraction for newly-weds on their honeymoons. Venice was now truly revealed
as the romantic city *par excellence*, where everything conspires to give delight:
nature, works of art, the character of the people, the very lay-out of the city
and its surroundings.

Two books did much to make travellers conscious of Venice's exceptional artistic
beauty: *The Stones of Venice* by John Ruskin (in three volumes published between
1851 and 1853) and *Le Voyage en Italie* by Hippolyte Taine, published in 1864.
Whilst Ruskin was teaching his readers to see and understand Byzantine and
Gothic architecture according to the original technique which he expounded in
The Seven Lamps of Architecture (published two years before *The Stones of Venice*) and
later in *Saint Mark's Rest*, he established a parallel between aesthetic flowering
and the ardour of religious faith, and saw the beginnings of decline when
ambition, greed and the desire for power caused material interests to prevail
over those of the spirit. For him then, the Baroque and even the Renaissance
were to be condemned for their 'profanation' of art.

201

This arbitrary, shortsighted judgment did not prevent Ruskin's writings from awaking several generations of passionate pilgrims to the splendours of Venice; they took his books with them as a traveller's breviary. Taine's work, on the other hand, stimulated curiosity and directed research towards the principle of environmental influence—the crux of his theories. It stands to his credit that he drew attention to the essentially Venetian character of an art which was the product of a body of geographical, historical, cultural and social factors. In Venice more than anywhere else—except perhaps Florence—art, city and life form an indivisible whole. What this boils down to is that we have to know every aspect of Venice, and even live there long enough to gain an insight into its distinctive features if we are to appreciate its art to the full.

Throughout the nineteenth century, whilst famous and obscure lovers were settling on the shores of the lagoon, having made their choice of the ' supreme city of love ', artists, art historians and amateurs were becoming ' Venetian by adoption '. Venice was no longer visited merely for the carnival and the licence which it allowed, as it had been in the eighteenth century; for one thing the carnival, ancient Venetian institution though it had been, dropped into disuse with the loss of prosperity and independence, but above all because Venice was now looked upon as a proud, majestic and lovely city. It was not to be criminally misused and reduced to the level of a town of pleasure as it had been by the tourists of the previous century.

*_**

Venice's beauty was grimly, almost tragically heightened by political events. Although the French and Austrian occupation was not so oppressive that it could stifle Venetian exuberance, the city's loss of liberty was so humiliating that its genius was paralysed. The noblemen, the bishops, the convents, even the *scuole* were no longer in possession of the resources necessary to support and encourage artists. The arrival of the agents and principles of the French Revolution put an end to the divisions of the class hierarchy; they were arbitrarily levelled in the name of an illusory equality. A stake in the struggle between foreign powers, the former Mistress of the Seas passed beneath the French yoke and accepted it, believing that it was a fair exchange for liberty. By the Treaty of Campoformio, however, the city was absurdly divided, with no account taken of geographical or social realities, between Austria and the Cisalpine Republic, which Napoleon created in 1797. Eight years later, another agreement signed at Presburg joined Austrian Venice to a newly established kingdom of Italy, but this was not to survive Napoleon's loss of power. When Venice passed once again under the Double-headed Eagle, she was subjected to a rigid process of assimilation—the more so because liberal tendencies were being openly confessed.

In Venice, as in other regions of Italy, patriots were tracked down by the imperial police and imprisoned—either in Austrian gaols or in the cells of the Doge's Palace. Discontent was rife in all classes of Italian society, which used every available opportunity to express its wrath and hatred. In the halls of the Correr Museum devoted to the history of the Risorgimento, it is easy to follow the evolution and progress of patriotic feeling. What appeared to be an event of purely economic significance—the laying of a railway line between Milan and Venice in 1837—was the stimulus for a violent outburst of Italian nationalism, and the voice of a young lawyer, Daniele Manin, was heard proclaiming Venice's political rights. He bore the same name as the last Doge, Lodovico Manin, and this was seen as

98, 99. Reliquaries in the Treasury of St. Mark's Cathedral. One of the great ambitions of Venetian Doges and noblemen was to collect reliquaries from all over the East and give them to St. Mark's. They hoped thus to obtain for their city the protection of the saints whose bones they possessed.

100. Painted wax head; Sacristy of the Redentore Church. There is a collection of these rather macabre heads, painted in lifelike colours and provided with beards and eyebrows like this effigy of St. Laurence, in the Sacristy of this church.

101. Reliquaries in the Treasury of St. Mark's Cathedral. The most remarkable among these exhibits is the piece of silver armour, containing the leg of a saint.

98   99

100   101

a symbol for the possible resurrection of the old Republic. Ten years later, during the ninth Congress of Scholars which met in Venice, Daniele Manin spoke—this time with greater maturity and a political experience more alive to the revolutionary ferment growing in every country. Arrested by the Austrian police and imprisoned as an agitator, Manin was released by a popular revolt which broke out on the 16th March, 1848, when Austrian newspapers informed the Venetians of revolution in Vienna, Dresden and Paris.

The Viennese rising was a short-lived one of course; the insurgents, workers and students, were quickly crushed by the army. But because revolution had also broken out in Milan and it was feared that Austrian troops could not maintain control in Venice, they were withdrawn. There was now a great outburst of jubilation in Venice, and as the foreign garrison was forced out, the Republic was proclaimed once again under the patronage of St. Mark, to counter the designs of the Carbonari and the extremists of *Giovane Italia*, who would have established a strictly revolutionary government. Liberal, moderate, cautious, Manin feared the excesses of a people in revolt once they gave way to their instincts.

But once Venice had been drawn into the liberating movement of the Risorgimento, local patriotism was submerged within the larger consciousness of being Italian. In the company of the Great Powers, the Italy of the Risorgimento was to figure as a power in her own right—a complete, united country. The Republic of Saint Mark was an anachronism in an age when the Italy of little principalities was a historic oddity. Even the most traditionally-minded Venetians recognized that an isolated Venice was no longer a practical proposition, and that even if it meant the loss of her independence for good and all, she could not hold aloof from the kingdom of Italy which was being formed in the liberated peninsula. The brief insurrection under Daniele Manin ended in 1849 with a disastrous siege, after which the Austrian regiments took possession of their barracks once again and the patriots went into exile.

From this time on, and throughout the succession of wars which made the kingdom of Italy united and independent, Venice's fate was merged with that of Italy and was never again to be divided from it. Venetian history was henceforth no more than an element in the history of Italy, like that of Naples, Milan or Florence. Italian nationalism had so completely replaced the individual Venetian consciousness that the plebiscite held by the Peace of Vienna in 1866 recorded only 69 votes against Venice joining the kingdom of Italy, whilst 674,426 were for it.

The end of her political independence did not, however, mean that the Queen of the Adriatic had lost her individual character; the Italian provinces were all possessed of their own distinctive personalities and these were too strong to be standardized. As a part of Italy, Venice preserved her originality, her traditions and her abiding spirit. If there is a city in Europe whose face and inner being have remained almost untouched by time, that city is Venice.

* *
*

Some saw the railway bridge connecting Venice to the mainland as a threat to her position as an island and feared that her beauty would suffer for it. There was equal anxiety more recently when an *autostrada* was constructed so that motor cars could travel to the very edge if not to the heart of the city. Alarming modernisation plans are put forward periodically with the object of increasing the comforts and amenities available to tourists. This should be seen as an outcome

102. Mosaic depicting a head (22″ × 16″); Museum of St. Mark's. This work, Eastern in origin or in inspiration, is one of the oldest in the Museum. The fragments which remain enable one to study the technical mastery of the artist, who succeeded in imparting a most moving expression to the face of his subject.

of the considerable change which has taken place in the traveller's psychology and behaviour.

During the nineteenth century, no one was discouraged by the difficulties and inconveniences of travel; if anything they contributed to the charm of the country through which one was passing. The traveller accepted them good-humouredly and took advantage of them to establish closer contact with the people and the country-side. He could wander about as much as he liked, and not being pressed for time was one of the pleasures of going abroad. Nowadays the traveller has to rush: he wants to see as many towns as he can in the least possible time. In Venice this state of affairs began with his reluctance to accept the ferry-boat journey across the lagoon —with the result that the railway was extended to the end of the Grand Canal. Today there is talk of a motor-road to satisfy Americans impatient to see the Piazza San Marco; this would permit traffic to pass over the Riva delle Zattere to the Customs House, where the statue of Fortune stands turning in the wind. What can we expect from the folly of these schemes ? There is every reason to fear the readiness with which tourist cities now make it their business to satisfy their visitors' every whim. There is already a tremendous surge of travellers, rushing between trains or making a brief landing from their pleasure boats, blocking the narrow streets and the *campi*. The travellers of the nineteenth century knew that beauty was to be won with love and patience—that it was no 'waste of time' to draw the journey out by enjoying every moment to the full.

In this book it is not our concern to say how Venice should be studied or observed, but the history of the Republic makes it obvious that the extraordinary accumulation of masterpieces within the city have contributed more than anything to its many-sided appearance. Each of the districts, called *sestieri*, has its individual character: Canareggio, Dorsoduro and Castello are almost different towns within the interior of the city. (Dorsoduro means 'hard back'. The district was given this name because its soil is harder than that of the other islands from which Venice was formed.) It takes many long walks to acquaint oneself with all the distinctive features of their streets and squares, the customs of their inhabitants, their trade and the styles of their houses.

These distinctive features are unfortunately tending to disappear. The Giudecca, for instance, has almost an atmosphere of poverty about it. (As its name indicates, it was originally the Jewish quarter, and was famous for its magnificent vegetation.) From time to time the more sensitive citizens of Venice and foreign enthusiasts—who are even more exacting in their concern for the authenticity and beauty of her monuments—have been incensed against innovations which are rarely successful. The Stucky Mills, built on the headland of Giudecca, caused some lively dispute, but they are on the fringe of the city itself and the eye has grown accustomed to seeing them.

Loving the variety of Venice means accepting that every period in her history has its contribution to make—provided of course, that this contribution is something beautiful and that the nature of its beauty does not destroy the harmony achieved in the work of previous centuries. When we examine the juxtaposition of styles extending from Byzantine to Rococo and even to Neo-Classical, we recognize how far elements as different, as opposed to one another as Gothic and Baroque can come to terms and merge within this harmony, but we cannot be sure that architecture which might suit Chicago or Brasilia would find a place on the Grand Canal.

The town-planning problems which have to be faced in Venice preclude, for example, the extreme solutions imposed by a city's destruction during a war. It is natural enough for Rotterdam, bombed as it was during the second world war, to have been rebuilt in the most modern, functional style. In Florence, which also suffered bombardment, the way in which reconstructed buildings harmonise with those of the Middle Ages has given rise to argument which has not yet ended. Venice, on the other hand, was fortunate enough to have been spared almost completely. The destruction of Tiepolo's ceiling in the church of the Scalzi was the only great disaster—to be regretted all the more because the great work by Ettore Tito which replaced it does not really tone with the extreme Rococo of the church.

We should love the diversity of Venice, her different quarters and surrounding islands, but in this diversity we should accept only those things which truly belong to Venice and could never have been created anywhere else.

* * *

This diversity recurs with even greater prominence and colour in the lovely islands which surround Venice herself. Situated halfway between Venice and the Lido, the little island of San Lazzaro of the Armenians has one of the most beautiful and ' romantic ' gardens imaginable. It was once occupied by a leper colony, but in 1717 the Signoria gave the island to the famous Manug Mechitar, the great holy man from the east who was driven from his monastery by the Turks when the Venetians lost Morea. Mechitar the Comforter settled with his Armenian monks in the wonderful garden, where little now remains of the white marble Renaissance cloisters. As theirs was a very hospitable order, the monks offered a cell to Lord Byron when he had grown weary of the pleasure-seeking and worldly life of the Venetians, and sought refuge in their haven of peace and silence. A rich library of manuscripts and incunabula was open to him and he was able to meditate in the little cemetery, overlooking the lagoon and the infinite expanse of sea and sky, where the kings of Armenia are still buried today. When the silvery bells of the monastery of Mechitar mingle their tones with the waves of the pink and golden sea, laid by the sunset like a splendid carpet from Venice to the Lido, the visitor is literally transported, out of space and time, into a world where all is light, transparent, serene and beautiful.

The calm of San Lazzaro sometimes seemed oppressive to Byron's impetuous, troubled spirit; he sought even greater solitude and found it on the Lido, where he would wander for hours along the beach. The Lido had not yet become a busy resort with a casino and large hotels; it was almost uninhabited—probably very much like the kind of marshy island which Venice had been in ancient times. It had a little town where the most important building was, and still is, slightly apart from the main built-up area. This was the Church of S. Nicolo, founded in 1044 by Doge Domenico Contarini. It was here, as we described earlier, that the ceremony of Marriage to the Sea was held every year on Ascension Day, following a solemn mass in memory of the Venetian victory over the Slavs. Among Venetian noblemen, the custom developed quite early of having a villa on the Lido where one could go to enjoy the bracing sea air. Like those of Murano, the villas were surrounded by beautiful gardens; these have now disappeared for the most part or lost their splendour. There are still a large number of houses, some dating back to the Middle Ages and the Renaissance, but most of them to the period when the Lido became fashionable—at the beginning of the nineteenth century. The visitor to the Lido who sees nothing more than watering-places and the large shady avenue of trees lined with big hotels does not know the real Lido. This is concealed behind the high, redbrick walls, overhung with the branches of eucalyptus and tamarind, in the silent little streets where old houses sleep the quiet sleep of things belonging to another age.

One of the great virtues of the islands of the lagoon, so seldom visited by tourists, is that they have repudiated modernisation; they have kept their character unchanged. When one grows weary of the crowds of foreigners, jostling one another in the streets of Venice, it is restful to cross the lagoon and find relaxation in Chioggia, a busy, colourful fishing port. It is by the wharves of Chioggia that the *bragozzi* are tied up. These are large, heavy craft, characteristic of the Adriatic and distinguishable by their sails, which are painted in the greatest variety of colours: ochre, yellow and red are the commonest. Images of saints are also represented in these primitive colours, together with ancient symbolic figures—suns, stars and lions—some of which undoubtedly date back to pagan times. Also to be observed on the prows of the *bragozzi* of Chioggia are the two yellow eyes painted on each side of the stem-post; these perpetuate a Mediterranean custom which was practised by the ancient Greeks.

The eyes were intended as a magical protection against all the dangers of the sea, but according to a rarely expressed though highly probable opinion, they were also given to the craft so that it could guide itself in case the helmsman should fall asleep. It seems equally possible that this precaution would have made the boat like a living being, capable of the free, independent choice of movement normally possessed by man alone. Chioggia was one of the most advanced areas of Venice; its strategic importance was asserted whenever the Republic was threatened by an enemy approaching from the sea—whether it was the Franks of King Pepin, the Genoese or the Turks. In order to strengthen the defensive system which closed the lagoon to invaders, a monk and cosmographer by the name of Father Coronelli proposed to the Senate that an immense wall be constructed from huge Istrian stone blocks, strengthened with bundles of piles and Pozzolana cement; it was to be proof against water, over four miles long, supported on a base 45 feet wide and rising to a height 16 feet above sea-level. These fortifications were called *murazzi;* when we see them today on the journey from Pellestrina to Chioggia, we can marvel that in 1750 when the period of commercial and political decadence was already under way, a work of this size was undertaken and completed. The expense was enormous and a burden on the already depleted treasury, but the result made it worthwhile. The advantage was not so much from the standpoint of sea warfare as to protect the approaches to the port of Chioggia from the storms of the Adriatic and the danger of becoming silted up, though when the French ships came to fire on Venice in 1797, they passed in front of the Lido ports, and the flagship, paradoxically called *Le Libérateur*, was forced back by their cannonades.

The seamen of Chioggia have tanned, muscular, weatherbeaten bodies and cheerful, noisy laughs. Goldoni delighted in imitating the quarrels of their wives, with their comic singsong accent and the imagery of their speech—which seems characteristic indeed of fishwives the world over. Perhaps the people of Chioggia do not give vent to their feelings as freely as they did in Goldoni's day, but they still show greater liveliness than the Venetians, and their spontaneous language has retained an almost mediaeval quality. Most of the fishermen of Chioggia now have motors on their craft in addition to the gaily painted sails inherited from their ancestors and faithfully reproduced from ancient models; yet they still retain their strength, their aggressiveness, their resistance to fatigue, hardship and rough weather, which enable us to recognize in them the essential features of the seamen who set sail on the galley of Pietro Orseolo to conquer Dalmatia, the comrades in arms of Bragadin, and the gunners of Morosini *il Peloponnesiaco*.

The island of San Francesco al Deserto takes us far from Venice both in space and time. Like San Lazzaro, it has devoted itself entirely to silence, meditation

103. Evening in Venice. The Salute Church and the opening of the Grand Canal are here seen from the campanile of the church of S. Giorgio Maggiore.

and prayer. It has no buildings apart from the monastery, whose precincts shelter the monks from the noise and curiosity without. Anyone visiting San Francesco al Deserto, with its rows of tall cypresses already visible from the distance like a rampart, has found a refuge from the clamour of the outside world.

When Saint Francis of Assisi retired here to live in complete isolation, the little island was marshy, devoid of all vegetation and frequented only by sea-birds; before the coming of the refugees from the mainland, these were slaughtered in vast numbers for food by the early inhabitants of the Venetian islands. Right up to the eighteenth century, hunting for sea birds was a favourite sport of the Venetians, as we can tell from many of the paintings by Guardi and Longhi. In the Middle Ages, however, this unhealthy little island attracted few visitors and was chosen for this reason by Saint Francis. Tradition has it that the birds were so numerous and so noisy that their cries disturbed the Saint at prayer. He accordingly gathered them about him and preached a sermon to them as he would have done to human beings. In this he entreated them to remain quiet whilst he was praying. The birds, adds the chronicle, understood and obeyed him; all Saint Francis had to do was give a sign and the cheeping, chirping multitude was reduced to silence until he had finished. Then they would carry on once again with their fluttering and their calls.

We are told that there was neither a well nor a spring when Saint Francis settled on the island, but hardly had he planted his stick than a clear, refreshing stream— the same one from which we can drink today—sprang from the earth. As for the stick, it sprouted into a cypress—the parent tree of all those now covering the island like a little forest.

Venice's character would be incomplete if among the rich gallery of her statesmen, soldiers, artists, poets, explorers, merchants, musicians and dramatists she lacked a Saint. In this respect, Venice seems to have been less favourable to contemplative life than Tuscany or Umbria. Always preoccupied with trade, shipping and warfare, the Venetians showed little enthusiasm for matters spiritual and hardly cared for a kingdom which was ' not of this world '. With the exception of one ' local saint ', St. Lorenzo Giustiniani, no Venetian holy men appear to have achieved sainthood, although monasteries were numerous. St. Lorenzo belonged to the great Venetian Giustiniani family. The Bellini portrait of him in the Accademia immortalizes his wasted face and ascetic profile. Significantly, it was on a remote island, unvisited by fishermen or even huntsmen and not in Venice itself, with all the chaos of her commercial and political intrigue, that the Umbrian saint found asylum when he fled human society. Even Torcello was too well inhabited, too preoccupied, in the midst of its splendid gardens, with worldly cares.

Today, however, we can see in Torcello what Venice must have been like in the days when it was known, not as Venezia, but Rivoalto. Of the former glory and prosperity which made it a kind of capital, Torcello has retained only its churches, its roughly built little palace and a few dilapidated houses inhabited by the poor. This, nonetheless, was the source of Venice's destiny, the cradle of the Republic at a time when the refugees from the mainland thought only of saving their lives and their few remaining belongings from the barbarians.

If we were to represent the islands of the lagoon with allegorical figures in the manner of the early painters, San Lazzaro would be a desert hermit of the East, Chioggia a sturdy seaman with a determined expression and powerful figure, San Francesco al Deserto a monk in a homespun habit and with bare feet, meditating against a background of sea and sky, and Torcello an old queen, fallen from her throne, plundered by her children yet still grimly proud. To these figures we should add that of the Master of Furnaces, whose molten glass flows

104. The Doge's Palace, seen from the Lagoon. This is the visitor's last impression of Venice, as his boat carries him away from the city and its serene and fantastic splendour.

211

in a river of fire before it takes shape at the end of his rod; he embodies the spirit of the glassblowers of Murano. Finally there is the young maiden, bending over her lace-making frame and shaping, with infinite patience, the wonderfully delicate architectural forms which have remained Burano's glory through the centuries.

We cannot really know Venice if we are ignorant of the nature of her humble, unobtrusive neighbours, who had their moment of glory in the history of Venetian politics, whose triumph was modest and shortlived, and who have become delicated to the practice of a single art, leaving it to the ruling island to conquer the Mediterranean basin and accumulate the richest merchandise of East and West in its stores and warehouses. Murano and Burano, indeed, give us some idea of what Venice might have been if it had not been her destiny to achieve the 'domination of the seas.' Without the genius of her statesmen, without the boldness, the fearlessness, the tenacity and keenness for profit of her merchants, Venice would also have vegetated in the half-light which overshadowed the twin islands.

Until the year 1000, it would have been difficult to say which of the island-sanctuaries would have prevailed—Rivoalto, where the fugitives of many mainland towns found their way, or Murano, which was specially favoured by the inhabitants of Altino. Maintaining independence of her neighbour, her power constantly increasing, the Island of Fire was able to preserve her autonomy, her laws and her administration up to about the thirteenth century, when she was finally eclipsed and absorbed by the Republic; she then became tributary to Venice, who appointed her chief magistrate, selected by the Senate—the *podesta*.

As often happens when a small state becomes dependent upon a large one, Murano left her ambitions behind and was satisfied to provide the Venetians with a kind of pleasure resort where the patricians had their houses concealed in the depths of huge, secret gardens. Murano became something of an intermediary between the Venetian palace and the mainland 'villa'; she was such a short distance away that within an hour's rowing one could enjoy her restful greenery, and the tranquillity conducive to reflection and learned conversation. The gardens of Murano quickly became famous throughout Italy for the haven they offered to scholars, men of letters and noblemen, who could meet one another there in learned discussion, and also for the many rare trees and plants which travellers brought from remote countries, to study them at leisure and feast their eyes on their strange colours and shapes.

The fact that in Italy, as in other European countries, the art of glassblowing conferred the title of gentleman on anyone who practised it, made the artists of Murano a veritable aristocracy; they wore swords and were considered fit to marry with the oldest patrician families of the Republic. The wonderful produce of the furnaces of Murano made an important contribution to Venetian trade. Venetian glass was indeed admired and valued everywhere, and during the Renaissance there was no court, no castle, no rich household which did not boast some masterpiece of Beroviero, Seguso, Salviati or one of the other great glassworkers—some of whose dynasties have lasted to the present day.

The reputation of the Mint at Murano was such that the Republic conferred on it the privilege of striking the *oselle* (literally 'hen-birds') awarded to distinguished men. The history of the *oselle* was a curious one: since time immemorial offerings and tribute in kind were customary (see Note 20), and on some occasions tradition prescribed an offering of sea birds. In the sixteenth century this custom became awkward and outmoded, but as it was impossible to dispense with it—so tyrannical was the power of tradition—Doge Antonio Grimani devised the scheme of replacing the birds with what were henceforth referred to as *oselle*, the medals struck at Murano.

Venetian painting received a powerful impulse from Murano at a decisive point in its evolution when it was in danger of coming to depend on the schools of the mainland—Padua and Verona in particular. Artists of strong, distinctive personality, the Vivarinis, appeared in the fifteenth century, giving Venetian style a new conception of its innermost nature and basic individuality. Murano is to be cherished then because its studios were the source of the modern forms which came to flower in the work of Carpaccio and culminated with Tiepolo. We should also recognize the true significance of the Romanesque cathedral of S. Maria e Donato, which is a fine example of Romano-Byzantine syncretism. Since there are now practically no Romanesque churches in Venice, the cathedral of Murano provides a transitional stage, a connecting link between the absolute Byzantinism of the Basilica of San Marco and the great Gothic churches of the Orders, the Frari, and SS. Giovanni e Paolo. This further confirms the importance of the islands of the lagoon within the knowledge we now have of Venetian art: the Veneto-Byzantine Basilica of Torcello, and the Romano-Byzantine church of Murano must necessarily be included among the wealth of essentially Venetian churches which we already know.

There is still one island which should not go unmentioned, though the traveller will find his visit there rather a sad one: this is the island of San Michele, which is occupied by the cemetery. As the population of Venice increased and the town itself became very much larger, the ancient custom of burying the dead within or around churches had to be dispensed with. Some patricians and famous figures in the history of the Republic retained the much envied privilege of having family vaults in their parish churches, and from generation to generation they bestowed rich gifts on them. But for those who did not belong to the elect, it became necessary for obvious reasons of hygiene, to establish a cemetery on an island near to Venice. The little islands of San Michele and San Cristoforo della Pace had been joined together by the labours of the monks of the Camaldulite Order, whose founder, Saint Romuald, built a monastery here in the tenth century. Driven from their refuge, the monks surrendered their island to the Venetian government, and it was there, as the town grew larger, that a cemetery and prison were established. The latter was used by the Austrians during their period of control—particularly for political detainees. Among these there was the famous Silvio Pellico, who left a moving account of his imprisonment.

About half a mile from the Fondamenta Nuove, we can distinguish the clear, pleasing outline of the Island of the Dead; there is nothing grim about it as it reflects its pearl-coloured walls and its cypresses in waters of jade. Every important ceremony in the life of Venice, whether it be a baptism, a marriage or a burial, is carried out on water, and gondolas are used to take the dead to their final resting-place. Yet ferry-boats of Charon though they may be, they represent an effort to dispel the sadness associated with them in a curious display of art and finery. Baroque lanterns of shining gilt, and allegorical statues of Time or Death surmount the hearse, with strangely telling effect. It seems indeed that even death itself must be confronted in an atmosphere of splendour, gaiety and theatrical lyricism. A burial in Venice is like a festive procession, and Baroque embellishment has rarely conceived such strikingly fanciful or picturesque figures as those represented on the funeral craft, as they drift slowly and majestically through the canals and across the lagoon towards the Island of the Dead—a far less gloomy one that often painted by Arnold Böcklin.

We should nevertheless avoid leaving the gay and lively city of Venice with the gloomy impression we might receive on catching sight of the cemetery. In point of fact, had we not known the sad purpose served by San Michele, we should never be able to guess it as we look across from the Fondamenta Nuove; behind its marble walls and the noble lines of its cypresses, we might more readily imagine one of the quiet gardens where the humanists discoursed on Plato and Aristotle, in the cool evenings, when scholars and lovely courtesans tuned their lutes to accompany the songs of poets. It was one of the conventions of late nineteenth century and twentieth century literature to look on Venice as a dead or dying city, pervaded by a mood of gloom. Maurice Barrès and Gabriele d'Annunzio found a morbid, intoxicating pleasure in this atmosphere, and Thomas Mann's *Der Tod in Venedig* took it to an extreme of obsession in which love and death inevitably had their part. Venice is not really like this, though on summer days the heavy odour of the canals and the energy-sapping heat cast what seems like an age-old mist over the façades of the old palaces, and emphasize the contrast between past splendours and the present modesty of the patrician dwellings now occupied by poor people. This poverty should not be viewed in the light customary in countries which are richer and more concerned with material comforts than Italy. For Italy indeed, the contemplation of beauty and the daily pleasure in a work of art, freely on show in the streets and squares of Rome, Florence, Venice or one of the little cities like Pisa, Siena or Orvieto, are more important than comfort. The greatest luxury is the knowledge and possession of the thing of beauty.

Venice itself is pre-eminently the thing of beauty which each can enjoy in his own way, according to his taste, his culture and the nature of his sensibility and understanding. This is therefore a many-sided city and subject to every kind of change; not only in the differing light of the seasons and the hours of the day, but in the minds of those who see her. She possesses to a degree that no other city can match the gift of meeting every man's desire, of granting him what he needs to ennoble his nature, to gladden him in the power of artistic possession, or simply in his love of life. For in Venice one lives more intensely, more deeply and more contentedly than anywhere else; every moment is bathed in her constantly changing beauty, renewed with every passing hour, whose wonders will remain unexhausted, even at the end of a lifetime of contemplation.

NOTES
Including selected works on Venice

[1] On the period of the invasions see Henri Pirenne's *Histoire de l'Europe des invasions au XVIème siècle*, Paris 1936. For the origins of Venice in general, P. Manfrin's *Le Origini di Venezia*, Rome 1902, and Gellio Cassi's *Il Mare Adriatico*, Milan 1915; D. Mantovani's *Le Isole della Laguna Veneta*, Bergamo 1925; A. Valori's *Venezia e le sue lagune*, Venice 1847. For the history of Venice from its foundation, refer to S. Romani's *Storia documentata di Venezia*, Venice 1925; Alberto Battistella's *La Repubblica di Venezia nei suoi undici secoli di storia*, Venice 1929; H. Krestchmayr's *Geschichte von Venedig*, Gotha 1920; E. Musatti's *Storia di Venezia*, Milan 1926; Auguste Bailly's *La Sérénissime République de Venise*, Paris 1959; Roberto Cessi's *Storia della Repubblica di Venezia*, Messina 1944; John Ruskin's *The Stones of Venice*, London 1851; Wilhelm Hausenstein's *Venezianische Augenblicke*, Dresden 1925.

[2] The distinctive shape of the gondola was dictated by the need to have a flat-bottomed craft which could be used in shallow waters. The shape of the iron at the prow has been variously explained. It counterbalances the weight of the gondolier, who rows in a standing position at the stern. The fact that the ordinary gondola is completely black has also given rise to divers fanciful theories. For its purpose, balanced as it is on an oblique axis, the gondola is the most perfect craft conceivable, and that is why it has not changed through the centuries.

[3] On the salt monopoly, which remained for a long time one of the most important items in Venetian trade with the continent, see P. Martinelli's *Del Commercio dei Veneziani*, Venice 1835.

[4] The word 'Doge' is a corruption of the Italian 'Duce,' which itself comes from the Latin 'Dux.'

[5] A. Maranini, *La Costituzione di Venezia dalle origini alla Serrata del Maggior Consiglio*, Venice 1927. See also B. Cecchetti's *Il Doge di Vene-*zia, Venice 1887, and E. Besta's *Il Senato veneziano*, Venice 1897.

[6] For relations between Venice and Byzantium refer to Charles Diehl's *Les Grands problèmes de l'histoire byzantine*, Paris 1943; Louis Brehier's *Vie et mort de Byzance*, Paris 1946; Vassiliev's *Histoire de l'empire byzantin*, Paris 1932.

[7] The Doge's headdress, the *corno*, was of cloth of gold. Some Venice enthusiasts would have it that the chief magistrate was given a *corno* of solid gold. The cap normally worn by the Doges, as their portraits show, was of silk or red damask.

[8] A. N. Papadopoli, *Le monete di Venezia*, Milan, n. d.

[9] Roberto Cessi, *op. cit.*, vol. I.

[10] Accusations were secretly placed in special boxes, but attention was only given to those which were signed. These were automatically followed up with an enquiry and, if necessary, action was taken against the accused. The name of the informer was kept secret throughout the trial, but once judgment had been given he received a large reward if the accusation was found to be correct. If it was not, he was heavily penalised. False accusations inspired by hatred or spite were thus prevented. The informer, who acted on his own responsibility and at his own risk, thus became an assistant to the judiciary.

[11] In English, 'Anthony of the Bridge.'

[12] In Venice the word 'piazza' is used only for the 'Piazza San Marco.' The diminutive 'Piazzetta' applies to the square between the Piazza itself, the Doge's Palace, the Library and the quay. There is also a Piazzetta dei Leoncini, which is situated north of St. Mark's Cathedral. All the other squares of Venice are called either 'campo' or 'campiello' according to their size.

[13] The Venetians had a strong belief in miracles and the supernatural, and, like other Italians, were inclined to be superstitious. Sailors and fishermen believed that storms were caused by demons and could be stopped by invoking the angels, especially the archangel Gabriel. According to a legend handed down by Doge Andrea Dandolo and quoted by Ruskin, the choice of sites for the churches of Venice was also dictated by miraculous or supernatural events.

' In accordance with his duties as Lord and Bishop of the Islands, Bishop Magnus of Altinum went from place to place to comfort the people and teach them gratitude to God who had delivered them from the cruelty of the barbarians. But Saint Peter appeared to him and commanded him to build a church in his name at the passage into Venice, or rather, the city of Rivoalto, where he would find sheep and oxen grazing; the Bishop did this and built the church of Saint Peter on the Island of Olivolo, where the cathedral of Venice now stands.

' Then the angel Raphael appeared to him, saying that he was to build a church for him in the place where he found a flock of birds gathered. The Bishop did as he was commanded and built the church of the Angel Raphael at Dorsoduro.

' Then our Lord Jesus Christ appeared to him, enjoining him to build a church in the centre of the city, where he would find a red cloud floating; and it came to pass that this was the Church of San Salvador.

' Then the Holy Virgin Mary appeared to him in all her beauty and commanded him to build a church where he saw a large white cloud lying, and this was the church of Santa Maria Formosa.

' Then Saint John the Baptist appeared to him, and bade him build two churches near one another in his own name and that of his father. This was done, and the churches were San Giovanni in Bragora and San Zaccaria.

' Then the Apostles of Christ appeared to him, also desirous of having their churches in the city, and they commanded him to build on the site where he found a gathering of eighteen cranes.

' Finally the blessed Virgin Justina appeared to him, and she called upon him to raise a sanctuary in the place where he found vines heavy with fresh fruit.'

[14] The two marble columns which stand between the Piazzetta and the quay, and between which it was the custom to carry out executions, also came from the East. There was a third column, but it fell in the sea when it was being unloaded and sank so deeply in the mud that it could never be recovered. The columns were erected by Nicolo Starantonio in 1172. As a reward he was given special permission (for games of chance were prohibited) to establish a gaming table between the columns. The east column, which is of grey oriental granite, bears a bronze lion which may formerly have been a chimaera or dragon. Its origins are obscure and subject to dispute; it has been severally described as Etruscan, Phoenician, Assyrian and Sassanid. The west column of red oriental granite is surmounted by a statue of Theodore, the old patron saint of Venice, commonly known as San Todaro, whose relics, like those of Saint Nicolas, were brought back by Admiral Enrico Contarini in the eleventh century from the town of Myra. The beast he is killing is a crocodile, which was sacred in Egypt. Theodore was martyred for destroying the animal idols of the pagans.

[15] The church of San Zanipolo (SS. Giovanni e Paolo) is as miraculous in origin as the old churches enumerated by Andrea Dandolo in Note 13. Tradition has it that Doge Jacopo Tiepolo, whose reign was from 1229 to 1249, saw the Oratory of Saint Daniel one night in a dream. It was standing on the site where the church was later to be built; the marshy fields round it were full of wonderful flowers of all colours, and doves were flying above them with golden crosses on their heads. Then two angels came down from the sky, swinging censers and singing, ' This is the place I have chosen for my Preacher Brethren.' When he awoke, the Doge went to the Senate meeting and told of his dream. As a result the Dominicans were granted the land in question and the money they needed to build the church we know today.

[16] The ' rio ' is a little canal. The diminutive term ' riello ' is also used.

[17] With its solid, imposing architecture, its heavy sculptures and the huge iron bars at its dimly-lit windows, the very sight of the Palace of the Lords of the Night must have been sufficient to strike fear into the hearts of the criminals who were taken there.

[18] Heroic events in Venetian history were recorded in the paintings of the great sixteenth and seventeenth century artists. These are to be seen in the main halls of the Doge's Palace. In the Hall of the Council of Ten, there is a painting by Bassano of *Pope Alexander III blessing Sebastiano Ziani*, the victor of Punta Salvatore in 1176, and another by Aliense of the *Surrender of Bergamo to the condottiere Carmagnola* (1427); in the Hall of the Pregadi or Senate, Palma the Elder has represented Doge Venier giving to Venice the mainland cities (Brescia and so on), which were conquered during his reign. In the Hall of the Scrutinio, we find Liberi's *Victory of Lorenzo Marcello in the Dardanelles* (1656), Tintoretto's *Victory over the Hungarians at Zara* (1346), Marco Vecellio's *Naval Victory over the Normans of Roger II*, Vicentino's *Capture of Cattaro by Vittorio Pisani* (1378), Sante Peranda's *Capture of Giaffa di Soria* (1123), and many others.

[19] Bailly, *op. cit.* pages 274-5.

[20] The following deserves to be quoted among the picturesque customs of Venice: when the Doge visited the church of S. Maria Formosa once a year, the priests gave him a hat of gilded straw, some sweet wine, and oranges on two basketwork trays.

[21] The famous Domenico Selvo had a Greek wife who was related to the Byzantine Emperor Michael VII and had an obvious influence on

his policies. Tradition has it that she bathed every morning in dew; this was collected for her at dawn in the meadows and gardens by a host of her attendants.

[22] See Villehardouin's *La Conquête de Constantinople*, published by Faral, Vol. I.

[23] *Bailo* was the equivalent of the English ' bailiff,' in its early meaning of ' judge ' or ' magistrate.'

[24] Mas Latrie, *Commerce et expéditions militaires, Collection des Documents inédits*, Paris 1880, vol. III.

[25] Bailly, *op. cit.*, Part Nine: *L'Age d'Or.*

[26] A. Sapori, *Mercatores*, Milan 1942, and *Studi di Storia economica medievale*, Florence 1947. Jules Scottas, *Les Messageries maritimes de Venise au XIV*ème *et XV*ème *siècles*, Paris 1938. Gino Luzzato, *Storia economica d'Italia*, Rome 1949, vol. I, and *Storia de commercio dell'antichità al Rinascimento*, Florence 1914. F. C. Lane, *Venetian Ships and Shipbuilders of the Renaissance*, Baltimore 1934. R. Pernoud, *Les Villes marchandes aux XIV*ème *et XV*ème *siècles*, Paris 1948. F. Heyd, *Histoire du Commerce du Levant au Moyen Age*, Leipzig 1885.

[27] Jean Alazard, *La Venise de la Renaissance*, Paris 1956, p. 73.

[28] Jean Alazard, *op. cit.*, p. 72.

[29] Jean Alazard, *op. cit.*, id.

[30] Emile Molinier, *Venise et ses arts décoratifs*, Paris 1889. Urbain de Gelthof, *Les arts industriels à Venise au Moyen Age et à la Renaissance*, Venice 1885. Vittorio Cian, *La cultura e l'italianità di Venezia nel Rinascimento*, Bologna 1905.

[31] Burckhardt, *Die Kultur der Renaissance in Italien*, Part I, Chap. 4.

[32] Jean Alazard, *op. cit.*, Chap. IX, *Venise villa fastueuse. Fêtes et luxe.*

[33] Jean Alazard, *op. cit.*, id.

[34] Giovanni Monticolo, *I capitolari delle arte veneziani*, Rome 1914. Broglio d'Ajano, *L'arte della seta in Venezia*, Rome 1902.

[35] Bailly, *op. cit.*, Part Nine: *L'Age d'Or.*

[36] Jean Alazard, *L'Art Italien*, vol. III.

[37] Marcel Brion, *Albrecht Dürer*, Paris 1960.

[38] For Machiavelli's ideas see Marcel Brion's *Machiavel, Génie et Destinée*, Paris 1948.

[39] Orestes Ferrara, *Le XVI siècle vu par les ambassadeurs vénitiens*, Paris 1954, and *Gaspare Contarini et ses missions*, Paris 1956. E. Alberi, *Relazioni degli Ambasciatori veneti al Senato*, Florence 1839-1863, 13 vol.

[40] Marcel Brion, *Catherine Cornaro, reine de Chypre*, Paris 1946.

[41] The best analysis of the Battle of Lepanto and its political consequences is contained in Orestes Ferrara's *Philippe II*, Paris 1959.

[42] For the various plans for a canal through the Suez Isthmus, see Fr. Charles-Roux, *L'Isthme de Suez et les rivalités européennes au XVI*ème *siècle, Revue de l'histoire des colonies françaises*, 1924.

[43] For Venetian agriculture, see Roberto Cessi's *Storia della Repubblica di Venezia*, vol. II, p. 106.

[44] Bailly, *op. cit.*, p. 244.

[45] This is shown by Giovanni Priuli's account, quoted in Romani's *Storia documentata*, vol. IV, p. 436.

[46] ' Few masters in the long history of art have been able to equal Giorgione in his ability to transpose emotional feelings into mental reveries and convey the expression of these reveries and emotions in pure painting; and even fewer have been able to use this ability with his supremely incorruptible innocence.' Jean Louis Vaudoyer, *La Peinture vénitienne*, Paris 1958.

[47] Marco Valsecchi, *La Pittura veneziana*, Milan 1954.

[48] Jean Alazard, *L'Art italien*, vol. IV: *De l'ère baroque au XIX*ème *siècle*, Paris 1960.

[49] A competition was held among the painters of Venice for a commission in the Scuola San Rocco. While his rivals contented themselves with offering sketches or drawings, Tintoretto had already finished a huge work and had it placed in the position selected by the judges.

[50] I have dealt at length with the importance of the church of la Salute in the history of Italian Baroque art, in my book on *L'Architecture religieuse de 1400 à 1800*, Paris 1960.

[51] The *bauta* was a large veil which covered the head and shoulders completely; the *tabarro* was a voluminous cloak, similar to a ' domino.'

[52] Ange Goudar, *L'Espion chinois*, Cologne 1774. Apart from the six volumes of his strange memoirs, he also wrote *Remarques sur la musique et la danse à Venise*, Venice 1773, and *Plan de réformes proposé aux cinq Correcteurs de Venise actuellement en charge avec un sermon évangélique pour élever la République dans la crainte de Dieu*, Amsterdam 1775.

[53] Philippe Monnier, *Venise au XVIII*ème *siècle*, Paris 1920, Chap. VIII: *Le théâtre Vénitien et la comédie italienne.*

[54] If a musical inspiration came to him during Mass, he would immediately leave the altar and rush into the Sacristy to write it down, then return to finish the Mass.

[55] *Vedute* were landscapes, either real or imaginary, or a mixture of the two.

[56] The marble slabs which are inlaid in the pavement of St. Mark's Square were known as the *liston;* people would arrange to meet in a certain square of the *liston.*

[57] Luigi Orteschi, *Delle passioni, i costumi e il modo di vivere dei Veneziani,* Venice 1859.

[58] See reference also in Chapter 3.

[59] Pompeo Molmenti, *Nuova Antologia,* 14th January 1904. Molmenti was the most learned, the most interesting and the most famous historian of Venice. Other works by him include: *La Dogaressa di Venezia,* Turin 1884; *La Vie privée à Venise depuis les premiers temps jusqu'à la chute de la République,* Venice 1882; *La decadenza e la fine della Repubblica veneta,* Venice 1897; *Il Decadimento politico ed economico della Repubblica veneta, Nuova Antologia,* 16th February 1907.

[60] Maximilien Misson, *Voyage d'Italie,* Amsterdam 1743.

[61] Giuseppe Antonio Constantino, *Lettere critiche, giocose, morali, scientifiche ed erudite alla moda ed al gusto del secolo presente,* Venice 1751.

[62] Madame du Boccage, *Oeuvres,* Lyons 1764.

[63] Carlo Goldoni, *Mémoires pour servir à l'histoire de sa vie et de son théâtre,* Paris 1787.

[64] Lady Mary Wortley Montagu, *Letters and Works,* 1837.

[65] Baron de Poelnitz, *Lettres et Mémoires,* Amsterdam 1737.

[66] Antonio Longo, *Memorie della vita di Antonio Longo veneziano scritte e pubblicate da lui medesimo per umiltà,* Venice 1820.

[67] Rosalba Carriera, *Diario,* Venice 1793.

[68] Vittorio Malamani, *Il Settecento a Venezia,* Venice 1891.

[69] This feverish search for pleasure was a source of astonishment to foreigners and other Italians alike. 'To bring laughter is a sublime talent,' wrote Casanova. 'Pleasure and intertainment are the best remedies for our ills,' asserted Rosalba Carriera. And Lady Montagu noted in her journal: 'Neither old clothes nor old loves are ever to be seen here... No one here is old as long as he is not bedridden.' Orteschi said: 'There is no night in Venice; eternal day shines there. The seven theatres and two hundred cafés in Venice, many of which do not close until dawn, encourage this busy nocturnal life. In the eighteenth century, the Venetians are incorrigible noctambulists.' 'No one gets dressed here until people are going to bed elsewhere,' remarked Goudar's Chinese spy.

[70] Also Lippomano, 10th December 1796: 'We no longer have even the comfort of the poor and the oppressed, which is to bemoan one's lot.'

[71] Malamani, *Il Settecento,* p. 166.

[72] Bailly, *op. cit.,* p. 326 ff.

[73] On this subject, see Giuseppe Cappelletti, *Storia della Repubblica di Venezia,* Book XIII, Venice 1855, and Leopold Curti, *Mémoires historiques et politiques sur la République de Venise rédigés en 1792,* Paris 1807.

[74] Romanin, *Storia Documentata,* Vol. X, and *Correspondence of Alvise Mocenigo,* April 1797.

[75] Vittorio Barzoni, *Rivoluzioni della Repubblica di Venezia,* Milan 1814.

[76] Alvise Mocenigo, letter of 29th May 1796.

[77] Attilio Sarfatti, *Memorie del dogado di Lodovico Manin,* Venice 1886.

[78] Philippe Monnier, *op. cit.,* p. 384.

INDEX

Figures in italics refer to illustration numbers